Indigenous Settlers
of the Galápagos

Indigenous Settlers of the Galápagos

Conservation Law, Race, and Society

Pilar Sánchez Voelkl

LEXINGTON BOOKS
Lanham • Boulder • New York • London

Published by Lexington Books
An imprint of The Rowman & Littlefield Publishing Group, Inc.
4501 Forbes Boulevard, Suite 200, Lanham, Maryland 20706
www.rowman.com

86-90 Paul Street, London EC2A 4NE

British Library Cataloguing in Publication Information Available

Library of Congress Cataloging-in-Publication Data

Names: Sánchez Voelkl, Pilar, author.
Title: Indigenous settlers of the Galápagos : conservation law, race, and
   society / Pilar Sánchez Voelkl.
Description: Lanham : Lexington Books, [2022] | Includes bibliographical
   references and index. | Summary: "Pilar Sánchez Voelkl offers an
   anthropological account of the early arrival and prominence of
   Indigenous peoples in the Galápagos Islands. Their history and everyday
   life reveal how multiple notions of nature, race, and society travel and
   meet, shaping the way conservation thought is translated into law"—
   Provided by publisher.
Identifiers: LCCN 2022019682 (print) | LCCN 2022019683 (ebook) | ISBN
   9781666906592 (cloth) | ISBN 9781666906615 (paperback) | ISBN
   9781666906608 (ebook)
Subjects: LCSH: Indigenous peoples—Galápagos Islands—History. |
   Galápagos Islands—Race relations—History. | Indians of South
   America—Ecuador—History. | Indigenous peoples—Social life and
   customs—Galápagos Islands. | Colonists—Galápagos Islands—History. |
   Quechua Indians—Galápagos Islands—History. | Nature
   conservation—Galápagos Islands.
Classification: LCC F3741.G2 S26 2022 (print) | LCC F3741.G2 (ebook) |
   DDC 986.6/5074—dc23/eng/20220601
LC record available at https://lccn.loc.gov/2022019682
LC ebook record available at https://lccn.loc.gov/2022019683

For Daniel and Antonio

Contents

Figures

Acknowledgments

I would like to thank my sons, Daniel and Antonio, for being the best travel companions I could have during the many years of study and work in Quito, New York City, Bogotá, and the Galápagos. In my first visit to the archipelago in 2008, Daniel and Antonio were only five and two years old. After years of sharing different places, experiences, and cultures, they became bright, strong, compassionate, creative, and loving teenagers. This work—with all the efforts and pleasures that came with it—is dedicated to you.

I will always be grateful to my wonderful advisor, Sally Merry, for her role in guiding, inspiring, and reflecting upon meaningful issues surrounding everyday life, law, and politics in the Galápagos Islands. She believed in me from the very first moment. She was thoughtful, generous, and patient while I navigated through different subjects, places, and interests while being a graduate student in the PhD program in anthropology at New York University. She could see the potential of making social research in the Galápagos. In 2014 Sally encouraged me to join the Anthropocene Conference at the University of California Santa Cruz. In the following years, she supported me traveling to make pre-field research on mainland Ecuador and the Galápagos. She later encouraged me in writing and publishing this book both in English and Spanish. Her work discipline, positive energy, and crucial contributions on legal pluralism, women's rights, and the cultural power of law in Hawaii and Boston have always inspired me. Sadly, she passed away in 2020. Thank you, Sally, for being such an inspiring woman and professor—the best advisor I could ask for.

I owe my theoretical knowledge of race and Latin America to Thomas Abercrombie. His witty prose, historical commentaries, and provocative analyses keep surprising me. I wonder what would have been his reaction to the end product of this process. I missed his comments and presence during the last years since his passing. I was also lucky enough to have Renato Rosaldo as my professor and advisor. He gave me the best advice I could have as a graduate student and as a mom, raising two little kids in New York. He inspired me as an anthropologist, professor, writer, and person while guiding me in the design of this project. His commitment to good ethnography and writing will always be stimulating. Emily Martin, Mary Louise Pratt, and Fred Myers were also great professors and thoughtful readers. Thank you to all of you; I truly feel humbled and honored to have such wonderful community.

I will always be indebted to two strong, supportive, smart women and leaders: Margarita Masaquiza and Martha Chango. They gave me the warmest welcomes I could have in both Puerto Ayora, Galápagos, and Salasaca, Tungurahua; they were open to my project and shared with me precious moments and knowledge. To Margarita, thanks for believing in me, for your endless enthusiasm and work, and for making me feel at home in the Galápagos Islands. Thanks to Daniel Masaquiza and Justin Scoggin for giving me the chance to volunteer at the Runa Kunapak School and the Tomás de Berlanga School library in Puerto Ayora. And to my students, I will always remember you—in particular, Fernanda Segura, for being a bright student who helped me a great deal with all logistical matters by the end of this process. To the members of the Salasaca Association and to all the people who helped me and shared their time and intriguing life histories, thank you. To Gaspar Masaquiza, Daniel Masaquiza, and Vicente Masaquiza, thanks for your kindness and illuminating conversations. To Maria Moya, Martha Chica and Sandra Ulloa, thanks for being my good friends in the islands.

My doctoral studies at New York University were made possible by funding from the following agencies to which I am most grateful: Fulbright, MacCracken and Colciencias. I also feel lucky to have engaged with this discipline which has offered me invaluable lessons and the remarkable gift of building a career from the passion for traveling and learning from different places and cultures. To my parents, grandmothers, and Uncle Gustavo, thank you for making me believe everything I dream is possible.

Introduction

Indigenous Settlers of the Galápagos

On the day I arrived at the Galápagos Islands in April 2017, I met Stella, a *mestiza* (non-Indigenous) elderly woman who sells newspapers at a stand in Puerto Ayora, the capital of Santa Cruz Island and the most populated city of the archipelago.[1] Every day, she travels by bus to the old ferry, which then takes her to Baltra Island where the central airport is located and where she can pick up daily national newspapers. For more than an hour, Stella and I shared the same seat on the ferry and then on the bus for the return trip to Puerto Ayora. Before telling me the story of her life and asking why I had come to the islands, Stella indignantly warned me about the way politicians on the mainland had always made derogatory remarks when they spoke of the inhabitants of the Galápagos, *los galapagueños*. As an example, she mentioned the comments recently made in the midst of a debate about a new reform to the conservation law (known as the Special Law for the Galapagos), which, since 1998, has governed nature and society in the archipelago.

Indeed in Quito the vice-president of the National Assembly discussed the reform, echoing an argument similar to the one used by Luis Jaramillo, delegate to the United Nations Educational, Scientific, and Cultural Organization (UNESCO), at the event which inaugurated the Charles Darwin Scientific Station in Academy Bay (*Bahía Academia*, Puerto Ayora), some sixty years before. The assemblywoman Aguiñaga said: "the earliest settlers [of the islands] arrived to fulfill their patriotic duty (*hacer patria*). But have we forgotten that it was a region where prisoners were sent? They were condemned to live in the Galápagos!" Ángel Vilema, her colleague, a native *galapagueño*, replied by pointing out that his ancestors were workers, not criminals, while mentioning the disdain for manual labor that characterizes the elites in the mainland:[2]

1

Is it my fault, *señorita* Aguiñaga, that my father has had to get up earlier than your father, that my mother has broken her back hauling fish and has cooked for 200 tourists, that my father has been a captain, sailor, guide and helmsman? And, I repeat, is it my fault that your family are idlers? (*Diario La Hora*, June 10, 2015).

The two speeches, that of Jaramillo in 1964 and of Aguiñaga in 2015, mirror a common narrative about the *galapagueños* that represents them as subjects who require correction, control, and surveillance. The stigma distorts the human history of the archipelago in which indigenous laborers from the central *sierra* (highlands), and not Europeans or prisoners, were the leading players. Not knowing of human pasts allows for the production of nonhuman narratives that revolve around nonhumans in the archipelago—like that about the famous, giant tortoise "Lonesome George" (*Jorge el Solitario),* who was turned into an icon of conservation worldwide (Nicholls 2007).

Meanwhile on that day, Stella continued describing her own life on the Galápagos, which began when she migrated from Guayaquil (a large city on the Pacific coast of Ecuador) to Santa Cruz Island in the mid-1980s. She spoke, for example, of the preponderance of men on the islands and added, "Many proposed marriage to me in those days." At the time, the city of Puerto Ayora had recently begun to be built. After several decades of watching how the city came into being, Stella could identify herself as a *galapagueña* and identify those others who were not—those who were later 'introduced' in the Galápagos.

The lively conversation with Stella suddenly took a turn when I told her about my interest in researching the history of the Indigenous colonization of the archipelago. For Stella, who is a *mestiza* (non-indigenous)*,* it seemed that the subject I had chosen was neither interesting nor important.[3] She repeated some of the surnames of well-known *colonos* (first settlers) of the island. She further warned me that the *Salasacas*, members of the Kichwa-speaking Salasaca Indigenous group from the slopes of the Tungurahua Volcano in the central Andean highlands of Ecuador's mainland, "were recent arrivals, who came after the [1998] law."[4] In this way, she suggested they were transgressors who stayed illegally after the conservation law started to enforce stricter population controls in the Galápagos Islands. She then spoke about the way local authorities "hunted them down" in their homes and near the marketplace where they usually looked for work as day laborers. She further described the persecution and deportation of *Salasacas* from Santa Cruz Island, as follows:

Every time a cargo plane arrives, the Governing Council (*Consejo de Gobierno*) hunts down the *Salasacas* in their homes or near the marketplace where they stand around waiting for a job . . . They ask for their papers and if they don't have them, they arrest them and deport them to the mainland. Today, they took 15 of them . . .

The *Salasacas* are recent arrivals. It was after the passing of the law, from 2000 onwards, that they came here. They used each other's IDs when they entered the islands—same photo, same identification card. Since they all resemble one another, it was easy to do that. Besides, all of them are called Manuel or Rosa Masaquiza" (Puerto Ayora, April 2017).

The *galapagueños* call these raids *batidas*. And, although the list of deportees is not public, it is known that—under the guise of enforcing the conservation law of the islands—local authorities usually persecute and deport Salasacas from Santa Cruz. On the other hand, like Stella, many of the *mestizo* islanders ignore and are not interested in knowing the history of the *Salasacas* in the archipelago. They rather speak of them as: "introduced," "illegals," or as "a plague" which recently hit the Galápagos. In so doing, they resort to the language categories of conservation science in order to create their own racial distinctions, where the *Salasacas* rather than settlers or "natives" are "introduced," "alien," or "invasive." And while a foreign visitor cannot easily detect the physical differences between a *mestizo* and an Indigenous person (so long as he or she does not wear their traditional ethnic dress), for the *mestizos* of the Galápagos, the *Salasacas* look different from them and they all look the same as one another. [5] Finally, it is true, as Stella observed, that Manuel Masaquiza and Rosa Masaquiza are by far the most prevalent names among the Salasaca people. In particular, the history of the surname Masaquiza illustrates the tensions between *mestizos* and Indigenous peoples and how oppressive forms of racism mark the relationship between the Salasaca people and the Ecuadorian state. To understand vernacular visions of race and social order is key to examine how conservation law is translated and enforced in the Ecuadorian archipelago.

When we were about to reach the bus stop at Puerto Ayora, Stella ended our conservation, urging me to talk to a teacher who had begun a campaign to change the name of an old settlement in the upperpart of Santa Cruz known up to now as "Salasaca." For Ecuadorians, that is clearly a Kichwa name that has been exclusively used to designate the ethnic group, its members living on the highlands and on the islands, and their native town in the central sierra on the slopes of the Tungurahua Volcano. Why was this district called "Salasaca" in the Galápagos? Why were doña Stella, the teacher, and other *mestizos* determined to erase the old district name in Santa Cruz Island? Who are the Salasaca people and how did they arrive at the Galápagos? Why did they become the subject of persecution and deportation by the local authorities in enforcing conservation law in the archipelago?

Indigenous Settlers

The Galápagos is known for its absence of Indigenous (aboriginal) human populations. Nevertheless, I chose to talk about "Indigenous settlers" in order to highlight the role of race in the making of history, society, and natural heritage on the archipelago—this because most of the earliest colonizers of the Galápagos were Indigenous peoples. A century later, the Kichwa Salasacas also played a critical role in the colonization of Santa Cruz Island. On the other hand, the stories of Indigenous settlers of the Galápagos help counter the way Indigenous peoples have been construed as collective agents tied to the land, passive recipients of government policies, or radically different persons with the assignment of reciprocity, animism, being one with nature, and temporal and ontological differences. In particular, the history of the Salasaca people speaks of the numerous times they had to reinvent themselves, their constant geographic mobility, and the ways they have engaged as agents of socio-economic and political change. Furthermore, by using "Indigenous," I intend to think through social and scientific categorizations and the cultural standards of belonging and citizenship, as well as the time frames which uphold them.

Three years before the young Charles Darwin visited the islands in 1835, a permanent human settlement already lived in the Galápagos. From 1832 to the early 1900s, Ecuador delegated human colonization of the Galápagos to two *hacendados* (large estate owners) who forcibly uprooted Indigenous laborers from the mainland and transplanted them as part of the *hacienda* system in order to exert sovereignty over the recently annexed remote archi-

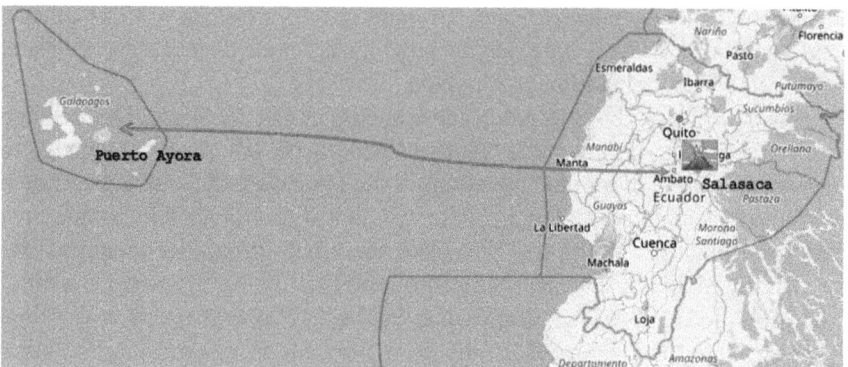

Figure 0.1.   **Ecuador and the Galápagos Islands. Salasacas of the Galápagos move between their native Salasaca (located on the slopes of the Tungurahua Volcano, between the Ecuadorian Sierra and the Amazon) and the Galápagos Islands (600 miles off the coast of Ecuador). Most of them live in Puerto Ayora on the most populated island, Santa Cruz. *Source*: Map created by P. Sánchez.**

pelago.[6] Most of them came from the Tungurahua province, located in the Ecuadorian central highlands of the Andes. They became the first inhabitants of San Cristóbal and Isabela Islands. Some Salasacas were part of these pioneer groups. Over the next decades, the population of the islands grew slowly. This drastically changed after the creation of the Galápagos National Park and the Charles Darwin Research Station in 1959, which had headquarters located in the desolate Santa Cruz Island. From the 1960s onwards, a second wave of migrants settled (voluntarily) in the Galápagos, specifically in this island. The Salasaca people (from the Tungurahua) were central players in the late colonization of Santa Cruz.

Today Santa Cruz Island is the site of the second biggest Salasaca community in Ecuador, after the Salasaca in the Tungurahua province.[7] At least three thousand people of Salasaca origin currently live on the island, that is, one in every five *santacruceños*. These numbers, however, are only an estimate. Accurate population data is difficult to obtain from census data due to the many islands' residents who evade surveys or do not give accurate answers, partly to avoid the potential discrimination that comes with identifying as "Indigenous" on the archipelago, and partly because they are afraid of revealing that they or people they know are "illegals" under the 1998 law.

The Salasacas

Despite their large presence and history in the islands, to this day, no written text, investigation, or research has documented the story of the Salasacas of the Galápagos. This is not the case with regards to Salasaca origins and the cultural identity on the mainland—the nature of which have been the subject of long-standing debates among Ecuadorian and non-Ecuadorian anthropologists (Peñaherrera y Costales 1959, Pérez 1962, Cassagrande 1981, Powers 1991, 1995, Garcés 2002, Corr 2013, 2018).

In continental Ecuador, the *Salasacas* are well-known for being one of the most traditional Indigenous groups. Wearing distinctive ethnic attire and speaking their own dialect of Kichwa, they are described as "fiercely protective of their territory and their cultural identity, proudly refusing to show deference to whites" (Corr and Powers 2012, 8). They are said to have "fended off encroachment by outsiders for centuries" (Cassagrande 1981, 267). Indeed, their territory, located on the slopes of the Tungurahua Volcano, was for a long time enclosed through the cultivation of *cabuya* (agave) plants, a type of cactus, that served as natural fences. In 1908, the *Salasacas* were even accused of "having allowed the *cabuya* leaves to grow too much" so that *mestizos* and other intruders could not trespass (Choque 1992, 88). When visiting Salasaca, Tungurahua, one of my interviewees—Rufino Masaquiza, a respected *yachak* (local historian or wise man)—reminded me: "In recent years, you would not have been welcome in Salasaca" (Interview, Salasaca, August 2018). In saying that, he pointed to the fact that I am identified as a *mestiza* who would be traditionally seen as an intruder in Salasaca.[8]

In contrast to the majority of Ecuador's native people, the *Salasacas* chose to remain Indigenous by creating an ethnic identity and keeping white and *mestizo* Ecuadorians out. In so doing, their native town "Salasaca" became a zone of "cultural refusal" (Scott 2009, 20) where Indigenous peoples could resist dominant culture and avoid the threat of *mestizaje* (racial mixing) (Corr and Powers 2012). However, in their routine migrations between Salasaca and the Galápagos, the same Salasaca peoples prefer to pass by as *mestizos* as soon as they reach the islands. At present, only a handful wear ethnic attire and speak Kichwa while on the islands. Meanwhile, the younger generations of *Salasacas*, born in the Galápagos, identify themselves as *mestizo* "*galapagueños.*" Regardless, local *mestizos*, like doña Stella, have learned to differentiate people of Indigenous origins as if they themselves had radically different origins.

Human and Nonhumans of the Galápagos

By and large, human history in the Galápagos tends to be silenced, creating space for nonhuman narratives to take their place. These have included the stories of the famous tortoise Lonesome George, the last of his species who did not manage to procreate, and more recently, his opposite: the prolific "Super Diego" who, at present, "is doing his best to save his species." These narratives further help to sustain the project of "remaking nature" (Raffles 2004, 12–20) that, in the Galápagos, means producing a nonhuman "evolutionary Eden," in which conservation not only protects the endangered species from invasive ones, but also their evolutionary history—that is, the purity of their lineages against populations of "impure" and misplaced genetic hybrids (Hennessy 2014).

Named after a US comedian, Solitary George came to be known for his sterile, anthropomorphized "love life." George was found alone in 1971 on Pinta Island. For decades, conservationists made multiple attempts to mate George with morphologically similar species in order to preserve his DNA within the Galápagos tortoise gene pool. However, they all failed. Despite George's initial apparent lack of interest, stories say he finally "hooked up" with three "fine" females from another island (without being able to procreate) and that he "was in love" with a herpetologist who, after many attempts, was the only one who could sexually stimulate him to collect his semen (Constantino 2007, 235–37). The search for a female tortoise "to put the spark back in George's love life" continued after the "beautiful twenty-six-year-old" zoology graduate student, also called "Lonesome George's girlfriend," retuned back to her home country, as George's biographer describes in detail (Nicholls 2007, 17–32). After many failed attempts, one US travel agency advertised George as "the world's oldest living gay turtle" (ibid.). When the tortoise passed away in 2012 before reaching middle age, he was eulogized in *Nature, The Economist,* and the *New York Times.* In a musical memoir, science reporters further wished George to "go and meet your tortoise lady on that island in the sky" (NPR 2015).

Nevertheless, "where George failed, Diego thrived." Diego, also called "the super-macho," "the father," and "the Don Juan" of the Galápagos, became George's opposite after being able to sire more than 800 offspring over the past forty years. He was described as an aggressive tortoise who used to antagonize other tortoises at the San Diego Zoo, but became the "star stud" of the new breeding center of the Galápagos when returned to the archipelago. Super Diego is still, however, considered the second most famous tortoise after George who ultimately came to be a testament to histories of extinction and man's destruction of the natural world.

Figure 0.2. Lonesome George at Puerto Ayora. After being the star of a highly successful exhibition at the American Museum of Natural History in NY, the stuffed body of Lonesome George returned to the Galápagos. Its body is now displayed at the Galápagos National Park and Charles Darwin Station offices in Academy Bay. *Source*: Photo: P. Sánchez, Puerto Ayora (Santa Cruz Island), September 2017.

Meanwhile, few stories are told regarding the human history of the archipelago. An important exception to this rule is the work of Ecuadorian historian Octavio Latorre. His books, however, tend to revolve around the tragedies, mysteries, and crimes in the Galápagos Islands (i.e. *The Curse of the Tortoise* [1992], which, while human, notably does not escape the legend of the tortoise) or a tale of the well-known Manuel Cobos (*Manuel J. Cobos: The Emperor of the Galápagos* [1991]), the *hacienda* owner who is officially recognized as the first colonizer of the archipelago. There are few mentions of the lives of the actual settlers of the Galápagos.

Tourist guides, movies, and documentaries prefer to recall the stories of various idealistic Europeans who unsuccessfully tried to settle on the archipelago. Over and over again, they repeat the stories of an eccentric German doctor with his mistress, and an Austrian baroness and her love triangle, who all fled from civilization to Floreana Island in the period between the two world wars, only to meet a tragic death in the Galápagos. The first legend refers to German doctor Friedrich Ritter—a vegetarian, dentist, philosopher, and disciple of Nietsche and Lao-Tse, who believed that to find one's Eden, one has to escape to live with Nature on an uninhabited island. His devoted girlfriend, Dore Strauch, suffered from multiple sclerosis and was originally his patient. She followed his decision to remove all their teeth in preparation for the trip, and their dreams to escape both their unhappy, childless marriages to live together on the desolate Floreana. After five years on the island and many conflicts with the Baroness, her lovers, and the Wittmer family (a German family who also settled in Floreana), Ritcher died of food poisoning. Before passing away, he cursed Dore, who then left the archipelago. The legend says that she possibly poisoned him.[9]

To the very same Eden arrived the "Baroness," Eloise von-Wagner Bosquet, with two men, one whom she claimed was her husband, and the other, a lover who was twenty years younger. She had a shop in Paris that she sold with the intention of building a luxury hotel for wealthy Americans on the island, but that was never built. Perhaps unsurprisingly, problems arose between the lovers until one day the Baroness and her husband disappeared with some of their belongings. The legend claims that they took a boat that headed to Haiti. Yet there was no record of such a yacht. Some think they were killed by the younger lover, who then hired a Norwegian fisherman to flee the archipelago. But the boat did not escape the Galápagos, reaching only Marchena Island, where the two sailors died of thirst. Except for Dore and the Wittmers, the group of hopeless romantics died in the same year in mysterious ways.

Such stories speak to tourists who connect with the mood of the adventurous European aristocrats discovering the ruggedness of these tropical islands—lost in the Pacific, wild, almost waterless, largely covered by rock, lava, and prehistoric creatures. They also reinforce the idea of the archipelago as a place not fit for human life. In turn, Ecuadorians take pride in these stories because they attest to their holding of a territory that is seemingly white within the limits of their Indian-*mestizo* nation. I suppose that is why whenever I asked about the early presence of Indigenous people on the islands, I was reminded instead of the stories of the Europeans who used to live on Floreana as well as of short-lived colonies of Norwegians and Germans who are thought to be a constituent part of the Santa Cruz Island settler society.

On the other hand, currently locals (both *mestizos* and Indigenous) are hidden from the view of thousands of tourists that visit the Galápagos (Quiroga 2009) as also are the tons of goods they require—which arrive weekly by cargo ships—and the waste they both generate. On average in 2019, more than five thousand tourists visited the Galápagos every week. Thirty thousand people permanently live on the archipelago. In such context, the Kichwa Salasacas are not only invisible but also highly stigmatized within *galapagueño* society. Before arriving in the islands, I read about them being "closed" (reserved) and hostile to strangers. In Quito, I was even warned by one of the scholars who had worked with Indigenous peoples of the central highlands that it would be nearly impossible to get access to either the Salasaca people on the mainland in Tungurahua or to the Salasaca colony in the Galápagos, which was controlled by the Masaquizas. Furthermore, once in Puerto Ayora, Santa Cruz, different *mestizos* told me stories that labeled the *Salasacas* as "savages," "introduced," and even as "aliens" to the national territory because "they are not even Ecuadorians, they're from Bolivia." Someone else, however, clearly stated that "they invaded San Cristóbal [Island] first," before reaching Santa Cruz Island. As such, the *Salasacas* who were traditionally known for being proudly Indigenous and creating a zone of "cultural refusal" in Tungurahua, ended up living in a zone of "cultural invisibility" (Rosaldo 1988) after crossing the borders of Indigenous and *mestizo* identities when migrating to the Galápagos.

The Disappearing *Colono*

Ever since the ratification of the 1998 "Special Law," the old categories that were used to classify people on the archipelago disappeared from the legal framework of the Galápagos. Until then, first settlers and their descendants, born in the Galápagos, were both officially and colloquially called *colonos*. Yet, after the passing of conservation law, they fell into a new category called "permanent residents." The rest are otherwise identified as "temporary residents," "visitors" (*transeúntes),* "tourists," or "illegals"—for those who exceed the official sixty-day visiting period on the islands. In sum, they are all "aliens" on the archipelago.

In this book, I use the term "disappearing *colono*" in two ways. The first emphasizes the removal of a legal category, *"colono,"* which *galapagueños* used to confer respect, recognition, and a bundle of rights to property and citizenship to those who sacrificed their lives, living in precarity and utter isolation, in order to *"hacer patria"* (follow their patriotic duty) by building an Ecuadorian colony in the remote archipelago. The second specifically applies to those *Salasaca* settlers who not only have been removed from the historical memory of the Galápagos, but also continue to disappear from sight by shedding their Indigenous identity, even though they are everywhere to be seen in the islands. By using this approach, I follow Rappaport (2014) when examining race and *mestizaje* in colonial Spanish America. Particularly, in the Galápagos, I try to think through why *Salasacas* are made to disappear when reaching the archipelago, how they fit in within local *mestizo* society, and the specificities by which conservationist classificatory practices emerged and their interplay with local distinctions of race to administer human populations in the Ecuadorian islands.

Between 1959 and 1998, the Galápagos Islands went through a rapid process of change, shifting between different property regimes, from being Ecuadorian state property governed by the *hacienda* regime, to becoming a World Heritage site—a common property of "humanity," ruled under the mandate of science. Science and *hacienda* regimes are nevertheless based on diverse understandings of race, society, and territorial ordering, each rooted in separate colonial legacies that organized social life differently in South and North America.

I will argue that as these systems interact, two acts of translation take place for the governance of settler society in the Galápagos. In the first, foreign scientists and state bureaucrats translate the findings of biology, evolutionary theories, and their own understandings of nature, race, and society to make laws and public policies. In the second, local authorities enforce foreign conservation law after translating it into their own understandings of race and social order. Following Merry (2006), foreign conservation ideas need to be translated in local terms and situated within local contexts of power and meaning in order to be effective. "They need, in other words, to be remade in the vernacular" (ibid, 1). In the Galápagos, this results—on the one hand—in the designation of *all* local inhabitants as "aliens" or intruders to the natural heritage site, the common property of 'humanity.' Moreover, they are stigmatized as the descendants of criminals in need of correction, as Stella complained. Under the category of "residents," the conservation regime further reminds them of their temporary, conditional stay in their homeland.

On the other hand, in the aspiration of both Ecuadorians and *galapagueños* to "whiten" themselves, Indigenous peoples, particularly the *Salasacas* of Santa Cruz, are made to become invisible. They not only suffer from the stigmas of being "primitive," "uncivilized," "predators," and "invaders" of the natural park, but they are also considered "outsiders" of both the Galápagos and the nation of Ecuador for having rejected state-making projects—notably *mestizaje*. The Salasaca newcomers thus became the main target of population controls, which aims to remove locals from the islands through deportation to mainland Ecuador.

I further argue that what underlies the initiative to erase the old district name "Salasaca" on the upperpart of Santa Cruz is the obsessive desire of *mestizo galapagueños* to hide, by all accounts, their own "indianness." Yet, the silencing on the islands of its human history and *mestizo* racism (manifested in self-contempt and concealment or denial of one's own Indigenous past within local families and within society at large), ultimately facilitate the expropriation of governance in a property, which belongs in theory to the citizens of the Galápagos and Ecuador.

Pachamama and Nature in the Galápagos

I first traveled to the Galápagos back in 2008 with my two young children while we were living and studying in the city of Quito, from 2005–2009. We hoped to learn from giant tortoises, endemic fauna, and Darwin's many observations at one of the world's most emblematic natural parks. Yet once there, I was surprised to find that the small village of Puerto Villamil (on Isabela Island) was inhabited by families who seemed to come from the Ecuadorian highlands, and to watch fighting cocks being raised in backyards with pink flamingos and marine iguanas crossing nearby. Then, while in Puerto Ayora, Santa Cruz Island, the large presence of Indigenous peoples, specifically from the Kichwa Salasaca community, was especially intriguing.

Tourists usually imagine the islands to be essentially uninhabited. This belief builds on images of the Galápagos as a site of pristine, pre-human nature, often through propaganda of charismatic megafauna, which is of usually giant tortoises (Ospina 2006); actual material and conceptual landscape transformations to craft a "natural laboratory" on the archipelago (Quiroga 2009, Hennessy 2014); and popular ideas about the Galápagos from science books (Beebe 1924, Grant and Estes 2009), nature documentaries, and tourism propaganda.

Even maps often tend to identify places across the archipelago through the endemic animal species that inhabit them. Such images evoke images of island "edens," Darwin's narratives (Beer 2009 [1983]), and the scientific valuation of the islands' isolation. But by 2008, when I first went to the Galápagos, more than 22,000 people were living on the archipelago. Ten years later, there were nearly 30,000 residents on the islands and around 275,000 tourists visiting every year. Santa Cruz Island, in particular, changed in a short time from a nearly-uninhabited island before the 1960s into the most densely populated one—a change spurred by the designation of the island to headquarter Galápagos National Park (GNP), the Charles Darwin Research Station (CDRS), and the tourism industry on the archipelago in 1959.

In my first visits to the Galápagos Islands, the large presence of Kichwa Salasacas in Santa Cruz and the complete invisibility and denial of the history and presence of Indigenous settlers on the archipelago was what struck me the most.[10] Yet, in those years, the political climate for Indigenous peoples in the mainland drastically changed. In particular, the Indigenous revolts of the 1990s led to the drafting of a new Constitution in 2008, which declared Ecuador as a "plurinational" and a "multicultural" state. Since then, the Salasaca people were recognized as members of the Kichwa nationality, the largest Indigenous nation in Ecuador, whose cosmovisión—summed up by the phrase *Sumak Kawsay* (roughly, "Buen Vivir" or "Good Living")—was meant to usher Ecuador along a new path, away from its long history of extractive and developmental economy (Acosta et al. 2011). With the 2008 Constitution, Ecuador also became the first country to grant legal rights to Nature (*Pachamama* or "Mother Earth"), considering non-human species subjects of rights and intrinsic value (Gudynas 2009). By 2012, the National Judiciary Council further announced the implementation of a pilot judicial court in the Galápagos Islands. Two court units were being implemented to ensure that environmental crimes were "treated at the same level of importance as human right crimes," as described by Ecuador to UNESCO in the 2014 State Report.

In that very same year, I decided to study the effects of the introduction of the Indigenous Kichwa Pachamama within Ecuadorian law and in the Galápagos courts. In particular, I was interested in exploring how Nature would "speak" on the archipelago and the ways the Kichwa communities on the Galápagos, particularly the *Salasacas*, were to be involved.

The islands seemed to be the "obvious place" to display the progressive ideas of the new constitution (Interview, Guayaquil, August 2016).[11] Nevertheless, bringing Andean Indigenous conceptions of Pachamama to the Galápagos referenced at once-contradictory notions of nature: one that indexed Mother Earth as a responsible agent in a collaborative enterprise in which humans and non-humans are mutually involved (Mignolo in Mangan 2002, de la Cadena 2015, Abercrombie 2016), and another that built on the Western distinction between nature and culture that is foundational to science, conservationism, and the discipline of anthropology (Latour 1993, Descola

[2005]). From the Western purview, the conservation regime that has long governed the islands aims to protect and restore the "pristine," "pre-human" habitat—that is, as it was when Darwin had found it.

With the aim of researching the first judicial court to defend the rights of Nature in the Galápagos, I made two preliminary visits to Santa Cruz in the summers of 2015 and 2016. However, following those visits, I could see that the project was more a matter of investigating the good intentions and grandiose dreams of a faction of *mestizo* "indigenist" politicians in Quito, or "ventriloquists" in the words of Guerrero (2003), who continued to act as intermediary spokespeople for Indians in Ecuador.[12] Indeed in the Galápagos, the Kichwa Indigenous collective was never consulted about the possible introduction of the Pachamama rights to the local courts or invited to participate in such reform. When I started fieldwork, four years after the official announcement was made, there were still no courts to address environmental crimes on the islands, nor on mainland Ecuador. Today, the project has been cancelled. Therefore, after I began my research but before I went to the field, both the subject of my research and the Nature court itself had vanished into thin air.

I thus decided to begin by focusing on the recovery of the historical memory of Salasaca first settlers, the *colonos*, of the Galápagos Islands. To that end, I conducted fieldwork in Salasaca, Tungurahua, by contacting the eldest settlers of Santa Cruz Island, who by then had returned to their homeland in the highlands, on the slopes of the Tungurahua. This was enormously facilitated by Martha Chango, Councilor of Salasaca, whom I met through a mutual friend who worked with an Indigenous women's organization in Quito. Between October and December of 2016, and also in August 2018, Martha and her family kindly welcomed me at their home in Salasaca. She further gave me a traditional Salasaca dress to celebrate with them on the Day of the Dead. When I arrived to the Galápagos, knowing Salasaca, Tungurahua, beforehand and, particularly, owning a Salasaca dress were very helpful in giving me access to the Salasaca Association and to Salasaca settlers in Santa Cruz Island.

While in Salasaca, I traveled to Ambato (nearby Salasaca in Tungurahua) and Quito to conduct archival research on the origins of the Salasaca people and the colonization of the Galápagos in the provincial and national archives. Then in the islands, I continued to collect the testimonies of some of the Salasaca settlers and their descendants. I thus arrived at the Salasaca Association and also visited the only intercultural school on the islands, the Runa Kunapak Yachay, which was an initiative of the Salasaca Association to provide education free from racism for children of Indigenous origins on the archipelago.

At that time, without our knowing it, Margarita Masaquiza (the president of the Salasaca Association) and I shared a mutual interest in reconstructing the historical memory of the Salasaca collective on the Galápagos.[13] That was a project which she and several other *colonos* (first settlers) and members of the association (including the first Salasaca town councilor, Jose María Masaquiza) had wanted to carry out for several years. They had asked for support from several mayors for the construction of a Salasaca historical museum in Santa Cruz. Despite their promises, however, the municipality did not include the project in its plans, nor assign any funds to it from its budget.

And so as soon as I arrived in the island, the association members gave me full support for my project. Margarita, in particular, was critical to my research. Margarita was the second Salasaca woman to reach Santa Cruz Island. She was a political activist, a representative and interlocutor of the community in the archipelago, and a facilitator of aid whenever a fellow Salasaca required it. In the third meeting we held, with her and a group of associates, Margarita invited me to help at the association and to assist her in political, social, or family activities. I thus started to work as a volunteer, at nights and during the weekends, for the Salasaca Association. Soon I also volunteered to work as a teacher for the Runa Kunapak elementary school. There on Tuesday and Thursday afternoons, I taught English to children of both Salasaca and *mestizo* origin.

After a couple of months in the archipelago, I became increasingly worried about getting a residency permit so I could remain on the islands for the full term of my field research. As a tourist, I could only legally remain on the islands for 60 days at most. Neither the association, nor the Salasaca school, could process the residency permit in a timely manner. I thus asked the Galápagos National Park to support my research. I imagined that the Park, which had assumed the challenge of governance in order to conserve the archipelago (a concern linked to controlling its human population) would be interested in learning more about one of the most important groups of settlers on Santa Cruz. Yet when I presented my proposal, the official in charge of the matter told me that the Park only endorsed research that would include "the taking of samples, biological research,"—in sum, "scientific data . . . never social studies." I had to look for support elsewhere.

Fortunately, during the following weeks, I found a volunteer, part-time job at the library of the Tomás de Berlanga school. This was the place where children of the conservationists, foreigners, and wealthy families on Santa Cruz tend to study. The volunteer position had been formally posted at the Gálapagos Governing Council so the residence permit could be processed promptly. Thanks to the school director, Justin Scoggin, I was not only able to work as the librarian, but could also stay on the islands until the end of the school year. Unexpectedly, this job allowed me to meet people engaged in the government of the Galápagos who were parents of students, and also U.S. tourists who came by weekly in a scheduled stop-over that the National Geographic cruise (the Endeavour II) makes at Santa Cruz. Some of them visited the library, which is the only one that the archipelago has, and donated books to children of the Tomás school.[14]

From then on, I worked every morning as the school librarian of the Tomás school, twice a week in the afternoon as the English teacher at Runa Kunapak, and at nights and over weekends at the Association. Throughout my fieldwork, I continued to conduct interviews with *Salasacas*—first settlers and recent migrants (the latter are considered "illegals" in the Galápagos because they arrived after the 1998 law). I also interviewed tour guides (who are either *mestizos* or foreigners), biologists working at the Darwin station, and *mestizo* settlers of Puerto Ayora. Finally, I conducted archival research at the Charles Darwin Research Station (CDRS) library. Its collections trace scientific research and the history of conservation management in the Galápagos from 1963 to this day. Memories, field notes, and publications, as well as obituaries, announcements, and social events, could be found in the CDRS flagship yearly publication, *Noticias de Galápagos*. Little by little I went through this collection, which turned into an important source for me to explore the islands from the perspective of mostly-foreign scientists who have studied the archipelago.

Lastly, as part of my study and as a reward for my work in the library, the Tomás de Berlanga school awarded me a free ticket on the Endeavour II. For over a week, I lived on the small cruise ship with a group of US tourists, travelling from island to island, learning about endemic species and theories of evolution while following the footsteps of Darwin. Yet as I traveled, I realized that despite having lived in Puerto Ayora for thirty or forty years, none of the *Salasacas* with whom I shared my time have had access to those emblematic places of the Galápagos National Park that I had the privilege of visiting.

Conservation Law and Racial Politics

This book offers the first historical and anthropological account on the early arrival and prominent presence of Andean Indigenous people in the Galápagos Islands and their relationship with the protected area. In order to understand why the *Salasacas* migrated en masse to the Galápagos and why they were made the target of population controls linked to conservation policy in the archipelago, this book first examines how *galapagueño colono* (first settler) society was made up and the way it is governed. Then, it studies the Salasaca people from their origins in the Andean highlands and along their journeys to the oceanic archipelago. In doing so, the voices of Salasaca settlers on Santa Cruz Island allowed me to examine, in the last chapters, how conservation law is translated and enforced—within local meanings of race—to govern society in the Ecuadorian islands.

The second section of this book brings an ethnographic perspective to the study of conservation law in everyday life. It starts by examining the interplay between science and *hacienda* regimes in order to link two seemingly separate spheres that order society and the natural landscape: conservation work and racial politics. I start by tracing how conservation ideas, which were conceived in the early decades of the 1900s United States, are expressed in both the Charles Darwin Station's mission as well as in the 1998 "Special Law." I examine how the moral discourse and hegemonic rule of conservationism gradually gained local consent, in spite of growing coercive measures imposed over the *galapagueños*. From a legal pluralist approach (Merry 1988, Santos 2002), I further study the way various agents obey and disobey, at once, different legal frameworks (state law, conservation law, and the heritage framework), each carrying contradictory notions about their rights in the archipelago. In turn, as I will show, the passing of conservation law further created a sphere of illegality with extra-legal subjects and practices flourishing in the aftermath of its ratification. I finally trace the way conservationist campaigns trespass the boundaries of the natural park, thus, interacting with alternate understandings of social order in settlement areas. In the interplay between science and *hacienda* regimes, locals resort to the lexicon and rationale of conservation science to designate which categories of humans—or absence thereof—have more rights to the Galápagos archipelago.

NOTES

1. For reasons of confidentiality, in certain cases throughout this book, I changed some of the names of and information about the people I talked with or interviewed.

2. From the Conquest onwards, the Spaniards who arrived in America refused to do manual labor in order to distinguish themselves from the *indios*, who they rendered their servants. This enabled them to depict themselves as aristocrats after they reached the New World (Abercrombie 1996). This contempt for manual labor goes on today as a sign of social status in Latin America.

3. A *mestizo* could be the product of racial mixing (between white Europeans, Creole Indians, and sometimes Africans,) or the product of cultural whitening (*blanqueamiento*), which requires Indigenous peoples to shed ethnic external markers—dress, language, customs—in order to adopt a *mestizo* identity. Although some physical characteristics are associated with Indigenous peoples, the vast majority of Ecuadorians and Andeans exhibit ambiguous phenotypes and identify themselves as *mestizos.*

4. Salasaca is both the name of the Indigenous community and of their native town in the Ecuadorian highlands in Tungurahua.

5. For example, a typical *mestiza* (like Stella) is a brown-skinned person (usually but not always lighter than an Indigenous woman). Another difference may be seen in her hair styles. The *mestiza* may have brown (or colored), curly, and short hair, while the Indigenous women usually have black, long (almost waist-length), lank hair.

6. More than a large estate, the *hacienda* in Ecuador was a property and a racial regime by which the Ecuadorian state delegated the administration of Indigenous populations to *hacienda* owners (Guerrero 2003). In 1832, the recently created republic of Ecuador annexed to its territory the Galápagos Islands.

7. It is estimated that the Salasaca ethnic group consists of twelve thousand people. Three thousand currently live in the Galápagos Islands, while the rest live in the province of Tungurahua of Ecuador's mainland.

8. The *yachak* felt confident with my visit as we were introduced by a mutual friend, a Salasaca leader within the collective.

9. These stories can be found on travel blogs and travel guidebooks of the Galápagos. For an insider's account, see Wittmer [1989].

10. Before starting my fieldwork at the end of 2016, I visited the Galápagos Islands as a tourist in 2008 and 2010, and later as an anthropologist in the summers of 2015 and 2016.

11. From an interview with one of the members of the Constituent Assembly, which drafted the new 2008 Constitution in August 2016.

12. Guerrero (2003, 277) uses the term "ventriloquists" to refer to white *mestizo* citizens of the upper classes who "put the words in the mouths of Indians and down on paper" in Ecuador.

13. I follow Jelin (2003, xv) in understanding the reconstruction of "historical memory" as a process that entails analyzing the presences, silences and meanings of the past. Memories are subjective, the object of disputes, conflicts and struggles, and must be looked at historically.

14. The Charles Darwin Station has a library but only with collections of scientific publications on the Galápagos.

Chapter One

Ecuadorian Colonization

At the beginning of 1832, three years before the young Charles Darwin visited the islands, no humans lived on the Galápagos. Situated 600 miles from the coast of Ecuador, the oceanic archipelago and its fauna evolved without land mammals. Alone with no predators, various species of giant tortoises, flightless cormorants, and iguanas more than five feet long—moving like "veritable dragons" along the island of Baltra (Beebe 2012 [1924], 243)—could evolve. The Galápagos was a no-man's-land.

Since 1535 Charles V, King of Spain, knew of the Galápagos after it was "discovered" by the Spanish priest and Archbishop of Panama, Friar Tomás de Berlanga. Nevertheless, throughout the whole period of Spanish rule (1535–1820s), the King never made an effort to occupy the islands, nor to bring them under the jurisdiction of any of the political-administrative institutions of the colonial government. As such, when the Republic of Ecuador was born in 1830, the archipelago continued to be officially regarded as a land that was *res nullius*—that is, theoretically a thing belonging to no one.

But in reality, this no-man's-land was being disputed by many men. Throughout its human history, diverse human groups used different techniques to claim ownership over the islands, including naming, mapmaking, sea battles, and the intensive extraction of its animal species. It was only through permanent colonization that Ecuador could finally secure possession over the archipelago. Nonetheless to this day, the Ecuadorian sovereignty over the Galápagos still seems fragile, particularly after the islands became a conservation territory in 1959 and the common property of 'humanity' (as per UNESCO in 1978), thus being governed by overlapping systems of law and various notions of race, society, and nature.

In what follows, I intend to start listening to the human pasts that have been silenced in the Galápagos. I examine the actors who have been involved for centuries in the dispute over possession of the islands, paying particular attention to the way the *hacienda* system worked. This property and racial regime became the central device for the recently created government of Ecuador to exercise sovereignty over the Indigenous lands and the population on the mainland, as well as the means to colonize the oceanic archipelago. Then I investigate the process of colonization of the four inhabited islands from 1832 and the moment of their annexation to Ecuador to 1959, in order to understand how first settler (*colono*) *galapagueño* society. was made up when conservationism arrived to the islands. I finally describe how local people created their own labels to identify themselves and to distinguish those who do not belong to the Galápagos. These were backed up by state law until the passing of the 1998 conservation law, which removed these categories to impose new legal ones that reflected Western understandings of nature and property, embedded in the making, use, and governance of heritage sites.

To talk about this silent history is not only useful to make room for human narratives, but also helps to highlight the significance of race in the making of society, history, and heritage in the Galápagos Islands. It further debunks misconceptions that index a white European "discovery" and colonization of the archipelago, that speak of *galapagueño* society as made up of exiled criminals, or that alternatively link *galapagueño* identity to the *mestizo* (mixed race) Ecuadorian coast while concealing the prominent role and presence of Indigenous highlanders in *colono* (settler) society.

NO MAN'S LAND, MANY MEN'S LAND

Pre- Columbian Times

The human history of the Galápagos has been traced back to the time when regional networks of trade were established for the exchange of the sacred *spondylus* (thorny oyster shells) between the peoples living in the coast of Manabí and Santa Elena and the civilizations of Central America.[1] The shells were (and are still) found at a depth of between three and sixty meters on the continental submarine platform, which runs from the Gulf of Guayaquil to that of California. Several studies suggest that the Galápagos must have been used as a common stop on the maritime trade route for the *spondylus*, which were heavily traded by the Valdivia culture that lived on the coast of Ecuador between 3,500 and 1,800 BC.

Vestiges of ancient Indigenous ceramics found in Bahía Ballena (Whale Bay) on the island of Santa Cruz attest to the existence of fishing camps in the Galápagos long before the Spanish Conquest (Heyerdahl and Skjolsvold 1956). However, archaeologists differ on the origins of these ceramics. In the

1950s, the first excavations were carried out in the Galápagos. In his study, Heyerdahl (1956) linked the ceramics to the period corresponding to the Tiwanaku, Chimú, and Inca empires, between 1200 BC to 1535 AD. A decade later, however, Lanning (1969) confirmed the pre-Hispanic and Ecuadorian origin of the ceramics, but differed from Heyerdahl about the period when they were made, estimating instead their origins in 1200–1400 AD.

Modern and ancient fishermen found in Whale Bay a good spot to establish their camps. It was also the place where the first visitors and settlers of Santa Cruz Island dwelt. From there, whaling vessels weighed anchor to hunt sperm whales right in their breeding grounds and in the deepwater-feeding areas to the west of the archipelago. From there too, pre-Columbian fishermen, ship crews, and the first inhabitants of Santa Cruz could move inland in search of the only source of fresh water on the island, which was located in the Santa Rosa district next to what was later known as Salasaca.

According to a group of Peruvian historians, the 'discovery' of the Galápagos actually took place in the travels made by the Incan royal families. They say that around 1465, Tupac Yupanqui (the tenth Inca), ventured to the islands and called them Ninachumbi and Huahuachumbi (Island of Fire and Outer Island in Kichwa). This theory was, however, widely questioned in the dispute regarding the right to sovereignty over the archipelago, which only arose after the wars of independence from Spain (1810–1820) and the emergence of independent republics on the mainland (Villacrés Moscoso 1985). On the basis of the memories of Tupac Yupanqui, Peruvian scholars claimed the right of Perú to sovereignty over the archipelago. Ecuadorian historians instead argued that the islands were earlier discovered by the Manteño Huancavilcas, who were the successors of the Valdivia peoples. What is clear from the archaeological traces found in Santa Cruz Island is that pre-Columbian Indigenous navigators knew and used the Galápagos. These human pasts have been silenced by more powerful narratives that sustain the pre-human, untouched nature of the archipelago, until the 1535 Spanish 'discovery.'

'Discovery' of the Galápagos

The official history tells us that, in 1535, the Spanish priest and Archbishop of Panamá, Friar Tomás de Berlanga, 'discovered' the Galápagos. It happened two years after the execution of the Incan leader Atahualpa (Huayna Capac's son and "the Last Inca"), by order of King Charles V, and in the very midst of a heated dispute over the treasures the Last Inca surrendered to his Spanish executioners. The year before, the King had ordered Berlanga to travel to what is now Perú in order to represent him in an investigation into the distribution of lands, gold pieces, and the *mit'a* tribute (a tax paid in kind through

Indigenous labor) between conquistadors Francisco Pizarro and Diego de Almagro. However, as it began sailing south, Berlanga's ship was dragged off course by the Panamá current, taking him and his crew to the desolate archipelago.When the friar arrived at the islands, he took note of the contents of these new lands, inhabited by massive numbers of "tortoises and *galápagos*," seals, iguanas "that are like serpents," and "birds like those in Spain but so foolish they do not know how to flee," as he soon thereafter reported to the King. At the time, the word "*galápagos*" was used to signal the resemblance between the tortoises' shells and the horse saddles used on the Iberian Peninsula. These were so big that "a man could sit on each one," according to Berlanga in a letter to Charles V on April 26, 1535 (Latorre 1996, 47).

The friar also told the King of their anxieties due to the scarcity of water. He described how, right after arriving at the islands, the thirsty sailors began to desperately dig wells, wishing to find water only to find it "was more bitter than that of the sea." Four days went by and on Palm Sunday (or Passion Sunday), Berlanga officiated the first Mass of the Galápagos and ordered several groups of two or three of his men to find out whether there was some source of fresh water on the land. Finally, he wrote, "it was our Lord who enabled us to find a stream," (ibid). Yet it was clear that drinking water was scarce on the archipelago. Two of his men and ten horses died of thirst that day. In the midst of his frustration and contrasting the islands to the abundance of new lands, water, and gold on the continent, Berlanga concluded this was not a suitable place for human habitation:

> I do not think that there is a place where you could plant a bushel of maize. It would seem that God once rained stones [on the land]. The soil you find here is like slag, it does not serve for anything, it is not even apt for growing a bit of grass (ibid., 48-50).

After six days there, Berlanga resumed his voyage to Perú. A short while later another Spanish vessel, commanded by Captain Diego de Rivadeneira, landed on the archipelago after being driven off course by the strong ocean currents of the Pacific upon departing from the coast of Perú. This time it was the Humboldt Current, which runs in the opposite direction of the Panamá Current. After his visit, Rivadeneira became the first to claim possession of the islands when he asked Prince Philip of Spain, son of Charles V, to grant him a royal grant (*capitulación*) to the land. He never received an answer (Luna Tobar 1997, 35).

It seems that the reputation of the islands as a barren, dry, desolate, and bewitched place protected them from human exploitation for the next couple of centuries. The islands did indeed appear to be under a spell, seeming to float on the sea, occasionally emitting smoke, mysteriously appearing and disappearing in the mist. They were also the scene of frequent shipwrecks and expeditions that met tragic ends (Latorre 2013, 16–18). In the midst of bewitchment, tragedy, and fascination, the Spaniards began to refer to them as the "Enchanted Islands" (Islas Encantadas). For a long time, it was said that several other European navigators futilely searched for them, making the Iberians laugh. They rather preferred to keep them a secret, claiming, "they were but shadows and not real Islands," as William A. Cowley later wrote in his diary in 1684 (Mitchell 2010, 33).

Despite the Spanish Crown's apparent lack of interest, the archipelago appeared on a world map for the first time, thanks to the navigators and cartographers who served the Spanish Catholic monarchs. In 1561, the islands were sketched in an anonymous Spanish manuscript (Latorre 2011, 39). Then in 1569, the Flemish geographer and cartographer Gerardus Mercator drew them on a map. A year later Abraham Ortelius, who was the royal geographer of King Philip II, included them in his Atlas, the *Theatrum Orbis Terrarum*, calling them the "Insulae de los Galopegos." However, in a later edition they bore their other name *"Islas Encantadas"* (Enchanted Islands). During this same period, a third variation can also be found in the chronicles of Cabello de Balboa, who called them the "Orphaned Islands" (Islas Huérfanas), since "they have not had a father to save them" (Luna Tobar 1997, 309).

The British surveyed the archipelago at the end of the following century, in 1684. Two Britons by the name of William arrived that year: Dampier, the famous "pirate naturalist," was responsible for the first published record of the flora and fauna of the Galápagos, while Cowley drew a more detailed map of the archipelago, giving new names to each of its islands. For example, he named "Quitasueños" (now known as Pinta) after Count Abington, "Santa Isabel" (now Isabela) after the Duke of Albemarle; "San Bartolomé" (or Carenero Island, now Santiago) after Earl of Abingdon; "Nuestra Señora de la Esperanza" (now Santa Cruz or Indefatigable Island) after the Duke of Norfolk; and in honor of his King, "Santa María de l'Aguada" (or "Salud," now known as Floreana) was renamed King Charles Island. More names would come after their annexation to Ecuador in 1832.

Appropriating the Galápagos

For Europeans, drawing the new territories, giving them names, and describing the contents of its lands were essential devices in the project of knowing the world and appropriating it (Pratt 2008 [1992]). Through travel and travel writing, they further constructed a "Eurocentered planetary consciousness" (ibid., 15–36). Travelers used maps and letters to speak of the fauna and flora of the Galápagos to different monarchs, thus revealing an ongoing dispute between different European powers over the control of this "no-man's-land." Tellingly, Spanish, English, Dutch, and French names overlapped on the islands as travelers traversed their waters, as can be further seen in subsequent records, like Guedeville's map (1716) and Vicente Fuerte's chart (1744).[2] Rumors and actual battles between English and Dutch corsairs and the Spanish Catholic navigators also played a role for some centuries.[3] Nevertheless by the early 1800s, the wars of independence in mainland diverted the attention of the Spanish king away from the archipelago.After their annexation to Ecuador, the Spanish creole elite renamed the Galápagos Islands again. They did so following the Spanish tradition by which naming not only served as a declaration of possession of the lands but also worked well to convert in an instant the new landlords into Catholic patron saints. For example, San Cristóbal Island (formerly called by the English after Earl of Chatham) came to be temporarily known as Santa Mercedes in honor of the wife of Flores, the first president of Ecuador. Likewise, what is now Isla Pinzón (or Duncan Island) was named Santa Ana, after the daughter of General Villamil, the first who tried to colonize the archipelago. In turn, King Charles Island became "San Carlos" in a local translation that, for a short time, also consecrated the English king.[4] Later, in 1892, to the Ecuadorian state, the Galápagos became officially known as "Archipiélago de Colón" (Columbus Archipelago). By this time, the islands of San Cristóbal (or Chatham) and Isabela (or Albermarle) had permanent human settlements. Some decades later, Santa Cruz (or Indefatigable) was colonized, eventually becoming the center of tourism and conservation and the most populated island in the whole archipelago.

In the end, human colonization was the only way by which Ecuador could ensure, after 1832, effective possession of the Galápagos. Nevertheless, the recently created republic could not enforce effective rules of restraint on access to and use of the islands. Therefore, for almost a century, the state property continued to be treated as a common pool resource by different actors.

To this day, disputes over the rights to the property are somehow reflected in maps, texts, cruise itineraries, and naturalist guides, which continue to alternate the different names of the islands—mainly, the ones that Ecuador gave to them in the 1800s and the ones given by the English buccaneer two centuries earlier.

An Open Space: Whalers, Aristocrats and Naturalists (1790s–1920s)

By the turn of the nineteenth century, the extractive use of the islands intensified with whalers and collectors capturing and slaughtering immense amounts of the Galápagos' specimens. Be it for industrial or scientific purposes, the exploitation continued long after the archipelago became state property of the nascent state of Ecuador. At the same time, the circuits of global capital started to redefine the value of Nature on the archipelago. They first turned its fauna into valuable objects for animal collectors of northern Europe and the United States. They then gradually transformed popular imaginations of the Galápagos as a cursed wasteland into images of a pristine, pre-human Nature, an edenic place to learn about science and evolution (Quiroga 2009, Hennessy and McCleary 2011).

Whalers arrived in the Galápagos late in the 1790s. Early expeditions to the Pacific started with six Nantucket whalers sailing to look for places to hunt after the drastic reduction of whale populations in the Atlantic. The British Admiralty followed, sending Captain James Colnett to explore opportunities further south. When arriving in the Galápagos in 1793, the captain was "charmed" with the abundance of sperm whales and fur seals (Whitehead 1985, 18). Once there, he prepared an updated chart of the islands and proceeded to rename them again.[5]

During the following decades, the islands turned into a central hub for the whaling industry with vessels coming from the US, Britain, France, and other countries. This lasted until the discovery, in 1819, of rich whaling ground to the northwest of Japan. Through that period the frequent expeditions turned the waters of Galápagos into a common-pool resource, open for the exploitation of whomever gained access, just as in Hardin's (1968) tragic prophecy. In only fifty years, "the enormous amounts" of whales that Colnett described were not there: *"almost none were seen anymore,"* as recorded in the logs of that period (Whitehead 1985, 19-21). Nevertheless, whalers continued their hunts up to the 1920s.[6]

The same industry was also responsible for the slaughter of more than 100,000 tortoises in the Galápagos. In just seven years (1861–1868), the logs of seventy-nine US whalers record 189 visits to the archipelago with 13,000 tortoises caught (Epler 1987). During that boom, every ship caught between 200 and 300 tortoises in each inlet. The giant animals were indeed very convenient for transport, capable of living for more than a year without eating or drinking. And, as U.S. Captain David Porter remarked, "when you kill them after that period, the flavor of their meat is greatly improved" (Grenier 2007, 78). Yet just in case food would become scarce, Porter let loose the first two goats on the islands in 1813.

In parallel to the whaling boom, the archipelago began to interest the men of science. By the end of 1780s, Catholic monarchs commissioned the Italian Alessandro Malaspina to pursue a five-year maritime scientific exploration. It is thought that the Galápagos Islands lay on his route. However, Malaspina's account of his visit to the archipelago is lost.[7] Soon after, a number of aristocrats and scientists of northern Europe followed. In 1795, Scottish naturalist Archibald Menzies arrived on board the *Discovery*. Later in 1824, the botanists

David Douglas and John Scouler went to investigate the flora of the Galá-
pagos. They found it very disappointing. Nevertheless, the abundance and
interesting nature of the animals compensated for the scarcity of plants.
Two months later George Anson, who had recently received the title of Lord
Byron, also visited the archipelago. Anson was sailing the *Blonde* towards
Hawaii in order to repatriate the corpses of the king and queen of Hawaii,
who had died on a state visit to his native England. During his stay in the
Galápagos, the English milord wrote:

> The place is like a new creation. The birds and beasts do not get out of our way;
> the pelicans and sea-lions look in our faces us as if we had no right to intrude on
> their solitude; the small birds are so tame that they hop upon our feet; and all this
> amidst volcanoes which are burning around us on either hand (Larson 2001, 57).

In the following decade, the Galápagos were annexed by the recently created Republic of Ecuador (in 1832) and visited by the most famous naturalist
in history, Charles Darwin (in 1835) on board of Her Majesty's Ship *Beagle*.
During his visit, what Darwin found "most striking" was: "to be surrounded
by new birds, new reptiles, new shells, new insects, new plants" (Darwin
2013 [1839], 398). He further noted:

> Most of the organic productions are aboriginal creations, found nowhere else;
> there is even a difference between the inhabitants of the different islands; yet all
> show a marked relationship with those of America, though separated from that
> continent by an open space of ocean, between 500 and 600 miles in width . . .
> Seeing every height crowned with its crater, and the boundaries of most of the
> lava-streams still distinct, we are led to believe that within a period geologically
> recent the unbroken ocean was here spread out. Hence, both in space and time,
> we seem to be brought near to that great fact—that mystery of mysteries—the
> first appearances of new beings on this earth (Darwin 2013 [1839], 222).

Indeed, as the work in the field of biogeography later showed (Mac Arthur
et al. 1967), the isolation and the relative absence of competitor and predator
species allow for unique evolutionary adaptations: the creation of new species. Oceanic archipelagos are therefore privileged places to observe evolutionary processes and examples of allopatric speciation. Yet the Galápagos
were unique. More than a "showcase of evolution" (UNESCO), they were the
site where Darwin discovered it.[8]

After Darwin's publication of *On the Origin of Species* in 1859, the Galápagos became a favorite place for collectors of northern Europe and the United
States.[9] World-renowned philanthropists, particularly Lord Rothschild—
followed by Vincent Astor and the Vanderbilts—supported numerous scientific trips to collect tortoises and other specimens. "Sav[ing] them for science"

before they went extinct, Lord Walter Rothschild (1983, 171) commented, reflecting the overall reasoning behind the natural history collector's quest and later, the purpose of conservationism. And so in 1901, the Lord hired Rollo Beck to visit the islands and bring back live and dead giant tortoises for him. Beck later returned in 1905–1906, leading the California Academy of Sciences' expedition that stayed for more than one year, gathering the largest collection taken from the islands with more than seventy-six thousand specimens.[10] Most of the Galápagos' dead animals ended up in the collections of the Royal Society, the Zoological Society of London, the British Museum, the Smithsonian Institute, Harvard University, and Stanford University.[11] Some others were sent alive to zoos in London, San Diego, and New York.

Meanwhile, from the coast of San Cristóbal Island, a couple of lonely state guards in charge of the *hacienda* workers watched the looting of the Galápagos specimens. In 1898, one of the guards denounced that the *Leander* and the *Whailen* took "in an unspecified amount" of tortoises and fur seals from Floreana Island (Latorre 1991, 34). He could not do anything but watch. With him were the Indigenous laborers who were part of the *hacienda*. Their presence was what ultimately allowed for the first shift in property regimes, transforming the Galápagos Islands from being a "no-man's-land" (*res nullius*) into becoming an Ecuadorian state property.

LAW, RACE, AND PROPERTY IN ECUADOR

It is often said that the earliest colonizers of the Galápagos were delinquents and convicted criminals exiled from Ecuador. In reality, most of them were actually Indigenous laborers who, prior to their arrival to the islands and since the 1830s, had been imprisoned for debts in *haciendas* located in the central *sierra* (highlands) of Ecuador's mainland. This could only take place under the *hacienda* regime (1832–1964), a racialized property system that reflected old Spanish colonial hierarchies and continue to inform social relations in present-day Ecuador. The arrival of conservationism to the archipelago later imposed another system of race on the Galápagos, based on Anglo-Saxon orderings. Today both visions of race interact on the islands in the administration of human populations.

Under Spanish Rule

Under Spanish colonial rule, the criteria of difference between "Indians" (Indigenous peoples) and Spaniards had to be solved in a way that allowed for the incorporation of natives with the objective of rendering them dutiful subjects, tolerable Christians, and forced laborers. While the English wanted Indigenous lands—but not subjects—in North America, the Spaniards needed "vassals," as the Spanish Crown officially declared them in 1542. In such context, questions regarding the humanity of Indians and their capacity for civilization were the center of heated debates in Spain that, for centuries, revolved around how natives should be treated in the New World.[12] If natives were fully human (for Spaniards, that is capable of Christianity), then enslavement or some other system of tutelary domination to give them the Catholic faith, such as the *encomienda*, would be wholly justifiable (Seed 1993, 640).[13] Conquistadors thus quickly agreed that although Indians were barbaric and idolatrous infidels, they did not have to be exterminated, but rather enslaved in order to be Christianized and be saved from hell.[14]

Just after a new territory was conquered, the Spanish king divided and handed out parcels of land and whole groups of Indigenous peoples, as property, among the conquistadors through legal means: the so-called *encomiendas* (labor grants) and *mercedes de tierra* (land grants).[15] In so doing, the crown granted the Spanish *encomenderos* the right to fully appropriate Indigenous lands and labor while collecting tributes among their subject populations. During the centuries that followed, land dispossession became fully institutionalized through legal instruments by which colonial officials constantly surveyed and expropriated the lands that belonged to the *ayllus* (sub-town units of Indigenous social organization), only to be sold to the highest Spanish bidders.[16]

At the same time, several royal decrees put in place a systematic process of redistribution of native peoples (*repartimientos de indios*) that involved the constant dissolution of communities and *ayllus* (Kolata 2013) whose members were arbitrarily assorted to various towns and municipalities and, particularly in Ecuador, across different *haciendas* (large estates) and textile mills (*obrajes*). Such process was enforced through the *perpetua reducción* of natives (literally, perpetual reduction, as missionaries called it) who were reduced and concentrated in the newly founded towns where they could be controlled, converted to Christianity, and acculturated into the Spanish 'civilized' way of life (*buena policía*) (Nader 1993). At the same time, their constant relocation allowed newcomers to occupy their lands while enabling the Spanish administrators to assert that when a settlement moved, its ancestral rights to the territory had expired (Herzog 2013). Moreover, officials wrongfully argued that during the Inca rule, Indians did not have property rights but only usage rights over the lands because they had long been engaged in massive population transfers.[17] By the end of such a process, the periodic inspection of lands (*composiciones*) became the most powerful instrument of native dispossession, while Indigenous peoples transformed from being the bearers of ancestral rights to being 'vassals' of the Catholic monarchs.[18]

The relocation of Indigenous peoples continued during the republican years. Land and labor grants were then given to "master citizens" (Guerrero 2003). Natives were constantly displaced and relegated to servitude in *haciendas,* textile mills, mines, towns, and households. They further became a constituent part of the landlord's private property. In such context, the Indigenous person came to be construed as linked to serfdom, to subsistence production, and as collective agents and holders of communal lands in the countryside who lacked autonomous judgment needed to make contracts or hold private property.[19] In contrast, Spaniards and later creoles (*criollos*), ascribed themselves as full citizens and 'moderns' (Latour 1993), civilizing agents in the Indies, and later as "whites" (as colloquially called), regardless of their skin color or mixed ancestry. [20]

In many ways, the colonial mindset of the Spaniards was different to the English one. For the Spaniards, natives were subjects and vassals. They thus became insiders of colonial society, although in the role of laborers, domestics, or field hands. In such a world, mixing came to be a routine recurrence—and could further result not only from sexual encounters but also from other sorts of activities. Social relations were thus to be informed not only by biological differences but, more importantly, by symbolic distinctions that relied on the choices of hybrid (*mestizos* of mixed race) individuals who could often navigate across different identities, eluding classificatory practices, and therefore defying the very nature of categorization itself (Rappaport 2014).

In contrast, natives in North America were never considered subjects of the English Crown (Seed 1993, 551). They were rather seen as outsiders, who had to be displaced and enclosed in reserves where they could be sovereign. As per the English logic, racial hierarchies were to be defined by skin color and blood, with natives being treated as 'aliens' in their homeland or, until 1924, as citizens of a foreign nation. These two rationales—the Spanish and the English logic—overlap in the Galápagos, as the case of the Indigenous *Salasacas* illustrate in the following chapters.

The Ecuadorian Hacienda

Permanent human settlements in the Galápagos could be established through the transplantation of the Ecuadorian *hacienda* system to the archipelago. The first colonies, in San Cristóbal and Isabela Islands, are, however, remembered as penal colonies. Furthermore, the Indigenous origins of the earliest colonizers have been completely silenced in the human history of the Galápagos. How did these groups of natives end up imprisoned and exiled to the Galápagos?

The *hacienda* system emerged in the years that followed the Independence of Ecuador in 1830. At the time, the creole elite (descendants of the Spanish conquistadors and the emerging creole rulers), together with members of the military and the Catholic Church, were negotiating the terms for governing the newborn republic. The three agreed that the *hacienda* regime would allow them to transfer the property of the Spanish Crown and the *encomenderos* (recipients of Indigenous labor grants) to the Ecuadorian state and the new landlord elite. Before long, the 500 *encomiendas* by which the territory and native people had been divided during colonizing took the form of *haciendas* within the republic.

There thus arose a class of landlords who owned big estates (*haciendas*) and textile mills (*obrajes*) and their opposite class: Indigenous laborers who were forced to work for a lifetime, attached to the property of said landlords. These two constitutive poles of such a caste system, the landlords and the Indigenous laborers, were the main characters in the earliest colonization of the archipelago that took place in San Cristóbal and Isabela Islands.

The Landlords

The new landlord elite was made up of full citizens of the republic, *"patrones ciudadanos"* ("master citizens" in Guerrero's (2003) words) who held all the positions of power—from their estates to the congress—including ministries and the presidency of the nation. At their *haciendas,* they were supposed to make the lands productive. Yet "rather than investing in machinery they retained as *pongos* (door keepers) the very same Indians who had formerly held the lands" (Abercrombie 1998, 494). The landlords were also in charge of civilizing the Indians, securing their reproduction, providing protection, and administering a species of justice (Guerrero 2003, 285). This often led them to interfere in the personal and domestic lives of their laborers and their families, and to preside over the Indigenous rituals their underlings celebrated.

Generation after generation, *hacienda* owners inherited that power and took turns holding offices in the government, acting as fathers of the nation and representatives or "ventriloquists" of the Indians whom they exploited (ibid., 277). Along the way, they adopted the aristocratic manner of their predecessors, which they believed their new status entitled them to—a posture of moral authority, a distant air, and the attribution of the rents produced by the labor of *indios* combined with disdain for manual work.

With the advent of the republic, measures to increase the state revenue as well as to enlarge the new landowning class patrimony were taken. On one hand, political discourse evolved, adopting a more progressive tone with the assimilation of modern economic theories.[21] On the other hand, state commissioners continued to survey the lands in order to list all those which were not yet recorded as private property. In the absence of title deeds, Indigenous lands continued to be expropriated, communal lands were often broken up, and the 'remains,' as it were— all of the *ejidos* (common grazing lands) owned by the colonial municipalities and Indigenous communities were auctioned off to the highest bidder.

As a result, during the republican era, the Indigenous population was further impoverished, driving most of those who were not yet under the tutelage of a "master citizen" into a desperate situation that forced them to ascribe to *haciendas* through debt peonage in order to survive. At the same time, it favored a stronger concentration of landownership, an increase in the available workforce, and ever-harsher conditions in the labor market (Guarisco 1995).[22] Fleeing to cities began to become a more feasible option only with the decline of the *hacienda* in the 1960s and with the progressive urbanization of Ecuador (which remained predominantly rural until the end of the 1980s).

Indigenous Laborers: Concertaje and Debt Peonage

From 1601 to 1918, the labor market in Ecuador was organized to control Indigenous manpower through a multitude of coercive mechanisms, starting with the *concertaje* (roughly, the willing agreement of the Indians).[23] In theory, the *concertaje* was a system of free and voluntary employment in exchange for a wage. In practice, it was rather a system of contracted debt which held Indian laborers (*conciertos*) attached to an *hacienda* under the threat of customary corporal punishment and prison. Indigenous workers were usually recruited by force, obliged to work endless hours, and subjected to the accumulation of debts to their bosses, which were impossible to pay and bequeathed to their children. In exchange for their labor, *conciertos* received access to a small plot of land called a *chacra*.

The impoverished Indigenous person was therefore bound to become a *concierto*, either as a *huasipunguero* (who lived with his family on a *chacra* of the *hacienda*), as a *peon* (a day laborer who might receive a higher wage but had no access to a parcel of land), or as a worker at textile mills or markets.[24] Meanwhile, they acquired a series of obligations that shackled them and their children for life to the landlord and to the *hacienda* system. Many of these debts were pecuniary in nature. For instance, Indigenous people turned to their landlords when they were in need of *suplidos* (advances in money or kind), *suplementos* (products like grains), and *socorros* of different sorts like food; cash payments for the ritual festivities of Corpus Christi, *Finados* (All

Souls' Day, or the Day of the Dead), Christmas, and San José; and textiles that were particularly important for *Finados* (Ibarra 1987, 85).[25] In the end, the *concierto* debts increased the valuation and market price of a *hacienda*, serving as a kind of added value to the property itself.

In order to meet their debt obligations to a landlord, both laborers and *huasipungueros* had to take on work at one or several jobs outside of the hacienda. Yet their mobility was regulated by laws that could sanction landlords who employed workers that had deserted other *haciendas*, or who were accused of trying to "seduce" *conciertos* from other *haciendas* to work for them. Until the mid-1900s, Indigenous *conciertos* in Ecuador wound up being regularly "reduced" to jails cells, causing a swelling in the ranks of those in the republic's jails. The Chief of Police of Ambato wrote of the following case in 1880:

> It sometimes happens that an individual, who has agreed to become a *concierto* or committed his personal work to serve on a *hacienda*, then commits himself to another person, for example, to carry goods from the coast. Since he has not complied with his obligations, the contractor sues for damages and the *concierto* is *reducido* to prison, due to the fact that he did not fulfill his first commitment and the owner of the estate where he was obliged to work suffered the consequences (ibid., 89).

As was stipulated in the Civil and Penal Codes, *conciertos* had to work facing the constant threat of being imprisoned or punished.[26] Alternatively, if the *concierto* fled to the urban centers and could not find a job, he could be sanctioned by laws against begging and vagrancy. Most of the natives in Ecuador therefore ended up ultimately locked in *haciendas*, *obrajes,* and Spanish households.

By the second half of the nineteenth century, the *haciendas*, public works programs, and agricultural sector of the coast increased the demand for the labor of Indigenous *conciertos* from the highlands. Concurrently, the *hacienda* landlords who were looking to colonize the Galápagos were actively recruiting *conciertos* who would be exiled and condemned to forced labor in the remote archipelago. The labor system was set up in order to meet the landlords' needs through the work of Indigenous laborers who had been linked to a private property and remained there, in perpetual debt. On the other hand, during this same period, several natural disasters hit the central highlands—particularly the Tungurahua province. The demand for labor on the Ecuadorian coast and in the Galápagos Islands was therefore met particularly by Indigenous peoples of the central highlands who were readily available—as debt prisoners or after being displaced.

COLONIZING THE GALÁPAGOS ISLANDS

The Possession Act (1832)

Five years before Darwin reached the Galápagos Islands, the Republic of Ecuador arose. Juan José Flores, the first president of Ecuador, was a Spanish *creole* who came from an aristocratic family and had distinguished himself in independence battles. Yet achieving the independence of the territory had come at a high cost. In 1830, the newborn Ecuador was saddled with a foreign debt of more than 1.4 million pounds to Great Britain, lent to support its revolutionary cause. Bankrupt and in crisis, Flores had to gain the trust of the nation's new citizens by constructing a much-needed sense of "imagined community" (Anderson 1983). Bringing the new Ecuadorians good news would particularly suit this interest.

In those years, General José de Villamil convinced President Flores to take possession of the ownerless archipelago. Villamil was a native of New Orleans, but moved to the Ecuadorian Pacific coast city of Guayaquil in 1811 to pursue his business ventures. During the 1820s, he became a founding father of the independence of the so-called Southern District, and a close advisor of the first president.[27] As Villamil saw it, colonization of the Galápagos could be pursued with soldiers who had rebelled against Flores. Exiling them to the remote islands and condemning them to forced labor could spare the rebels a death sentence on the continent. In the archipelago, they could work for Villamil in the production of a red dye from the orchil lichen that grew there. The proposal reached a receptive audience. For Flores and his allies, it was the perfect opportunity to deal with several urgent matters: first, effectively and permanently colonize the new territory—that is, in *corpus* (body) and *animus* (with heart)—in order to claim Ecuadorian sovereignty; second, to cast away the enemies of the first Ecuadorian president while bringing a mood of victory to the new citizens.

The government wasted no time in announcing the annexation of the Galápagos. In February of 1832, to formalize the possession, Colonel Juan Ignacio Hernández reached King Charles (San Carlos, later, Floreana) Island aboard the schooner *Mercedes,* accompanied by Villamil and his partners, the Chaplain Eugenio Ortiz and a first group of eight poor exiles. Soon after, they all celebrated Mass, raised the flag of the new republic, and thus the general proclaimed the islands as belonging to Ecuador, praising the Ecuadorian governance for "bringing the light of society [civilization] to shine for the first time in that fertile territory" (Luna Tobar 1997, 65).[28] A year later, another eighty-eight unfortunate soldiers joined, trying to become the first permanent colonists in the Galápagos. They were followed by a further two hundred, recruited by Villamil himself at different times whenever he returned to the

mainland. Among them were some artisans and laborers who had been imprisoned for debt in the highlands, more opponents to the government, as well
as prostitutes, criminals, and vagrants arrested on the streets of Guayaquil.

As a result, by 1835, the population of Floreana had risen to more than
300. Most were "people of color, who have been banished for political crimes
from the Republic of Equator," as Darwin reported in a little-known diary entry when he visited the archipelago (Darwin 2013 [1839], 220). Yet Villamil's
business venture and that first attempt to colonize the Galápagos failed within
a short time. Neither the orchil dye enterprise nor his efforts to sell beef fat
and meat to the whalers worked. Nor was he able to convince ship captains to
pay a tax for sailing the waters of Ecuador. In the midst of isolation, financial
ruin, and a lack of fresh drinking water, Villamil abandoned the island and
left his workers.[29] Some years later, when Villamil returned to Floreana, he
found that barely eighty people remained. He managed to convince a few of
them to move to San Cristóbal Island with the idea of starting a new venture
there. However, most of them preferred to return to the mainland. In addition
to this, the general soon started to face new challenges. He was appointed as
Ecuador's ambassador to the United States in 1853 with the mission of leasing the islands to US investors. Meanwhile in the Galápagos, fewer than forty
habitants remained on San Cristóbal Island.

To be fair, the colonel, the chaplain, and the Spanish *vecino* (full master
citizen— Villamil in this case) had tried to be faithful to the traditional ritual
by which the Spaniards founded thousands of cities and towns on the continent in the colonial era. Along with the seedbed of soldier colonists, the key
agents were there, representing the army, the clergy, and the state, each playing their part in the act of possession of the new territory. A Mass was held,
the flag was raised, and the lands where the first colony would be established
were distributed between the 'respectable' citizens. Yet a critical piece was
missing in this act of possession: the large numbers of Indigenous people
that the Spanish (and their descendants, the *criollos*) needed in order to put
together functioning *haciendas*, create public infrastructure, and do the hard,
manual labor needed to build new towns and cities.

The Earliest Colonizers

Despite General Villamil's failure, transplanting the *hacienda* to the Galápagos seemed like the natural way to colonize and exert sovereignty over the
recently annexed territory. So by the end of the 1860s, the Ecuadorian state
tried again. On Floreana, the Spaniard José Valdizán founded his *hacienda*
with a labor force of almost a hundred men for enlarging the grazing fields
and boosting the production of beef on the estate (Latorre 2013, 64). Valdizán

also extended his productive enterprises to other islands, mainly for the extraction of orchil dye and the production of tortoise oil.

This time most of Valdizán's group were *conciertos* from the highlands—many of them facing imprisonment for their debts in *haciendas* and *obrajes* (textile mills). A few years later, he added to the group some criminals taken from the jails in Guayaquil (Grenier 2007, 84). The population of the island thus reached more than 150 people. However, there was a marked hostility between the highland workers and the convicts. While the former had been described as hospitable and hardworking, the latter were resentful about being forced to live an orderly life and felt trapped in the middle of the ocean (Latorre 2013, 61–70). After working there for eight years, a group of convicts rebelled and killed Valdizán. Don José's naive hope that he would redeem such criminals by mixing them with honest workers is explained as the reason for the failure of Ecuador's second attempt to colonize the Galápagos. By 1880, according to the log of the British ship *Triumph,* Floreana was completely deserted. Meanwhile, thousands of heads of cattle freely roamed all over the island, although many were later decimated by wild dogs.

Yet a hundred of Valdizán's laborers did remain on the archipelago, moving to San Cristóbal after arranging work with a different *patrón*: Manuel J.

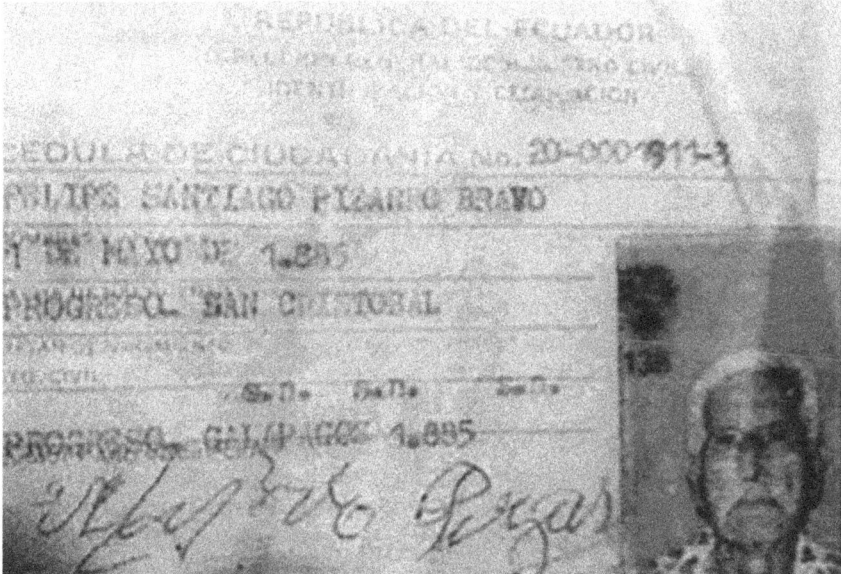

Figure 1.1.   First generations of native *galapagueños*. For example, don Felipe was born on May 1, 1885, in hacienda El Progreso. The Pizarro Bravo family is thus acknowledged as *colonos* in San Cristóbal Island. *Source:* Photo provided by his granddaughter: Evelin García Pizarro.

Cobos, who had recently settled in this island to pursue a new *hacienda* enterprise (Bognoly and Espinoza 1905, 87). Additional laborers came after—mostly Indigenous people from rural Tungurahua who had been recruited by Cobos (Latorre 2011, 223). Two decades later, in the late 1890s, Antonio Gil also arrived to likewise found a *hacienda* on Isabela Island. Nevertheless, colonization of the archipelago only truly prospered through Cobos's *hacienda* on San Cristóbal Island. The first generations of native *galapagueños* were born in those decades, at hacienda El Progreso.

San Cristóbal Island

Manuel J. Cobos, owner of the hacienda El Progreso in San Cristóbal Island, is credited for the colonization of the Galápagos. Cobos is described as "a capable and responsible citizen," and an entrepreneur of boundless energy with a strong wish to make a fortune and a sound sense of how to exploit any business opportunity—be it legal or illegal. At the same time, he was known as the "tyrant Cobos" due to his lack of ethics, cruelty, and indifference to human suffering (Latorre 1991, 25).Before reaching the archipelago, Cobos had already amassed a large fortune with the products he exported from the archipelago (like the orchil lichen, hides, fish and tortoise oil). [30] He had also pursued businesses with a partner in Baja, California, taking with him nearly 300 Indigenous laborers from the Ecuadorian highlands to Mexico.[31] Yet Cobos was not a regular businessman. He was charged with several crimes, especially for being the owner of the hacienda El Progreso at a time when he proclaimed himself the "emperor of the Galápagos." During that time, the landlord shot five laborers to death, ordered another six to be whipped to death, and exiled fifteen men to desolate islands where they died of hunger (Bognoly and Espinosa 1905, 96). Among the frequent crimes Cobos committed on the islands were rapes of women—married or single—and pre-pubescent girls (Latorre 1991, 61).

Some of the first workers recruited by Cobos were, in fact, delinquents and criminals. In doing so, Cobos honored an agreement he had made with prison authorities to secretly transport a group of urban delinquents, rural rustlers, unemployed foreigners, and street children who were tricked into traveling with them.[32] The idea was that forced labor on the islands would turn them into model citizens. However, the censuses completed during the time the hacienda El Progreso was in operation show that the illegal prisoners were actually a minority of the earliest settlers in the archipelago. This is clear in the 1886 census, which only listed six prisoners (*confinados*) among the 200 inhabitants of San Cristóbal Island.

In reality, the large majority of San Cristóbal colonizers were Indigenous day laborers and *hacienda* laborers, or "*indios conciertos*" (59 percent), who had been imprisoned for debt (Latorre 2013, 83) in the highlands of Ecuador. Cobos enlisted them to work for *El Progreso* after buying their debts from other landlords. Some others were artisans and the rest were independent employees or government officials (Guevara 2015). By 1891, the census listed all of the inhabitants of the island as *conciertos*. Most of them were men.

Those nearly thirty years of tyranny bore their fruits. The dignitaries who visited the island (for example, Alex Mann in 1910 and Nicolás Martínez in 1911), agreed on an estimate of an annual production of 500 tons of sugar, as well as to large amounts of *aguardiente* and rum which were distilled from the sugar. To transport the sugarcane, the Cobos' empire counted on a system of roads that were several miles long and a railway which ran through the estates of El Progreso. In a parallel venture, Cobos maintained a permanent staff of workers (*aceiteros*) who extracted oil from sea lions, marine turtles, Galápagos sharks, iguanas, codfish, and even whales. He also established an inter-island network of workers for the extraction of lime, orchil dye, timber, and sulfur. He owned up to fourteen thousand heads of cattle on San Cristóbal alone and grew *yuca*, plantains, potatoes, maize, beans, vegetables, and coffee—the latter on plantations of more than ten thousand acres. Finally, by the 1890s, he introduced agave (or century) plants, known in Spanish as *cabuya blanca,* to build natural fences across the *hacienda*. He entrusted this task to a group of laborers who were *Salasacas*.

Early in 1904, the decline of Cobos's kingdom began. In that year, a group of ten laborers rebelled and murdered the landlord. In accordance with their plans, they quickly destroyed the accounting books and finally freed themselves from the debts which bound them to the *hacienda*. They also emptied the barrels of *aguardiente* there in order to avoid any kind of excesses. The group then fled to the mainland in a sloop which followed the wind until it reached the Colombian port of Tumaco. But lacking money and contacts, the fugitives from the Galápagos could not go into hiding and were imprisoned and deported back to Ecuador. When they reached Guayaquil, more than eight thousand persons waited on the waterfront to watch the protagonists of what would become one of the most famous trials in Ecuador. Two men were sentenced to death while the others involved were found innocent.

With a revolver tucked into his belt, Cobos had created a *hacienda* which transplanted a model of property with its two opposing classes: that of the landowners (of Spanish descent) and that of the Indigenous workers. Yet in contrast to the mainland, the *hacienda galapagueña* did not arise from the appropriation of Indigenous communal lands, but from the appropriation of a property which, until then, belonged to no one. It did replicate, however, the vision of race and system of debt peonage that thrived in the highlands. In the islands, the Indigenous laborers were nevertheless deprived of the produce they grew in their *chacras* (food plots). The isolation and the absolute dependence of the officials of the national government on Cobos explain the excessive cruelty reached at *El Progreso*.[33]

Isabela Island

In Isabela Island, the laborers recruited by Antonio Gil for his *hacienda*, Santo Tomás (1870–1935) found better luck, given that the working conditions were better than those of their counterparts at El Progreso in San Cristóbal.[34] The second landlord of the Galápagos forcibly recruited most of his *conciertos* on the streets in Guayaquil, taking advantage of a decree the government issued in the 1870s which authorized the forced recruitment of unemployed people in Ecuador (Grenier 2007, 85–86). Yet in 1904, of the nearly 500 persons who lived in the archipelago, only 14 percent worked for Gil at the Santo Tomás. As time passed, the population of Isabela never surpassed 150 and even fell to only 70. Some decades later in 1946, the small agricultural colony on Isabela Island was surprised by the sudden arrival of 250 convicts deported from the mainland by the government of Velasco Ibarra. With the presence of those convicts, the population of Isabela reached 400 in the following decade, but by the end of the 1950s, most of the convicts had died—victims of the government's total abandonment of them. Lacking basic services like water, sanitary installations, and food, the convicts ended up dying of hunger or because of the tortures to which they were subjected. An example of this is the building of the so-called Wailing Wall (Muro de las Lágrimas), which had no apparent purpose but led to the death of many of the convicts in Isabela Island. Some who had served out their sentences were not even able to return to the continent because the state did not provide any means by which to do so. "Let them return any way they like! They would have to swim!" (Rodas and Vicanco 2012, 190, citing Linke 1958). In 1959, the penal colony was finally closed, following the signing of the agreement between the Ecuadorian government and UNESCO. This allowed for the building of a permanent international scientific base on Santa Cruz, the neighboring island. At that time, 200 people lived on Isabela, of whom 61 were convicts (ibid., 203).

Over the course of a century, the model of colonization of the Galápagos was based on the exile of Indigenous men from the central highlands, particularly from rural Tungurahua (as the censuses of 1932, 1949, and 1958 confirmed). Yet a major problem of this strategy lay in the fact that the absence of women meant that there continued to be a low birthrate on the islands (Grenier 2007, 194). Consequently, the so-called original families of San Cristóbal and Isabela Islands developed their own strategies—for example, the interchange of partners for almost three decades, from 1920 to 1950 (Ospina

2001, 9-10). The lack of women is, nevertheless, seen as the main motive for regular conflicts and "anomalies" to arise in these first colonies, "since it did away with the essential laws of Nature, that is, the correct balance between the sexes" (Latorre 1991: 60).[35]

Yet for the Ecuadorian state, the *haciendas* of Cobos and Gil in San Cristóbal and Isabela Islands were very profitable ventures. Not only did they enable the permanent colonization of the archipelago, but also—at least until 1959—they allowed for the recognition of Ecuador as sole sovereign state for the Galápagos. By 1959, when the conservation regime arrived to the islands, around 1,800 people lived in these two islands. Most of them (1,590 people) lived in San Cristóbal, which turned into the seat of the provincial government and what is known today as the cultural capital of the *galapagueño* society. Another 300 settlers lived in Santa Cruz and Floreana Island. To colonize these two islands, the government of Ecuador pursued a different strategy. It first tried to promote, in the 1920s and 1930s, the migration of European families. However, these small colonies did not prosper.

Santa Cruz and Floreana Islands

Colonization of the most desolate islands, Santa Cruz and Floreana, is often attributed to the late arrival of Europeans—particularly Norwegians and Germans. Even today, visitors "get the wrong impression that they [the Europeans] make up a large portion of the local population in these islands. In Santa Cruz, this is due to the proximity of that minority to the port . . . and, possibly, to the popularity of "German's Beach" (*Playa de los Alemanes*) (Lundh 2002, 354). Some other famous touristic sites on Santa Cruz—such as Pelican Bay, Academy Bay, or Tortoise Bay—were named by these early, short-lived settler groups, like that of the Norwegians, or by passing visitors such as those collectors from the California Academy of Sciences.

For the Norwegians, the Galápagos became popular in 1907 after the shipwreck of the *Alexandra*, which left one of its lifeboats with its survivors making it to Floreana Island. The book and articles published by August F. Christensen (the son of a leading whaler who became consul of Ecuador) and three young journalists (who visited the islands in 1922) was widely read by the general public in Norway. Meanwhile in Ecuador, the government was eager to persuade Europeans to settle in their islands. They needed to grow their colony in the archipelago, but no Ecuadorians were willing to voluntarily settle in the dry, inhospitable, 'cursed' archipelago.[36] To persuade new settlers, two laws were ratified offering land grants and a fifteen-year tax exemption. They demanded, however, the new settlers to become Ecuadorian citizens (Hoff 1985).

Figure 1.2.   Norwegians' books of the Galápagos. Two books describe the Norwegians' adventures in Galápagos: Alf Harbitz's "The Crew of the 'Alexandra' Ship" (1915) and Ola Mjanger's children's book "Settlers in Galapagos" (1936). *Source*: (Hoff, 1985, http://www.galapagos.to).

Between 150 to 200 Norwegians tried to permanently settle in the archipelago during the 1920s. The first group came with Christensen's Galápagos colonization project. The project received an overwhelming response from the public when it was announced. Christensen then picked only thirty people—mostly young candidates with higher education—who sold their houses, land, and winter clothing to travel with him to the archipelago by the end of 1925. Yet upon arriving on Floreana Island, the adventurous travellers had to confront the isolation, the lack of news, mail, and electricity, and the constant uncertainty of when they would receive the much-needed supplies from the mainland. They also faced a severe drought in their second year on the island after the abundant El Niño rains. Even worse, they soon realized they did not enjoy exclusive rights to whaling in the archipelago as the Ecuadorian government had promised. The whaling project was thus dissolved before making a single catch. Moreover, they found out that the abundant wild cattle that roamed Floreana Island were difficult to catch and almost impossible to keep fenced in. Within a couple of years, none of the first Norwegian settlers stayed in the Galápagos, even though they knew that other groups of Norwegians headed for Santa Cruz and San Cristobal had already arrived. Once again, by 1927, Floreana was left completely abandoned (Latorre 2011, 20). Some years later, the German doctor Friedrich Ritter, Dore Strauch, the Wittmer family, and the Baroness and her lovers got to the island. However, except for Dore and the Wittmers, all of them died in mysterious circumstances in 1934. The Wittmer family stayed on Floreana and owns several luxury cruises today.

Another group of eighty-three Norwegians made it to the archipelago with the Randall Expedition, but with the plan to engage in agriculture on the archipelago. They built fourteen houses in what they called the "Norwegian Camp" (*Campo Noruego*) at the highlands of San Cristóbal. Again, after a short while, almost all of the settlers returned to their homeland. Failure of this second colony is attributed to the resistance of Norwegian settlers to farm and eat local food products. Instead, they tried to plant the Scandinavian seeds they had brought with them, only to find that they were devoured by ants, pigs, and other roaming animals (Lundh 2002, 109).

Finally, two other ships carrying eighty-six Norwegians arrived on Santa Cruz Island around those same years. The group was surprised to find that the island was not completely abandoned. Some Ecuadorians were there farming in higher elevation areas close to Salasaca and Santa Rosa districts (Hoff 1985). Once there, the Norwegians built a fish cannery, seven houses, a pier, and steel rails that connected the pier to the cannery. Nevertheless, after fifteen months there, the overall mood was far from optimistic. The lack of fresh water and the utter isolation were very depressing. They also became increasingly aware that the tales of fantasy of the islands told by the Norwegian press had nothing to do with reality. In fact, "the islands were as dry as heeps of ash and suited only for iguanas, sharks, and a handful of *niggers*," as Sigtvart Tuset, one of the settlers, wrote in his diary (ibid., italics added). In few years, the cannery failed, leaving only two of this group in Santa Cruz by 1932.[37]

Like Darwin, the Norwegians described Ecuadorian settlers in Santa Cruz Island through their own racial terms, labelling them as "blacks," "niggers," or "colored people." Most of them were, in fact, various shades of brown and already building their own caste distinctions in the islands through their choices of occupation, the person they married, status, or relative wealth. If otherwise labelled as *mestizos* (of mixed race), the Europeans regarded them all as inferior and preferred not to associate with them in any way. Hoff, who collected the Norwegian settlers' memoirs, reflects on this:

What was it, then, that broke up this [the Norwegian] colony? Probably the main reason was that originally few of them were indeed farmers and fishermen . . . And by and large they were only prepared to cultivate 'Norwegian' food. Other reasons were the minimal advance knowledge about geography, culture and language . . .

Many of the colonists regarded non-Whites as inferior, especially the *mestizos* (anyone of mixed native American blood) who were in the majority . . . Such an attitude built greater barriers than all the barbed wire stretched across *Campo Noruego.* Spanish, primitive schools, an inferior public health service, Catholic religion . . .

These were problems never considered before . . . After all, was not the original idea to build a Norwegian colony? Nobody had prepared them for living next to Catholics and *blacks*!" (ibid., italics added).

Figure 1.3. Family of *colonos* (first settlers), Santa Cruz, Galápagos. 1935. *Source:* Photograph: Rolf Bloomberg/ Archivo Blomberg.

Furthermore, the Norwegians failed to build the solidarity networks that were key for settlers to succeed in isolation, as many of the testimonies of the Salasaca settlers in Santa Cruz speak of.

During the Second World War, the Santa Cruz population grew significantly due to the arrival of more than twelve thousand US Marines that temporarily occupied the neighbouring island Baltra (or Seymour). Just four days after the Japanese attack on Pearl Harbor, the US Marines arrived there to build a military base that included an airport, a pier, 408 buildings, and thirty-two miles of paved roads (Harrison 1947). The presence of the US Marine Corps during those years boosted the demand for fresh food while bringing cash into the mostly barter economy of the archipelago. Ecuadorian military and civilian authorities followed. At the same time, the small village of Academy Bay, close to the pier, was regularly getting more visitors. All this attracted new settlers to the island, even though water was even scarcer there than in the other three inhabited islands (San Cristóbal, Isabela, and Floreana).[38]

Some of the first permanent inhabitants to arrive on Santa Cruz were the descendants of *hacienda* workers from San Cristóbal Island. Many others were "mountain farmers from Ambato," the capital of the Tungurahua Province, close to Salasaca, in the Ecuadorian highlands, as Hoff (1985) recalls. *Colonos* (first settlers) of Santa Cruz initially settled in the higher elevated areas and found the towns of Santa Rosa, Salasaca, and Bellavista. Yet most gradually moved closer to the pier as business opportunities arose; for example, catching lobsters that were abundant on the island sea shores and free diving to gather sea cucumbers (while being connected through a hose to an air compressor on the boat's deck—please see Bloomberg's picture at the cover.). The small village by the pier, Academy Bay, grew apace particularly after the building of the Darwin scientific station, early in the 1960s. There the city of Puerto Ayora started to be built, starting in the mid-1970s.

COLONOS OF THE GALÁPAGOS

In 1959, when the conservation regime arrived to the Galápagos, four of the nineteen islands that make up the archipelago had permanent human settlements. Most of the first settlers of the islands had rural, Indigenous origins, and a great part had come from Tungurahua in the central Ecuadorian highlands. The pioneers arrived to San Cristóbal and Isabela Islands under the 'tutelage' of two *hacienda* owners, following the model by which the Ecuadorian state delegated the administration of Indigenous populations across the national territory. *Hacienda* owners not only controlled Indian labor but were also supposed to civilize the Indigenous peoples who inhabited and were part

of their private property, thus playing out a confusing mixture between pater-
nalistic attitudes with the more frequent role as despots and tyrants. However,
after the decline of the *haciendas* of the Galápagos in the mid-1930s, the
Indigenous laborers were just left abandoned. They then started to build a
different identity—one that is definitely marked by their history of isolation.

A second wave of settlers arrived to the islands following the creation of
the Galápagos National Park and the Charles Darwin Station. Most of them
settled in Santa Cruz, turning this island from being one of the most desolate
into becoming the most populated one. In fifty years, it went from a population of almost 300 people in 1959 to over 15,700 in 2015, while the total
population of the archipelago grew from 2,100 inhabitants to 25,000. An
important part of these *colonos* (first settlers) of Santa Cruz were Indigenous,
particularly, Salasaca people of the Tungurahua region.[39]

Despite the rapid population growth, people of the Galápagos clearly
identify first settlers of every island and their descendants. Until 1998, the
Ecuadorian state recognized these families as *colonos* of the archipelago.
Colloquially they are also known as *"carapachudos,"* a name that indexes
their living in oceanic isolation, 600 miles off the coast of Ecuador, enclosed
like the endemic giant tortoises of the Galápagos, living under their own carapaces (*carapachos*). In contrast, locals call people who don't belong to the
Galápagos (including Ecuadorians from the mainland): *"afuereños"* (foreigners). For their part, 'white' visitors (particularly Europeans and people from
the United States) have an additional label; they are known as *"colorados"*
(reddish—from the sunburnt hue of their skins).

All in all, the term 'foreigners' (*afuereños*), as used in the Galápagos, is not
only used to denote people from another country, it further includes everyone
coming from an outside world, from the mainland—those who cannot understand what it is like for *carapachudos* to have lived, enclosed, inside their
archipelago. The feeling of difference comes from that:

> lonely fight to humanize a hostile territory in the cruelest solitude and abandon-
> ment. The *afuereños,* recently arrived, and those from the continent don't un-
> derstand this past; they don't value it; they don't know the rights of privilege of
> those who came first and, with their sacrifice, made the prosperity of the islands
> possible (Ospina 2001, 8).

Among locals, the most respected *carapachudos* are those who come from
the "original," "pioneer," or *"colono"* first families. Such labels entail having
earned the respect of others in recognition of their sacrifice after living in the
dry archipelago in a state of almost total abandonment from the Ecuadorian
government.[40] In particular, the *"colono"* category further extended to all
people who settled in the Galápagos before the passing of the 1998 conser-

vation law. But after the law, all *colonos* (first settlers, natives, and their de-scendants) became aliens in the archipelago, falling into the category of "per-manent residents," as they are now legally known. In turn, all new migrants who have settled on the islands after 1998 (including mainland Ecuadorians) would be "illegals" in the archipelago unless they were to get married to and live with a "permanent resident" for ten years or more.

Meanwhile on the mainland, local politicians and popular imagery usually denote the *galapagueños* as the descendants of 'convicts,' thus completely ignoring the way the labor system systematically criminalized Indigenous laborers in Ecuador. Such narrative is useful to maintain a vision of race in which Indigenous populations are considered uncivilized peoples in need of correction. From that perspective, to cede (in 1959) the administration of land and settlers in the Galápagos to a group of white, foreign scientists fit into the *hacienda* logic. The new patrons were supposed to make the islands produc-tive while carrying the civilizing mission. But the US and north European scientists who arrived in those decades were patrons of a different kind. For them, settlers of the Galápagos were not insiders of a nascent society—as the Spaniards considered the dominated populations—nor were they the servants of the new property but "aliens," "colored," and "poor people" who did not understand the purpose of science. They needed to be controlled and 'enclosed' in delimited areas outside their natural property. Tellingly, local language indexes this sentiment in the way *galapagueños* speak of their need to go to the "outside" (*afuera*) to the continent, as if trapped in the remote archipelago.

NOTES

1. The *spondylus* were used as a ritual object—as food of the gods, currency, per-sonal adornment, or a feature of sculptures, funerary offerings, and religious rituals.

2. For example, in Guedeville's map (1716): *Mascarín, del Tabaco, Isla del Diablo* and *San Bernabé*. In Vicente Fuerte's chart (1744): *Las Dos Hermanas*. And, in other documents of the time, *San Clemente, de los Paños, Santo Tomás* and *Santa Teresa* (Latorre 2011, 213–16).

3. By 1692, for example, the Jesús, María y José (Jesus, Mary and Joseph), a 600-ton ship with forty cannons, spent the whole month of August surveilling and exploring the archipelago, after noticing the presence of the corsairs (Latorre 2011: 40). Rumors about possible English attacks grew over the following century. These finally led the Viceroy of Lima, at the request of Bogotá, to send Captain Antonio María del Valle to the archipelago in January 1800 with one hundred men to prevent any corsairs from establishing a base there. A short while later, a skirmish between three English pirate ships and two ships of the viceroyalty also took place to the west of Isabela Island (ibid., 42–3).

4. In 1892, the Congress of Ecuador changed the name of San Carlos (or Charles) Island to Santa María. However, it is now colloquially known as Floreana.

5. He also set up a mailbox on a beach of King Charles Island (now known as Floreana) so that whalers, sailors, and those passing by the Galápagos could send messages to other members of the transnational maritime network, which already embraced all of the seas.

6. According to the *Times Herald,* the logs of the US whalers record the catching of more than fifty-five thousand whales in the Galápagos between 1791 and 1920 (Luna Tobar 1997, 55). If we take the British whale hunts into account, the number is much higher.

7. This may be understandable when taking into account that the scientific practices of Catholic Spain favored the practice of secrecy and the tradition of scribes over the printed word, so that most of its studies and archives were inaccessible to other Europeans (Cañizares-Esguerra 2006, 14–45).

8. The work of earlier navigators and other scientists were also central to the development of Darwin's theory. For example, in 1846, following Darwin's instructions, Thomas Edmonstone visited the archipelago, making separate collections for each island. In 1868, Simeon Habel also collected birds, reptiles and insects that were analyzed by Osbert Salvin in Vienna who, at the time, corresponded with Darwin (Sevilla 2017, 30). However, later accounts of Darwin tend to stress his image as a true scientist, acting on his own in the discovery of nature.

9. An exception to the rule was German geologist and geographer Theodore Wolf who collected and advanced a systematic exploration of the islands' fauna during the 1870s. He was, however, doing science from the "periphery," as he was based on the mainland in Guayaquil (Ecuador), with scarce funds and no support from any European center of knowledge nor any North American institution, thus depending on *galapagueño* settlers for every one of his periodic visits (Sevilla 2017, 30–8). His collections were unintentionally lost.

10. In honor of this expedition, the place where the Charles Darwin Station was built in 1964 took its name: "Academy Bay."

11. In 1871, zoologist Louis Agassiz—a strong believer in creationism—cruised the archipelago in an effort to disprove Darwin's theories. He and his son both collected for Harvard University. In 1875, W.E. Cookson also collected in the islands but for the British Museum curator, Albert Gunther. On board of the *Albatross,* Baur and Adams did likewise for the Smithsonian (1888 and 1891). And in 1898, Heller and Snodgrass went to collect with the Hopkins-Stanford Galápagos Expedition. In the 1920s, the New York Zoological Society supported naturalist and marine biologist William Beebe who, being the first curator of birds at the Bronx Zoo, visited the islands twice to collect tropical birds, and to gather more data in support of evolution (Grant 2009). Allan Hancock went for the first time in 1928 and several times from 1931–1938. He later bequeathed his collections to the University of Southern California. In 1929, Gifford Pinchot visited the islands, as also the Cornelius Crane Pacific Expedition of the Chicago Field Museum of Natural History did in the very same year. Finally in the 1930s, the Vincent Astor Expedition went to explore Santa

Cruz Island, William K. Vanderbilt visited twice, and so did the Templeton Crocker Expedition and the Academy of Natural Sciences of Philadelphia (in 1936 and 1937).

12. The well-known debate between the friar and *encomendero* San Bartolomé de las Casas and the colonizer Fernández de Oviedo illustrates this point.

13. On the contrary, if they "lacked the use of reason" (if they were 'incapable'), "lacking capability altogether" ('beasts'), they could not be Christianized, and would "be brought under the political authority of the Spanish Crown through the title of the Papal donation" (Seed 1993: 140).

14. See, for example, the writings of López de Gómara (1552), Ginés Sepulveda (1550) and even José de Acosta (1590).

15. Colonial authorities secured labor and land usurpation not only with the use of violence but more importantly with the introduction of Iberian laws, moral arguments on property and propriety, as well as forms of arguing and evidence giving that justified native dispossession and the appropriation of wealth in the courts of the New World (Herzog 2013).

16. Land dispossession became institutionalized with the introduction of *"composiciones de tierras,"* a legal instrument by which colonial officers singled out all properties that were "insufficiently worked" or unoccupied. Spanish judges decided, of course, what "sufficient" or "proper" use meant (Herzog 2013, 316). Their criteria was more than problematic; they presumed Indians did not need as much or, as in Locke's theory, they believed natives "did not pursue agricultural pursuits" (Herzog 2013, 321). Natives who held "too much" were often accused of "abusing royal goodwill" and usurping public property.

17. During the Inca empire, the labor and tributary system in the Andes was also based in the constant relocation of people.

18. *Composiciones* worked in the colonial period, just as they did for Castilian kings from the 1560s and onwards in the Iberian Peninsula, following the Christian conquest of Muslim territories.

19. The inalienable character of communal lands negated the possibility of separation (Radin 1987, 1852) of Indigenous persons to land—and rural labor. These ideas conveniently ignore that property rights were an integral part of Inca society, that Incas made contracts and owned private property—although concentrated in the hands of provincial aristocracy and royal families (Kolata 2013, 54), and that significant transfers of property were made by Indian *caciques* to the church as a way to secure the destiny of their souls after death (Abercrombie 1998). Moreover, Indigenous peoples were imagined as a radically different person to whites and *mestizos* with the assignment of reciprocity, animism, being one with nature, temporal and ontological difference (Abercrombie 2016).

20. Spanish *criollos* (or creoles) were people born in the colonies but of totally (or at least largely) Spanish descent. The Spanish Crown often passed over *criollos* for the top military, administrative, and religious offices in the colonies in favor of the Spanish-born *"peninsulares."*

21. For example, theories that defended economic liberalism as a mark of civilization (Guarisco 1995, 86), laws which promoted agrarian capitalism in the region (Platt 1982), and later on, programs aimed at developing the "Third World" (Escobar 1995).

22. The end of the *ejidos* made Indigenous families face a grave problem: obtaining access to lands where they could graze their animals. That meant that they had to intensify the work on their *chacras* (food plots) in order to lease grazing lands or pay with their work to a landlord for the pastures, water, roads, firewood, and straw they required. Sooner or later, the productive crisis disrupted the *chacra,* above all with the advent of the second or third generation of the family, which resulted in the fragmentation of the property and a larger gap in the production needed to satisfy the basic needs.

23. The boom in *concertaje* took place after the decline of the *m'ita* (the ancient Inca institution of obligatory labor on public works), which the Spanish Crown took over, allowing it to continue in force up to the eighteenth century, compelling native men to pay tribute with their work. The *mitayos* had to work ten months every year, usually far from their community or birthplace. In the territory of Ecuador, those laboring in the *m'ita* were mainly employed to grow crops, tend cattle and sheep, and produce textiles for an *encomendero* or a *hacienda* owner.

24. The *concertaje* system in Ecuador was thus not limited to rural production but also to textile industry and commerce in urban settings.

25. All these were deducted from the laborers' daily wage, along with the cost of any damages the workers may have caused to the cattle, sheep, crops, or fences. Moreover, goods sold to *conciertos* at the *hacienda* 'store' with money lent to them by the *patrón* (landlord) were exorbitantly priced. Finally, the *concierto* was forced to pay for the costs to participate in ritual *fiestas* of the community; for example, if he was named as an acting leader or host of the *fiesta*, he became responsible for the expenses of the ceremony.

26. Despite being formally abolished in 1833, whipping continued to be a common practice in Ecuador through the turn of the twentieth century. The *majordomos* routinely engaged in punishments that included whipping, public scourging, or simple beating. The sanction "would not be complete if the *indio* [Indian], when he stood up, did not thank his victimizer, with the well-worn phrase, "God bless you, master" (Martínez 1916, 47; in Ibarra 1987, 91).

27. Villamil was also regarded as the founder of the Ecuadorian Navy, since—thanks to him—the government acquired its first warship, the *Patria,* where its first officers and crewmen were trained.

28. With that first group of soldier colonists also came the first barnyard animals and several heads of cattle, sheep, horses, dogs, and pigs.

29. Villamil's laborers were left in the charge of general Williams, who became the first tyrant of the Galápagos. The growing brutality of Williams and his overseers caused the colonists to revolt, forcing Williams to flee to the mainland in 1841.

30. He sold these products in Panamá in exchange for contraband merchandise that entered Ecuador at the port of Chanduy. This illicit activity was the reason why president García Moreno ordered his arrest in those years. To avoid his detention, he fled to Mexico.

31. Cobos bought up with his partner, José Monroy, large tracts of forest in Baja, California, to extract their orchilla dye. A few years later, he began to ship groups of laborers from the Ecuadorian highlands from the port of Guayaquil to Mexico, always

stopping at the Galápagos for provisions. In three voyages Cobos transported a total of nearly 300 men to work on that enterprise.

32. Some of the delinquents had never been convicted, though they were deported all the same.

33. There were eight officials in San Cristóbal: the territorial head, the secretary, and six policemen. They all had to submit to Cobos's orders, since they depended on him for their housing, food, water, and transport.

34. For example, they had the right to exploit individual parcels of land for sustenance farming.

35. The difference between sexes gradually narrowed. The number of men, however, continued to be larger until the 2000's (Gavilán and Ospina 2000; Arboleda 2001).

36. Until the 1960s, Ecuadorians seemed to agree with the way Herman Melville [1854] depicted the Galápagos as cursed, dry, evilly enchanted isles. This idea is also present in a local legend. It tells tortoises can tell the good or bad intentions of humans in the Galápagos after watching so many human tragedies throughout their long lives. Depending on their intentions, the islands are a curse or a paradise (Latorre (2013 [1997]: 3–6). The lack of water is the curse of the giant tortoise (ibid).

37. Kristian Stampa and Gordon World remained in Santa Cruz after the rest of the group left. Trygge Nuggerud was the only one who stayed in San Cristóbal after Randall's expedition. During the following decades, some new European families arrived; among them were the four Angermeyer brothers, captain Herman Lundh, three other Norwegian families, a Danish couple, a German, and an Alsatian family. Nevertheless, after the Second World War, only the first two remained on the island (Lundh 2002). Hoff (1985) mentions the Kubler family, Gordon Wold, Sigurd Graffer, Jacob Hersleb Horneman's family, the Guldberg family, and the Kastdalen family. Most of their children, born in the Galápagos, eventually left.

38. Fresh water was scarce but accessible in San Cristóbal Island through *El Junco*, the only fresh water lagoon in the whole archipelago. In Isabela, the water was drawn from the subsoil through cracks. The main water source in Floreana Island is a natural pond that fills up with the rain water during the rainy season. In turn, Santa Cruz Island had one little spring in Santa Rosa (close to Salasaca) in the highland.

39. Aside from Tungurahua, the provinces of Loja, Manabí, and the cities of Guayaquil and Quito also became sources of migrants.

40. In Santa Cruz, they further make a distinction between those who live in the higher elevated areas of the island, the "*chacreros*" (closed to the *chacras,* or small agricultural plots) and those who live by the pier, "*de la playa*" (from the beach).

Chapter Two

Science Takes on the Galápagos

For more than a century while on the islands, the Indigenous laborers fought to survive in the midst of isolation as on the mainland the successive governments of Ecuador persevered in their efforts to sell or lease the archipelago. In 1830, the sovereign Republic of Ecuador was born with a foreign debt of more than 1.4 million pounds sterling. Year after year, the debt owed to Great Britain grew. The sale or lease of whole parts of the country's territory— particularly, the Galápagos islands and the Ecuadorian Amazon—seemed, at the time, reasonable. There were, however, additional pressing needs for the newborn republic that prevented the sale of these regions.

In the meantime, at the international level throughout this period (1830– 1959), the conservation or "Nature movement" reached its height. Particularly for the Galápagos, there was a growing wish on the part of scientists and wealthy families of the United States and northern Europe to turn the islands into a living museum to render homage to Darwin and teach the world about evolution. Claiming the archipelago for science thus became a matter of priority on the agenda of scientists, wealthy people, and politicians, as well as officials of the newly established United Nations Educational, Scientific, and Cultural Organization (UNESCO) and the International Union for Conservation of Nature (IUCN).

These historical and political conditions paved the way for yet another change in the property regime, transforming the Galápagos from being a state property into becoming a conservation territory (1959) and a common heritage of "humanity" (1978). The creation of heritage and an imagined collective that owns it, was constitutive of a new kind of racialized system of property based on the valorization of whiteness and its merging with novel forms of ownership. In this case, 'white' elites (local and foreign) joined to claim their rights to access, use, and control a World Natural Heritage. From

51

there on, science and *hacienda* regimes have overlapped on the islands to govern the Galápagos' nature and society.

On the one hand, the initial aspirations of the local elite in Quito to do business with the archipelago and somehow belong to a powerful nation, along with their absolute indifference to Indigenous laborers left abandoned in the archipelago, are indicative of their desire to whiten themselves and the whole nation. It can be observed in the negotiations that the Ecuadorian government held with France; in the conceptions of civilization and racial subordination of local people that were made clear on the day the Charles Darwin Scientific Station was inaugurated on Santa Cruz Island; and, finally, in the agreement that allowed the property to become managed by foreign entities that framed Ecuadorian colonization as the major threat for nature protection. On the other hand, the interests of powerful families and scientists in the United States shaped the agenda of transnational agencies to the point of creating new regimes to own, administer, and inherit properties in foreign countries. In this new scheme, 97 percent of the land of the Galápagos Islands was designated for the making of a natural park for the 'humankind,' while settlers of the Galápagos were confined to the remaining 3 percent. They further became stigmatized as the descendants of convicts, trespassers of the park's area, or people who did not understand what the Galápagos is nor the purpose of conservation.

THE GALÁPAGOS FOR SALE (1830S–1940S)

Between 1844 and 1944, Ecuador undertook eleven different negotiations aimed at ceding the Galápagos in exchange for a reduction of its foreign debt with its main creditors: Great Britain, France, and the United States (Villacrés Moscoso 1985). Some other attempts were made with other countries. Meanwhile, up until the end of the 1930s, different scientific military expeditions visited the islands, motivated not only by their interest in nature but also by the mission to observe and appraise the property offered by the Ecuadorian government.

At the time, just after the wars of independence in the region (1820s–1830s) took place, the acceptable terms for the alienation, sale, or leasing of territories began to change. The disaggregation of a territory was increasingly regarded as a lack of "decorum" and a violation of the "honor" of any civilized nation (Luna Tobar 1997, 198–99). On the other hand, at the turn of the century, the invasion and use of force to take possession of the territory of another nation became seen as an act of barbarity, which violated the spirit of modern states. Diplomatic means, moral arguments, and legal frameworks of a multilateral nature had to be developed for the creation of new property regimes at the global level.

The Role of Perú

Throughout this period, Perú played a fundamental role in preventing the Ecuadorian government from selling the Galápagos. Until recent times, the tensions arising from border disputes and fears of an invasion were latent in Ecuador. Perú believed that it had a right to own lands across the southern frontier of Ecuador as well as the Galápagos archipelago. It argued the islands were part of pre-Columbian Inca possessions. Based on the chronicles of Spanish Sarmiento de Gamboa (1572), Perú insisted that the tenth Inca, Tupac Yupanqui, had discovered the islands in 1465. The historians of Ecuador, however, rebutted this theory by arguing that the inhabitants of the highlands of Perú—especially the Incas—were not sailors. Moreover, "the nobles (called *"orejones"* [those with big ears]) of Huayna Capac (the eleventh Inca), did not know how to swim" (Luna Tobar 1997, 18). By contrast, the Manteños-Huancavilcas were expert navigators who may have traveled to the Galápagos on rafts before the Inca invasion of their territory (Holm 1986). There was no doubt that pre-Hispanic peoples had discovered the islands, but Ecuadorian historians insisted they rather came from the coast of present-day Ecuador.

The controversy went much further. Over and over again, aiming to protect the disputed property, Peruvian diplomacy denounced the rumors and plans of Ecuador when trying to sell or lease the Galápagos. At the end of the 1830s, the diplomats denounced the Ecuadorian president (Flores) when proposing to surrender the archipelago to its main creditor, Great Britain, in order to pay off part of its debt (Bognoly and Espinosa 1905, 54–5). Perú warned other countries about the risks that such a transaction would entail, particularly, an increase in unchecked smuggling and a fall in the trade revenues in coastal provinces. France and Spain supported this campaign. Two decades later, Perú complained upon learning that Great Britain would lease the archipelago in exchange for freezing Ecuador's foreign debt payments. With the support of France, Spain, and the United States, the Peruvian delegates managed to block the transaction.

They also challenged the negotiations that General Villamil undertook in Washington, DC, in the 1850s as the ambassador of Ecuador. Twenty years after the general had been granted lands and a labor force of rebellious soldiers to found the *Compañia Colonizadora de Galápagos* (Colonizing Company of the Galápagos) on Floreana Island, the Ecuadorian government charged him with the mission of obtaining a loan of three million pesos from

US investors in exchange for exclusive rights to exploit guano on the islands. His foreign mission was backed by the parliament of Ecuador which, with the ratification of the law of 1851, gave the executive a free hand in "selling by leasing" (*enajenación por arrendamiento*) of the archipelago. In 1854, Peruvian diplomats warned the minister of foreign relations in Lima about this move and gathered a coalition among the governments of Spain, Great Britain, Chile, and France so that they could jointly issue an energetic protest against Ecuador's efforts. In the letter sent, Chile reminded the young republic that it should begin to behave in accordance with the norms of conduct of a sovereign, free, and independent nation.[1] Furthermore, they claimed that:

> Subjected to the protection of the United States, Ecuador will have the appearance of an independent state for a time, and afterwards, will begin to be a colony of the United States (Varas in Luna Tobar 1997, 100).

It was, however, Washington which decided to end the negotiations with the argument that the monetary compensation would not be enough. Their rejection of the proposal to exploit guano in the Galápagos was further reaffirmed by the findings of scientists on board Alexander Agassiz's first expedition. They found that the extraction of guano was hardly possible due to the enormous colonies of birds found in the islands. "Neither by throwing stones or shooting at them did [the explorers] manage to drive away those animals, who seemed as impassive as domestic animals" (Luna Tobar 1997: 106).

During the next decades, Peru's claims to the ownership of the Galápagos and their complaints about the attempts by different Ecuadorian presidents to sell or lease the archipelago had a huge impact in the public opinion and led to indictments against those who were selling out the homeland (*los "vende patrias"*). It too had an impact on neighboring countries which disapproved of the conduct of the Ecuadorian government to the extent of preventing the sale or lease of the Galápagos.

An Offer to France

Reflecting the wishes of his class, Flores, Ecuador's first president, was a staunch admirer of France and in some manner hoped Ecuador could establish a link or become part of that nation. For that reason, when in 1844 Iturburu—the French consul in Guayaquil—proposed the acquisition of the archipelago to France, the Ecuadorian government supported him. In the opinion of the consul, the deal would not be difficult, considering "the poverty of the country's finances . . . and the private situation of its head of state [Flores] . . . who is vain and prodigal by nature" (ibid., 76). To assess this offer, France sent its first scientific military expedition to the archipelago.

In the 1860s, President García Moreno also wrote to the French government about "Ecuador's wish to unite itself to that grand and generous nation" and thus become the base of France's colonial empire in the region and seat of an imposing maritime power (Moscoso 1985, 87). According to him, national citizens thought of France as "a prosperous and strong nation, which is of our same race" (ibid., 176). By contrast, the United States was perceived as a "dangerous" nation.

Efforts to negotiate the sale of the Galápagos Islands (along with the Ecuadorian Amazon) with France continued in the following decades. The executive branch justified its offers with old arguments. It argued that both the islands and the Amazon were "empty lands" (*baldíos*) which belonged to the nation—that is, in theory uninhabited lands, even though by then the same state had exiled several hundred Ecuadorians to the Galápagos and knew quite well that the Amazon was used, inhabited by, and possessed by Indigenous peoples since preconquest times. Ultimately, nothing came of these negotiations.

Finally, at the end of the nineteenth century, France made an offer of one hundred million francs to build a port in the Galápagos. The French government also studied the possibility of establishing a coaling station on the islands.[2] These offers took place precisely after the French heard a rumor about the hopes that a syndicate of three major European nations had for the acquisition of the Galápagos. To support its position, the French delegates made use of a minute issued in 1888 by the chancellery of Ecuador, which confirmed that it would be the favored nation in any negotiation.

However, by that time, the Ecuadorian Congress had already received multiple proposals. The parliament had further created a commission to study each offer. In 1891, the experts concluded that some of the offers "were injurious to the government of a nation which is zealous of its decorum." More importantly, they underlined that the intentions of such foreign countries were usually "disguised as [an interest in] scientific investigations but really aiming at the alienation of the archipelago" (Luna Tobar 1997, 159). Nevertheless, the Ecuadorian government continued the negotiations, increasingly aiming to reach an agreement instead with the United States.

The United States: The Galápagos for the Security of the Continent

At the end of the 1880s, the United States began to show an interest in the Galápagos. Several arguments were used to challenge Ecuadorian sovereignty over the archipelago. For example, the US Secretary of State, James G. Blaine, first questioned the nationality of General Villamil, who he claimed was a citizen of the US and also the first to claim possession of the archipelago (even though it was for Ecuador). Yet Villamil had been born in New Orleans, but at a time when the state of Louisiana was still part of the Viceroyalty of New Spain and not a territory of the United States. Later in 1883, Blaine argued through the commissioner George Earl Church that the archipelago should again be declared a "no-man's-land," since only herds of wild cattle inhabited it. This time President Flores—then in his second term—reacted by sending a letter to the *New York Herald*. He believed such status would automatically expose the archipelago to the invasion of any European naval power. Another argument for territorial claim that was used several decades later pointed at the early presence of US whale hunters in the waters of the Galápagos. The United States claimed they were the first to discover the archipelago. In the end, none of these arguments worked.

It was precisely the article in the *New York Herald* which ignited one of the biggest scandals in Ecuador when in 1896, three young members of the opposition reprinted it in the local press (*La Prensa Libre de Quito*), adding the remark: "The Galápagos for Sale: Who bids the most?" President Eloy Alfaro persecuted the authors. After confessing his guilt, one of its authors, Rafael Polit, was imprisoned and ordered to be sent to the Galápagos so he could "ensure that Alfaro did not sell the islands" while being there (Luna Tobar 1997, 153).

Even so, Alfaro and his successors continued to negotiate the leasing or sale of the Galápagos. They knew that the country's armed forces were too weak to defend the archipelago. Moreover, the presence of the state on the islands was practically nonexistent.[3] Ecuador's sovereignty over the territory was only being guarded by those Indigenous laborers who had been exiled to work there in the *haciendas*. Selling or leasing the islands thus seemed like a better option than losing them at any time to some foreign power. Also, the need to build the public infrastructure of the country and defend its southern frontier continued to be urgent.

In 1899, the United States made its first bid to buy the Galápagos, made in person by the Secretary of State, John Hay. That was the start of a round of negotiations between the two countries, which—from the standpoint of the US delegation—was marked by "the intention of Ecuador to conduct a virtual raid on the United States Treasury, and the passion with which representatives of the Department of State sought, always in vain, to advance their version of the Navy's interest" (Challener 1973, 106). For example, while the US diplomats valued the archipelago at one million dollars, President Alfaro insisted that it was worth twenty million. Later when US Minister Sampson offered to protect the archipelago from any external danger—at no cost—in exchange for Ecuador's cession of the island of San Cristóbal (or Chatham), Ecuador asked instead for a loan of ten million dollars with the island as a warranty.

The US government rejected the proposal and confirmed that it would make no bid under those conditions.

The two governments finally reached an agreement in 1909. The US seizure of Panama had taken place by then. The same General Alfaro who had persecuted the young Polit during his first term and had condemned his predecessors' efforts to sell or lease the archipelago accepted an offer from the United States. The agreement was based on leasing the Galápagos to the US for a period of ninety-nine years in return for a loan of fifteen million dollars. Alfaro hoped to use the money to enlarge the railway network, which had recently linked the highlands and the coast on the mainland, and finance other public works projects.[4] However, the Ecuador Congress objected to the deal and the Military Junta as a whole vetoed the transaction on the basis that it clearly violated the "honor" and "decorum" of a civilized nation. The announcement, published in the most widely read newspapers in Ecuador, stated:

> Fortunately, the logic is inflexible: if you accept a principle, you accept its consequences. If the Congress or the Executive Branch were able to lease the Archipelago of Galápagos, it would also have the power to lease any of the provinces of the Republic or all of them together . . . May God deliver us from leasing that territory, sacrificing our morality and honor.
>
> May God deliver us from turning the United States into the supreme arbiter so that it may settle the controversies among the republics of South America . . . *What would Chile and Colombia think of our conduct, or the republics of Argentina, Brazil, Bolivia and Venezuela . . .*
>
> If they seize the archipelago from us, Ecuador's honor remains unscathed and it will still have the right to protest before the civilized world, to state that in this, the 20th century, the United States or Japan are returning to the period of Conquest, the period of pillage and barbarity. But if Ecuador, prompted by fear or greed, cedes the archipelago to the United States, it would be dishonored forever and would not be able to proudly raise its head to figure among the civilized nations (italics added, Luna Tobar 1997, 197–99).

It was clear that the republic's reputation in the eyes of its peers was at stake. By the turn of the century, to sell parts of its territory would mean to sacrifice the morality and honor of the state and also expel Ecuador from the group of "civilized nations." Moreover, it was feared that the United States wouldn't honor its promise to respect the sovereignty of Ecuador during the term of the leasing contract and it would wind up as an island republic or "another Texas." Monsignor González Suárez warned: "If we have to die as a nation in the face of an inexorable adversary, let us die intact and not be mutilated first in that shameful partial death" (ibid., 200). Once again, the transaction for the leasing of the Galápagos could not be finalized.

For its part, the US government was going through an expansionist phase under the administrations of Presidents William McKinley (1897–1901) and Theodore Roosevelt (1901–1909). Its diplomats often invoked the terms of the Monroe Doctrine to warn Ecuador that the islands could not be occupied or controlled by any country other than the United States. US concern increased when a German syndicate offered to buy the archipelago from the Ecuadorian government in 1918. It increased even more so during the inter-war period, with rumors about a deal between Ecuador and Japan, Italy, and Germany.[5]

The US press stoked these fears by calling several times for the acquisition of the archipelago in the name of hemispheric security. In 1911, the *New York World* further suggested that it might be convenient to provoke an emancipation movement among the incipient inhabitants of the Galápagos to attain the independence of the archipelago. Later on at the end of the 1920s, the US press insisted on the advantage of acquiring the Galápagos in order to improve the security of the continent because, given its strategic location, it would be "an indispensable point of support for the formidable dividing line between two worlds and two races, the yellow and the white" that will "force the Orient to keep within its boundaries" (quoting van Loom 1929, ibid. 1997, 227). Finally, by 1941, a few days after the attack on Pearl Harbor, the government of Ecuador begrudgingly agreed to the cession of Baltra Island (Larson 2001, 175) so that the archipelago could become "the impregnable fortress for the defense of the Panamá Canal" during the Second World War (*Time* Magazine 1942, ibid., 273).

While Base Beta or "The Rock" was installed on Baltra Island, the president of Ecuador—President Velasco Ibarra—resumed negotiations. In his opinion, the Galápagos were "useless" (*"de nada sirven y para nada sirven"*). Managing to lease them was instead "a sure formula for obtaining millions of dollars" and saving the country from bankruptcy (Norris 2004, 58–9). At that time, however, the United States was already demanding that the period of occupation should extend to ninety years, while Ecuador was only willing to grant one of thirty years. In the end, the US State Department made it clear that it would not pay any compensation to Ecuador and the cession of the archipelago should be an act of good will by Ecuador for the benefit of the security of the continent.

On April 1, 1946, World War II ended and the negotiations with the United States had broken down. The marines, however, remained in the Galápagos. On that day Velasco Ibarra demanded that the United States vacate Baltra and a month later, he issued a decree for the establishment of a penal colony on Isabela Island. In the following months, more than 250 criminals were deported to this island in order to push for the departure of the contingent of US Marines.[6] Meanwhile that year, some 120 settlers were living in the higher elevated areas of its neighboring island, Santa Cruz, and another 1,000 lived on the other three inhabited islands (Lundh 2006, 14). In 1948, the US military base was finally dismantled.

By the end of the 1940s, it was clear to the United States that the way to control or profit from the archipelago would not be achieved by means of a bilateral agreement for its sale or leasing. At the same time, during the decades prior to the war, the US interests on the islands had begun to expand to other fields, beyond the said security of the continent.

Hunters, Conservationists, and Millionaires

Between 1890 and the 1930s, the tacit alliance between science, government, and the elite was consolidated in the United States. Theodore Roosevelt's extravagant hunting expeditions that embodied an ethos of "the commerce of power and knowledge in white and male supremacist monopoly capitalism" (Haraway 1985, 21) are one indication of it.

In the waters of the Galápagos, such alliance began with the expeditions of Spanish priests and English buccaneers who, with their field notes, established "mutual engagement between natural history and European economic and political expansionism" (Pratt 2008 [1992], 37). Later came the collectors of specimens whose journeys were financed by English aristocrats. And then at the turn of the century, came the yachts belonging to US millionaires who often visited the islands, lending their cabins to groups of scientists who were investigating and observing the Galápagos fauna. On their return voyages, they also carried live animals that were supplied to zoos in the United States. Although the First World War halted scientific explorations for a number of years, US naturalists kept busy processing and classifying the more than ten thousand specimens they had recently collected in the Galápagos (Larson 2001, 145).[7]

Meanwhile in the United States, the "white hunter" filled natural history museums with objects collected in regions of the periphery, which were dedicated to educate the public on conservation, masculinity, race, and eugenics (Haraway 1985).[8] At the same time, aristocratic families with patriotic leanings were devoted to the enjoyment of nature, traveling, and hunting. In that period, hunters' societies (like the "Boone and Crockett Club") and groups of descendants of men who had received distinguishing honors in the war (like the "Society of Colonial Wars") arose. Their leaders were to become the pioneers and activists of the conservation movement. They included, for example, Madison Grant (a friend of president Franklin Delano Roosevelt and a major architect of the racially restrictive immigration policy in the

United States in the 1920s), Gifford Pinchot, and C. Hart Merriam (founder of the National Geographic Society) (Spiro 2008). Others in that cohort were J.P. Morgan, William K. Vanderbilt, H.F. Osborn, and John D. Rockefeller III who became the patrons of science as well as leaders of conservation, eugenics, and monopoly capitalism (Haraway 1985, 54).

Between the 1920s and the 1930s, the yachts of Vincent Astor, William Vanderbilt, Kermit Roosevelt, Templeton Crocker, G. Allan Hancock, and Harrison Williams sailed through the islands.[910] Gifford Pinchot himself, known as the "father of conservation" and a government official in the administrations of both Roosevelts, visited the archipelago in 1929 as part of an expedition sponsored by the Smithsonian Institution. At the end of the following decade, president Franklin Delano Roosevelt also went, along with scientists who made collections for the Smithsonian, while he fished in the Pacific aboard the USS *Houston*.

As a result of these visits, a group of wealthy US families proposed the acquisition of the Galápagos Islands for its use as a game preserve (Parks and Rippy 1940, Luna Tobar 1997, 225). The plan was published in the *Chicago Sunday Tribune* in 1930 in an article entitled "How to buy the Galápagos?" To do that, the editorial suggested forming a group of four hundred sportsmen whose money could finance the acquisition. A wildlife reserve, a scientific station, and an occasional refuge for military and civilian vessels could be created there. The *Tribune* further suggested that the US government contribute with federal funds and act as a mediator to persuade the Ecuadorian government in the making of a natural sanctuary which, in the end, could be a good business for both countries. All of that eventually happened. To quote the editorial:

> To preserve these places for future generations, a group of wealthy sportsmen has thought about the possibility of buying the archipelago . . . Mr. Gifford Pinchot of Pennsylvania has suggested that the islands be turned into a refuge for wildlife. The *Tribune* has asked the government of the United States to buy them as a reserve to protect wildlife, a scientific and meteorological station and an occasional safe harbor for military and civilian vessels.
>
> Apart from that, there is a recent suggestion, by Mr. C.F. Kettering, head of research at General Motors and Eugene F. McDonald, president of the Zenith Radio Company, that a group of wealthy men think about buying the Galápagos from Ecuador in order to donate it to the nation. It would be a magnificent gesture and of enormous importance for the United States.
>
> A group, made up, say of four hundred wealthy sportsmen, could buy the islands, probably without much difficulty or sacrifice. It would not be difficult to find a low price and an easy deal. The Ecuadorian port of Guayaquil could expect an increase of its commerce and the whole western coast of South America would be more accessible to tourists and American investments. (Alfaro 1930, 16–17).

As the notion of heritage now expresses, the property envisioned by this group of sportsmen could be inherited by future generations. Although the acquisition plan did not bear fruit, three decades later the private initiative of powerful men able to activate the necessary networks (between science, the universities, the aristocracy, and the government) proved to be a crucial factor in the success of this international venture.

The Roosevelt family was particularly interested in the Galápagos, especially in acquiring Isabela (or Albemarle) Island. Franklin Delano Roosevelt's interest went back a long way. His great uncle, Captain Amasa Delano, had stopped off at the island several times on his voyages to China early in the 1800s.[11] The president's mother, Sara Delano, had also visited Isabela when she was a girl. He was himself captivated by the island when he visited there in the summer of 1938. Following the tradition of men of his class, the president went hunting during his visit.

Figure 2.1. President Franklin D. Roosevelt seated on the well deck of USS Houston (CA-30) with a shark he caught in Sullivan Bay (on the southeast of Santiago Island). A sailfish is being hoisted up on the left. Galápagos Islands, July 1938. *Source*: NHHC Series, NH Series, NH 93163, Archives Branch, Naval History and Heritage Command, Washington DC. Photo: Otto Schwartz, USS Houston Association, 1982.

On his return from the Galápagos, Franklin D. Roosevelt proposed the establishment of a sort of collective protectorate over the archipelago. When the Ecuadorian government rejected the idea, the president looked for an alternative by making use of the Pacific Development Company of Delaware which, with the support of federal funds, would try to establish alliances with private landowners on Isabela Island in order to obtain a concession for fishing in the waters of the Galápagos (Humphreys 1981, 122).[12] In spite of being presented in Ecuador as a development project for the island, the initiative caused a big commotion among public opinion and those close to the president, Arroyo del Río. The press and the Peruvian Congress also criticized the proposal (Luna Tobar 1997, 283–6). In the end, neither the idea of the protectorate nor of the sale or concession bore fruit. In addition, with the start of the Second World War, the only project that was able to succeed was the installation of the US military base on Baltra Island (1941–8). President Arroyo del Río was nevertheless accused of ceding Baltra in exchange for bribes and personal benefits (de la Torre 1993, 31).

By the 1950s, discussions about the Galápagos no longer revolved around the security of the hemisphere or the possible sale or leasing of the archipelago. Instead, they focused on concerns about the extinction of the endemic species on the islands and the desire to turn them into a living memorial to Darwin apropos of the celebration of the 1959 upcoming centenary of *On the Origin of Species*. A redefinition of the value of the property had already taken place.

A Decent Republic

Ecuador continued to own the Galápagos Islands due, first and foremost, to the presence of laborers-settlers on the islands who, after being uprooted from the highlands under the *hacienda* system, played a role in protecting the national government's possession for over a century. For its part, the Ecuadorian government focused on maintaining these settlements at the minimum cost. The use of law and the concern to build the country's respectability and reputation were also significant in preventing the sale or lease of the archipelago.[13]

In 1913, the Ecuadorian Parliament issued a first decree to prohibit the executive branch from signing contracts which would allow foreign nations or natural persons to establish colonies on the archipelago; it further ordered that three-quarters of its population had to be Ecuadorian nationals or, in their absence, foreign colonists must be naturalized in the country. It then forbade public notaries from endorsing petitions for the granting of public deeds in the name of foreign companies. Later in 1930, it further declared the territory as a state property, ignoring any private claim to the ownership of lands that were not cultivated. In so doing, it recognized the rights of the laborers who had already distributed the lands after the decline of the *haciendas*. According to some of my interviewees, each tenant took all the land he could possibly enclose—for example, within his possibilities of building a fence or another type of enclosure.[14] Finally, when the Second War ended and after noticing that the United States was delaying the evacuation of Base Beta, President Velasco Ibarra issued another decree to create a penal colony on Isabela (the very same island that Roosevelt dreamt of buying a few years back).

On the other hand, the creole elite's hope of selling the islands to France and even turn the nation into a French colony seemed, at the time, possible and legitimate. The same was true of the alternative of selling whole parts of the territory, including its inhabitants—as in the times of Spanish America. Financial pressures, an urgent need to pay off the foreign debt, the little value given to a land with little fresh water in the middle of the Pacific, as well as the country's inability to defend it (along with a large part of its mainland territory) were all justifications for initiatives towards those ends. Hence, although the Ecuadorian parliament had warned—since 1891—that scientific expeditions might be a façade for projects to alienate the Galápagos, successive administrations continued to negotiate its sale or leasing, even up to the middle of the following century.

Yet at the same time, Ecuador was also concerned to act as a sovereign and decent republic according to the new norms of civility. Each of the nations of Latin America was going through the same process: having to build their reputation after independence from Spain. In addition, harsher sanctions started to be imposed on the disaggregation of a nation's properties, on the cession of a territory to become a colony of another power or, later on, on the invasion or forcible seizure of foreign territories. In that context, Peru's claims to the possession of the archipelago paradoxically favored Ecuador's retention of it. By denouncing the government of Ecuador every time that it offered the islands, the Peruvian delegates, along with its peers, exploited public shame to civilize the conduct of the new republic. On the internal level, those who accused the successive presidents of "selling out the country" were also effective in blocking scandals and the alienation of the archipelago.

As such, the use of shame, rumors, gossip, and scandal helped to prevent a change of ownership of the Galápagos. They further worked to civilize the nation (and the continent as a whole) by controlling its rulers in their impulse to sell part of the national territories. They later worked, too, at the global level to facilitate the ratification of multilateral agreements and to monitor compliance (Merry 2006).[15] This started with the emergence, after the Second World War, of new property regimes and diverse forms of neoliberal governance that reshaped the access, control, and use of territories and their natural resources (de Castro et al. 2016)—and more recently, after the 2010 Convention of Biological Diversity, the commitment of 192 state parties to enlist and protect nature reserves within their territories, following the IUCN mandate on what nature is and should be. They agreed on the urgency of such a task, thus designating whole areas as: world heritage sites, strict nature reserves, wilderness areas, natural monuments, habitat/species management areas, protected landscapes/seascapes, or national parks. These areas should all adhere to the rule of international treaties and conservation agencies irrespective of their specific type of governance or the territories on which they are located. In that sense, the agreement by which Ecuador gave away the management of the Galápagos for the protection of nature was an unprecedented move in the history of imperial geopolitics.

FROM GAME PRESERVE TO A LIVING MEMORIAL TO DARWIN (1930S–1959)

The proposal made by US millionaires to buy the Galápagos was followed by a series of diplomatic moves aimed at convincing the Ecuadorian government to establish a legal framework for the protection of the fauna on the archipelago. But during the next decades (between 1930 and 1959), the plans envisioned for the Galápagos project changed. From being thought of as a place marked out as a game preserve, it instead turned into the site to commemorate Darwin's 'discovery' of evolution.

In Memory of Darwin's Visit (1930s)

Back in the 1930s, scientists started to foresee the islands' potential for the *in situ* study of evolution. In 1932, one of the naturalists who visited the Galápagos on board the expedition financed by Templeton Crocker was the first to call them an "[e]volution workshop and showcase" (Larson 2001, 166). Another scientist thought they would serve as an "outdoor biological laboratory" in one of the "most amazing natural laboratories of natural processes on earth" (Hennessy 2014, 58, citing Barrow 2009, 176). Yet, the scientific impulse was ultimately prompted by the desire to commemorate the centennial of Darwin's visit to the Galápagos (1935) and the publication of *On the Origin of Species* (1959) with the creation of a natural sanctuary and, later, a living memorial for Darwin.

US explorer Victor Wolfgang von Hagen took the first steps in such project, although trying to pursue it in a solo campaign. He did send invitations on the part of "Darwin Memorial Association" to notable scientists in northern

Europe and the United States for the celebration of the one hundredth anniversary of Darwin's visit to the archipelago. But no one showed interest. He also formally announced the event in a brief commentary in the *New York Times*.[16] Then he headed to the islands.

Once there in September 1935, he erected the first bust of the famous naturalist on the pier of Puerto Baquerizo Moreno in San Cristóbal Island. Here is how he recalled the *galapagueños* who attended the ceremony on that day:

> It was a simple ceremony. A few idle *galapagueños*, half teethed and half clothed stood by, mainly for the wine that was to follow. I made a short speech in Spanish; the commandant, who did not know any more about Darwin than

Figure 2.2. Invitation to the Charles Darwin centenary celebration. "The Darwin Memorial Association has the honor to invite Dr. John Merriam [Director of the Carnegie Institution] to take part in the ceremony celebrating the centenary of Charles Albert Darwin on the Archipiélago de Colón." Galápagos Islands, September 17, 1935. Source: (www.galapagos.to)

he did about Wedgwood, accepted the monument in the name of Ecuador (von Hagen 1941, 171).

von Hagen himself financed the voyage, the monument, and all the efforts that followed to achieve the goal of protecting the Galápagos. On the mainland, he awarded medals and diplomas to the president of Ecuador and other senior officials of the government on behalf of the "Darwin Memorial Association" and devoted himself to sponsoring cocktail parties, meetings and fiestas, and coordinating a group of local professors known as the "Scientific Corporation for the Study and Protection of the Natural Riches of the Colón Archipelago." The group succeeded in lobbying the Ecuadorian state to adopt the 1936 protectionist decree which declared the Galápagos a "national reserve." The government further accepted that foreign cooperation, in the form of a committee of experts, could oversee the protection of wildlife on the archipelago in the future.

Yet outside of Ecuador, von Hagen's lack of scientific credibility (having no institutional affiliation and no evidence of specific degrees of academic training) rapidly turned him into an outsider in the discussions that began to be held regarding the future of the archipelago (Hennessy 2014, 63–8). He had already contacted scientists of international renown (like Harold Coolidge and Julian Huxley) in order to get their support for creating a scientific station to honor the memory of Darwin on the archipelago. But after some investigations, the scientists thought von Hagen was more a "promoter" than a true scientist who would not be able to lead a scientific station (ibid.). Furthermore, they found that the association he had founded never officially existed. He was later linked with the illicit sale of Ecuadorian archival from Quito that had disappeared and appeared in a London's book shop. As a result, he became a "persona non-grata" in Ecuador. Nonetheless, through von Hagen's efforts, the project to establish a natural sanctuary in memory of Darwin began to be heard of.

The Galápagos Project

The Galápagos project had to be halted with the outbreak of the Second World War. The United States nevertheless managed to secure its presence on the archipelago through the establishment of a military base on Baltra Island. The project was only resumed by the mid-1950s after Austrian ethnologist Eibl-Eibesfelt conducted fieldwork in the archipelago. Shocked by the devastation of its fauna, he wrote letters to the IUCN and UNESCO to ask for immediate intervention. The defacement of the landscape by visitors who came in yachts, the killing of fur seals, and the persecution of sea lions by fishermen—both local and foreign—were some of his greatest concerns. In

Baltra he particularly was shocked to find that where William Beebe had observed plenty of large land iguanas, he could only find one single carcass that had been shot some years before, during the U.S. occupation of the island.[17]

His concern reached UNESCO's first Director, Julian Huxley. A decade earlier, when the Second War finalized, UNESCO emerged with the mission to structure a new world order around the promise of peace through international cooperation in education, culture, and the sciences. Huxley himself was responsible for the incorporation of the "S" for science in the institution's name because, he argued, "culture without science doesn't make sense" (Holdgate 1999, 22). For its first delegates, it was, nevertheless, not obvious to consider the preservation of rare fauna and "unspoilt scenery" as part of the organization's mission. About this commitment, Huxley expressed:

> Delegates asked me what seemed to me silly questions: why should UNESCO try to protect rhinoceros or rare flowers? Was not the safeguarding of grand, unspoilt scenery outside its purview? However, with the aid of a few nature lovers I persuaded the Conference that the enjoyment of nature was part of culture and that the preservation of rare and interesting plants was a scientific duty (ibid., 22).

Following a sort of Malthusian approach, Huxley further insisted that if the organization were to face the problems of the modern world, it must deal with pressing issues such as the recognition of the idea of an optimum population size and the conservation of wildlife. The latter required setting aside particular spaces so that other (nonhuman) species could be protected and privileged.

Besides, the Galápagos Islands were especially appealing to Huxley. Since the 1930s, he had expressed an interest in island wildlife and, particularly, in Galápagos science. During that decade, Huxley financed David Lack—by then an amateur bird observer—to study finches on the archipelago. He later drew on Lack's data to write his 1942 treatise *Evolution: The Modern Synthesis* and his 1953 monograph *Evolution in Action* (Larson 2001, 178). Moreover, he was the grandson of T. H. Huxley, better known as "Darwin's bulldog." And he had become the leading authority reconciling Darwin's theory with Gregor Mendel's ideas on heredity. Presumably, he also had already heard of the endeavors that von Hagen pursued in Ecuador to protect the islands' fauna in Darwin's name. Backed by the elite networks of science and politics, Huxley could embrace the Galápagos project as part of UNESCO's institutional agenda.

After receiving Eibl's letters, Huxley joined forces with his colleagues Harold Coolidge and the Belgian scientist, Victor van Straelen, to pursue a territorial claim over the Galápagos. Coolidge was member of the Boone Crockett Club and had hunted and studied African animals in the Belgian

Congo. There he coincided with van Straelen, and the two made concerted efforts to found the world's first gorilla sanctuary in what would become Congo National Park. With Huxley, the three conservationists had recently worked to create the IUCN to strengthen the conservation movement worldwide, which then spawned the World Wildlife Fund (WWF) for the protection of endangered species. A full, credible network was thus starting to forge, enabling the use of scientific knowledge to justify governance of foreign territories that were classified as of a valuable nature.

The next year, UNESCO sponsored Eibl and US ornithologist Robert Bowman for an exploratory mission to the archipelago. They were sent out to choose a site for the biological station, to make a preliminary "census" of the animal population, and to suggest protective measures (as described in Eibl's 1958 accounts, titled "Wonders of a Noah's Ark off the Coast of Ecuador"). Upon returning from the field, the scientists urged for the safeguarding of the fauna and flora of the archipelago at the fifteenth International Congress of Zoology in London, which for the first time in its history, had a section on conservation. As a result, the Committee for the Galápagos was formally created, with J. Huxley as its head. van Straelen, H. Coolidge, D. Ripley, Jean Dorst (director of the French Museum of Natural History), Sir Peter Scott (who was later head of the WWF), Jean-Georges Baer (then-president of the IUCN), and Luis Jaramillo (Ecuadorian delegate to UNESCO) also became members. R. Bowman began service as the Secretary for the Americas on the committee. The objective of the committee was clear: to "save" the archipelago of the Galápagos and, at the same time, to turn it into a "living memorial" to Darwin and a "museum of evolution in action" (Huxley 1954, 9).

A Living Memorial to Darwin (1950s)

There is no doubt that the Galápagos was the right place to observe and learn about the processes of evolution. For one thing, given the remoteness of the archipelago, the number and variety of ancestors of native species is more limited than in other places, which means that "the laws of evolution are much easier to distinguish than in the rest of the world, where the complexity of natural phenomena and the multiplicity of ancestors complicate inextricably the tracing of relationships" (Dorst 1961, 30).[18] For another—and on a more nostalgic note—the fauna and landscape of the Galápagos promised to transport visitors to another time, one that claimed to offer a picture of pre-human, pre-historical life in a place that could testify to the existence of a pristine nature on earth in the present time. This is how Bowman described the island of Fernandina when he returned from his field study there:

Only after several days of intimate contact with the weird world of Fernandina did I overcome my initial impression that the physical and biotic elements were in temporal and geographic discord with the outside world. Where else on earth can one find enormous herds of ocean-venturing dragon-like iguanas, reminiscent of pre-historic times?

Where else does one find a member of the typically Antartic penguin tribe living in comfort directly on the Equator and feeding on the small fishes that teem in these "tropical" waters? . . . Where else can one find a giant of the cormorant family of birds with wings so reduced that, in mockery of the evolutionary process, they render the bird flightless? And all of these biological productions are staged in a setting one might imagine to be more typical of the coolest parts of Hell or an adolescent planet (quoting Bowman 1960, Hennessy 2014, 77).

Only in the Galápagos. Beyond that, it was the perfect time for science to pay tribute to Darwin and the revolutionary concept of evolution. "To take advantage of this anniversary to create the station…would doubtless be the best homage to the father of the brilliant theories of evolution," declared Dorst, who was appointed second president of the Charles Darwin Foundation (1965–70) and later vice-president of the IUCN (Dorst 1961, 8). The destiny of the Galápagos seemed obvious.

But first to achieve that, the Committee for the Galápagos had to convince the Ecuadorian government. Public opinion in Ecuador at the time distrusted the United States. That was clear, for example, from the Ecuadorian reaction to a rumor that spread in 1960 about a group of US migrants on their way to the Galápagos to establish a settler colony there. According to the *LA Times* (Oct. 13, 1960), this not only prompted a protest in front of the US Consulate in Guayaquil but also ended up in 400 Ecuadorians—"many of them Indians"—being sent to Santa Cruz and San Cristóbal Islands in order to keep population numbers in favor of nationals (Hennessy 2014, 84).

The Galápagos committee thus decided to resort to the umbrella of the IUCN and UNESCO to undertake the project as an issue of transnational governance rather than a matter of US imperialism. They created the nongovernmental Charles Darwin Foundation (CDF) under Belgian law to pursue fundraising, publicity, and the signing of agreements with the state of Ecuador. Members of the former Committee for the Galápagos were appointed as its founding board members, naming Van Straelen as the visible head of the project and first president of the CDF (1959–1964). Following this, the Belgian scientist paid a visit to Ecuadorian President Velasco Ibarra to share his previous experience as founder of Congo National Park. According to the CDF, the president was highly impressed (*Noticias de Galápagos* 1990). The scientist showed that nature on the Galápagos Islands was of great value to science, and consequently, the islands could also generate valuable capital for the Ecuadorian state.

Throughout the negotiations between the Ecuadorian government, the CDF, and UNESCO, there was no mention about any monetary compensation involved. For Ecuadorian officials, the islands—as well as the Indigenous laborers who lived there—had no value and sovereignty was difficult to defend. They could, however, foresee the possibilities for economic development that this arrangement could generate, as the discourses at the inaugural event of the Darwin station illustrate.

THE CREATION OF THE GALÁPAGOS NATIONAL PARK AND THE CHARLES DARWIN STATION

The Signing of the Agreement (1959)

In July 1959, under emergency Decree-Law 17, the government of Ecuador agreed to designate the archipelago as a 'national park' and ceded its administration to a foreign institution: the Charles Darwin Foundation. It thus awarded the CDF's board the power to decide on the size of the park's property; the natural reserves or monuments it would have; and the species of fauna and flora that would be controlled, eradicated, or safeguarded. In addition, it granted the scientists the right to establish a legal framework to regulate the way to govern nature and society in the whole of the archipelago with the cooperation of Ecuadorian military and civil authorities for the enforcement of this legislation.

Paradoxically, the Catholic Church was a witness to the moment when the men of science and the representatives of the government of Ecuador met to designate the Galápagos as the place to commemorate the origin of evolutionary theories and modern secular thought. In the words of Huxley at the 1964 Symposium on the Galápagos International Scientific Project:

> It was on the Galápagos in the early autumn of 1835 that Darwin took the first step beyond the fairy-land of creationism into the coherent and comprehensible world of modern biology; for it was here that he became fully convinced that species are not immutable—in other words, that evolution is a fact (Huxley in Bowman 1966, 3).

From then on, science and the *hacienda* regime agreed to join hands in the endeavor to fabricate a living memorial to Darwin. Conservationists were to impose the European nature/culture divide on the new subject territory so

Figure 2.3. The Signing of the Agreement. Professor Victor Van Straelen signs the agreement to create the Charles Darwin Foundation with the Ecuadorian Minister of Foreign Relations in Quito. The Catholic Bishop was present as a witness. Source: Illustrated by M. Salinas. Based on the photo published in 1964 in *Noticias de Galápagos*. 913.

that they could start the work of reordering nature to turn the cursed islands into an allegorical place to understand the origin of species. In so doing, they established the Western ideology of nature protection, fueled by the appreciation of "wilderness" (Cronon 1992, Whiston 1996)[19] and the belief the work requires the separation of "Nature" from humans, both spatially and temporally.[20]

Within a couple of years, the park's borders were defined. Following the English logic, first settlers and natives of the Galápagos were labeled as outsiders who had to be enclosed in reserves where they could be sovereign. As a result, 97 percent of the archipelago's land became part of the natural sanctuary. The remaining 3 percent was allotted for urban use and as agricultural buffer zone. In this scheme, the Ecuadorian government ensured that locals would provide the labor and services required by scientists, tourists, and state bureaucrats so that the enforcement of conservation law and the making of a pristine evolutionary landscape could take place. And although the borders were supposed to enclose 'Nature' and not humans, from the way *galapagueños* colloquially speak, it seems that the park's borders actually enclosed them.

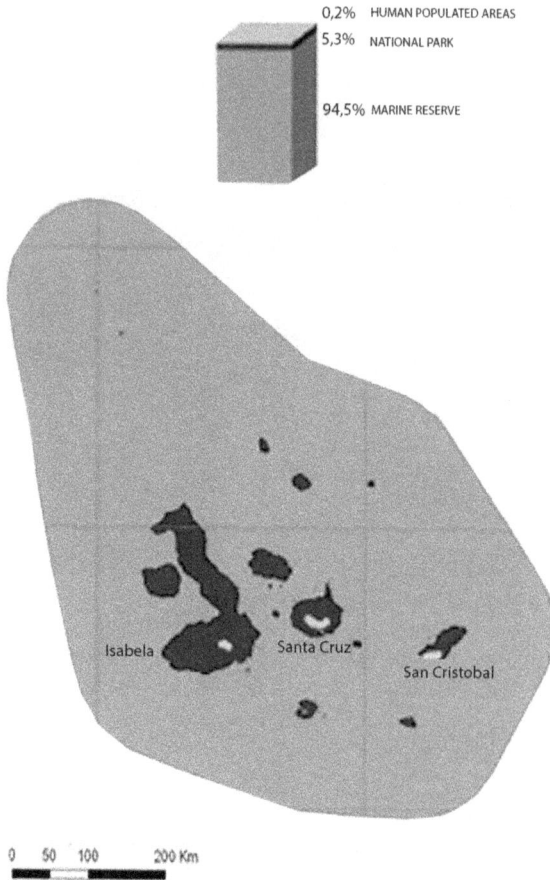

Figure 2.4. Protected areas (in black and dark gray) and areas used by humans (mostly agricultural zones, in light gray). Three percent of the archipelago's land (or 0.2 percent of the total park's area, including the marine reserve) was designated for settlers (urban use and agriculture). *Source*: Map created by Mauricio Salinas.

The Inauguration of the Darwin Station (1964)

After the agreement was signed, the building of the scientific station, directed by Professor van Straelen, was set into motion. Following Eibl's 1958 recommendation (in which he refers to the islands only by their English names), Chatham (San Cristóbal) and Charles (Floreana) were to be ruled out as possible sites to locate the station. Eibl thought they were already spoiled by colonization. Albemarle (Isabela), for its part, still had a prison colony.

Meanwhile, Indefatigable (Santa Cruz) Island was ideal, since it was the least populated and was situated in the center of the archipelago where many of the more interesting islands (like Duncan and Barrington) were at easy reach.

Although the main problem of the islands—and particularly of Santa Cruz—was the fresh water supply, Eibl observed that "the settlers collect rain water on their roofs and store it in large tanks," in sufficient amount to cover their needs all year round (Eibl 1958, 26). Besides, Santa Cruz was next to the small island of Baltra, which had a 1,800-meter-long asphalted landing strip and a deepwater dock, both built at the time it was occupied by the United States during the World War II. The essential infrastructure was in place to now serve the men of science.

The first suitable option for the site of the research station was located in Academy Bay, two kilometers away from the small settlement of Puerto Ayora. At the time, very few people lived there. Most of the settlers of Santa Cruz had established homes in areas of higher elevation on the island. The second option was even closer to Puerto Ayora, which could be useful to facilitate the provision of food and services to the incoming scientists. Yet this option was soon rejected because it was located too close to the human settlement and to a salt lagoon where "settlers come to get salt and are a source of constant disturbance" (ibid., 27). Some years later, Dorst reflected on the site that was ultimately chosen for the Darwin station:

> The fact that it is close to inhabited places, without their being in too close a proximity to them, would enable us to exploit all of the advantages of this situation, avoiding at the same time the many material and psychological drawbacks which would arise from an excessive promiscuity (Dorst 1959, 10).

Local manpower was, however, critical to advance the building projects overseen by the earliest directors of the station, among them: a laboratory, the director's house, workshops, an electricity plant, dormitories, storerooms, roads, a meteorological station, a seismographic station, a pier, slipway, breakwater, and a "chalet" for visiting scientists (Snow 1964). For their part, UNESCO, the World Wildlife Fund, the New York Zoological Society, and the Royal Society of London bore the cost of the installations as well as the salaries of its earliest directors. The place was not only meant to be a center for scientific observation and experimentation but also a mandatory site for "every biologist who should, once in his life, undertake a pilgrimage to the Galápagos, where one of the greatest successes of science was born" (Dorst 1963, 147).

Finally, in January 1964, amidst the cacti of Academy Bay, around 500 people assembled for the inaugural ceremony. Huxley, van Straelen, and Charles Darwin's grandson were there, along with sixty scientists (who had sailed from San Francisco), ambassadors, UNESCO delegates, and more than 100 representatives of the government and the armed forces of Ecuador. To transport them to the ceremony, the United States provided a large transport plane and Ecuador, a Dakota airliner. Several helicopters were sent there for interisland journeys, along with the vessels *Pine Island* and the *Golden Bear*, the latter a training ship of the California Maritime Academy. In addition, cases of the finest champagne were carried from California, together with the group of scientists who took part in the "floating symposium" of the Galápagos International Scientific Project. The ship sailed southwards to the port to join "the most important social event in the history of the Galápagos," in the words of a reporter from the San Francisco Chronicle, another of the invitees (Perlman 1964, cited by Larson 2001, 194).

The inauguration of a permanent international scientific base in the Galápagos began with speeches by Dr. van Straelen, the recently appointed president of the Darwin Foundation who represented Western science, and General Gandara, the head of the local militia who represented the governing junta of Ecuador. They were followed by Cristóbal Bonifaz, Ecuadorian Ambassador to France, and Luis Jaramillo, its delegate to UNESCO, who spoke of the national government's position before a crowd of islanders, members of the Ecuadorian armed forces, and (English-speaking) scientists.

Bonifaz began by thanking the UNESCO for its "scientific and moral support" for the creation of a "living museum of evolution." He also emphasized: "it is logical to suppose that in this well-known center of fishing on the Galápagos, this scientific endeavor will have immediate industrial advantages" (Bonifaz 1963, 3). Up to that time, the islands had been a favored site for whale hunting and later for tuna catching by big Japanese and US vessels. Meanwhile, from Ecuador's annexation of the Galápagos in 1832 to that period, its coast guard had futilely watched the fishing of its waters by third parties and the routine "looting" of thousands of specimens by foreign scientists and millionaire tourists. The only initiative the national government in Quito had taken was to assert its sovereignty over the archipelago through the transplantation of the *hacienda* (with its Indigenous laborers) for agriculture livestock production. It was thus natural that when the station was inaugurated, the government of Ecuador assigned the administration of the recently created Galápagos National Park to its Ministry of Agriculture and Stock-Rearing. This determination would eventually result in a contradiction, since the ministry would not understand why there was such interest in preserving an "unspoilt" scenery in the archipelago (Latorre 2011, 253).

For his part, Jaramillo, the Ecuadorian delegate to UNESCO, restated his commitment to the project "for those who, in one way or another, [conduct] daily work for the progress of mankind," while at the same time, he described the islands that were hosting them as a place which "at times had been a refuge for convicted criminals, at others, of ultra-civilized bohemians" who were looking for "a sort of return to the sources of man's origins" (ibid.).

In his speech, Jaramillo reinforced the Ecuadorian state commitment to UNESCO's "evolutionary humanism" (Huxley 1954) while using a familiar tone when speaking of the islands and their inhabitants. On the one hand, there was the civilizing mission of science and white foreign scientists.[21] On the other, the territory was inhabited by two kinds of men who—in line with the Social Darwinism of Herbert Spencer (1864)—could be easily placed at two opposite poles of cultural development. On one side there were the barbarian, more primitive, local inhabitants—the supposed offspring of "criminals" expelled from Ecuador. On the other, on the summit of the island, there were the "ultra-civilized" Germans and Norwegians who still received by far the most attention in official accounts of the human history of the Galápagos.

The sense of progress in Jaramillo's words involved conceptions of race and civilization, which were rooted in anthropological thought after the encounter of Europeans with colonial subjects during the era of transatlantic, scientific imperialism. In constructing this cultural and racial ladder towards civilization, anthropologists borrowed evolutionary ideas and classificatory practices from the science of ecology. These were used to recast human groups in a way that advocated for the superiority of the white race and its civilization.[22] These ideas were later put in action in the United States, in policy-making for population control, family planning, and racially restrictive immigration laws.

The reverse applied, ecological thought was shaped by anthropology and other social sciences; for example, Darwin found inspiration in Malthus' ideas (on how to avoid the increase of poor populations) to write *On the Origin of Species* in 1859 (Martin 1991, 500). This was also true when he adopted Spencer's phrase "the survival of the fittest" for later editions of his foundational text (Endler 1986, 28).[23]

From this perspective, the reframing of nature followed by the territorial claim over the archipelago expressed Western racist ideology, based on a heightened self-consciousness of European superiority. Because of their scientific expertise, it justified the need for Western conservationists to manage the Galápagos. They knew how to make efficient and rational use of resources to maximize nature's output or otherwise reach its equilibrium point (Worster 1994, 202, Drayton 2000).[24] Conservation law responded accordingly by framing, some decades later, the quest to protect nature in the Galápagos in relation to the way society was to be governed—that is, in terms of a typical Malthusian problem.

In the words of the Ecuadorian delegate, the foreign hierarchy was further conflated with the racial inequalities that had long been established by the *hacienda* order. The "convicts" that Jaramillo spoke of were actually Indian laborers who had been systematically enslaved and criminalized in Ecuador by a racialized system of labor. Yet in reality, most of those who were listening to the speeches of the scientists, politicians, and army officers in the cactus grove were neither European families nor the descendants of *colonos* or pioneer families of San Cristóbal and Isabela Islands.[25] Instead, the majority of the attendees were rural families who had recently settled in the higher elevated areas of Santa Cruz, attracted by opportunities made available with the construction of the Darwin station, the increasing arrival of tourists, and the greater demand for food.[26] In five years, from 1959 to 1964, the initial 300 that lived in Santa Cruz became more than 700 "souls" (Lundh 2001, 37). Many of these new settlers were originally from Ambato, Tungurahua, in the highlands (Hoff 1985). They gathered on that day in Academy Bay to hear the announcement of a new scheme of governance, a seemingly much needed order, which was yet another racially contingent form of property.

When the inaugural ceremony ended, the scientists embarked on a five-week-long exploration of the archipelago. Thanks to the helicopters which were made available to them, they were able to land in places that had never been known to Western science, like the inaccessible summit of Culpepper Island (now Darwin Island) and Cape Berkeley in the northwest part of Isabela. Afterwards each group returned to California with their animal collections and scientific equipment (Snow 1964, 4).

THE HUMAN PROBLEM

From the outset, the two scientists (Eibl-Eibesfeldt [1958], Bowman [1960]) who gave their recommendations to achieve the essential conditions for the establishment of an international scientific laboratory in memory of Darwin warned the scientific community about the problems that human colonization had to their mission. "On the whole colonization conflicts with nature protection. How can both interests be reconciled?" Eibl asked. His Ecuadorian colleague, Miguel Acosta-Solís, recommended that the local government "should prohibit further colonization" because the protection of nature should be primarily concerned with the preservation of species for aesthetic enjoyment and scientific study rather than utilitarian exploitation (Bowman 1966, 282–5). Besides, according to the director of Darwin´s station, the settlers completely misunderstood the purpose of UNESCO, rather imagining it to be another "United Fruit" coming to the region:

The UNESCO has to pay attention on what they are doing. I think most of new settlers in the west of Santa Cruz came there on a false reasoning—false for us at least. They simply imagine the UNESCO to be a big commercial company, like the "United Fruit" or something like this, they simply moved in, thinking that if one hectare was worth 1 *sucre* then, it would soon be 100 or 1000 *sucres* worth!

This is the type of thinking of those poor people. Of course, the government is responsible for that awfulness . . . We can't do much with that irresponsible people in the government, they don't even know apparently what the Galápagos are! (Bowman to Coolidge, quoting Leveque 1960, in Hennessy 2014, 89).

For conservationists, both *galapagueños* and representatives of the Ecuadorian state did not know what the Galápagos were. The station's mission was therefore oriented toward educating the locals while making laws in order to control human interference with pristine nature. Furthermore, for the CDF, the task "demanded routine surveillance, with a view of reporting infringements of laws and regulations, rather than scientific research" (*Noticias de Galápagos* 1969, 14). In such a context, the work of the scientists involved monitoring locals who were perceived as a threat. The problem was thus seen as "intimately connected with Ecuadorian policy on colonization and land settlement" (ibid.).

Soon, there was a clear demarcation of the limits of the park, with green and white stakes being permanently placed across its borders. This ended with the customary way to claim a land in the Galápagos, which was the establishment of a fence around it. "The more barbed wire one could afford, the more land one could claim" (*Noticias de Galápagos* 1972, 25) In 1968, the Ecuadorian government further sent a delegation in order to solve, once and for all, the problems of what became "illegal" land claiming, as it trespassed the borders of the park's area. In addition to this, the Galápagos National Park (GNP) began to patrol the park. Its prime task was defined as the protection of the wildlife in the archipelago, while reporting directly to the Ecuadorian government in Quito. As such, both the foreign conservationists and the Ecuadorian political and economic elite of Quito came to be responsible for the protection of the natural property.

In 1972, "human exploitation" was identified as the major threat. In particular, scientists at the Galápagos Science Conference pointed at the lack of control over population growth in the archipelago, noting that immigration from the continent had already tripled and there was "a very high birth rate" at the local level (*Noticias de Galápagos* 1974, 15).[27] By the 1980s, when six thousand people already lived in the Galápagos, the scientists stressed that the islands were "ill-adapted to human settlement, unsuitable for agriculture and livestock" (Curry-Lindhal 1981, 9). They also recognized that "no dialogue has been established between the local people, the park, and the station" (ibid.).

By the end of the next decade, the 1998 Special Law responded to these Malthusian concerns by framing local population growth and immigration as more harmful to the environment than the increases of the numbers of tourists and cruises visiting the Galápagos. It transformed *colonos* and people born in the Galápagos into "permanent residents" while restricting immigrants' entry and allotted time of stay (turning those who exceeded the permitted stay into "illegals," despite their status as Ecuadorian nationals). In order to enforce this, the CDF required Ecuadorian authorities to persecute and deport back to the Ecuadorian mainland those who remained illegally in the islands. At the same time, no limits were imposed on the increases in cruise or land-based tourism. Instead, the park started to schedule the cruises' itineraries in a way that tourists wouldn't see many groups or boats on the water at any particular visitor site; an optical illusion of fewer tourists was created rather than an actual reduction in numbers. For their part, local authorities were charged with enforcing the law specifically targeting Indigenous migrants—mainly "illegal" *Salasacas*.

NOTES

1. In part, Chile's strong opposition may have been due to its own interests in the negotiations over the Galápagos. In 1897, Chile offered Ecuador a warship in exchange for the cession of one of the islands. In 1905, it further offered to build a port there and lend its support for the protection of Ecuador's sovereignty. During the same period, Chile also sent several scientific expeditions to the archipelago to assess its value.

2. At different times, Great Britain and the United States were also interested in establishing a coaling station on the archipelago.

3. It took until 1917 for an Ecuadorian president, Alfredo Baquerizo Moreno, to visit the archipelago. To honor him, the name of Puerto Chico—the capital of San Cristóbal Island—was changed to "Puerto Baquerizo Moreno." Nevertheless, the presence of the Ecuadorian State in the Galápagos continued to be practically non-existent until 1928, when the management of the archipelago was put in the hands of the Ministry of Defense.

4. Alfaro also thought of using eight million dollars to improve public sanitation in Guayaquil, which was scourged by epidemics; three million for the railway of Alausí and Cuenca; two million for Ambato-Curaray railway; and two million for Quito—and one million for Ibarra (Luna Tobar 1997, 196–7).

5. One of the rumors said that a secret agreement between the Japanese and Peruvians had been reached to facilitate Japan's bid for a fishing concession in the Galápagos. Another one circulated about the presence of Italian and German spies in

the region, and the possible annexation of the islands by Germany when Hitler was in power. Yet by 1939, the only Germans who lived in the Galápagos were the Wittmer family and the Angermeyer brothers (in an article titled "Galápagos Grab by Nazis Feared," in *The United Press,* 1939—in Luna Tobar 1997: 200).

6. The penal colony on Isabela was definitively closed in 1959, shortly after the Ecuadorian government signed the agreement for the creation of the Galápagos National Park and the Charles Darwin Scientific Station on the archipelago.

7. Between 1897 and 1906, seven scientific expeditions to the Galápagos Islands sailed from San Francisco Bay alone. The scientific institutions of the United States had more specimens from the Galápagos than from any other place in the Pacific.

8. Native peoples were also included in the regular exhibitions of natural history museums and World's Fairs until early in the 1900s (Griffiths 2002, 46–85).

9. For the New York Zoological Society, Harrison Williams financed William Beebe's famous expedition in 1923. His accounts published in his book *Galapagos: World's End* (1924), became a best seller.

10. Grant also authored the book *The Passing of the Great Race* (1916), which Adolf Hitler referred to as "my Bible" (Spiro 2008, xi).

11. Captain Amasa Delano published an account of the fauna of the islands after his visits to them in 1800 and 1801. (www.galapagos.to).

12. This probably referred to former workers of Antonio Gil who took over his lands after the collapse of *Hacienda Santo Tomás* in 1935.

13. Settlers were completely abandoned by the state and entirely subjected to the *hacienda* master rule. The presence of the state was minimal with a handful of guards living in San Cristóbal Island. The Ecuadorian Navy rarely visited the archipelago.

14. In 1928, due to their need of cash, many of the settlers sold their lands in San Cristóbal Island to a Spanish landlord, Lorenzo Tous, who invested in coffee production.

15. The use of shame still works in gaining compliance for the signing of treaties, such as the Convention on the Elimination of All Forms of Discrimination Against Women (*CEDAW*) (Merry 2003) or, more recently, the deployment of a variety of programs and reform strategies through the development of quantitative indicators of global governance (Merry 2016).

16. He also convinced the Ecuadorian government to issue a series of Galápagos stamps (with Darwin's portrait, tortoises, and iguanas) that would be sold at the time of the centennial in order to raise funds for the Galápagos project. These were, however, printed too late.

17. President Roosevelt once intervened when informed that GIs were running iguana races, taunting feral goats, and shooting animals in the military base of Baltra Island. In 1944, Roosevelt sent a memorandum to his secretary of state: "I have been at this for six or seven years and I would die happy if the State Department could accomplish something" with regards to the protection of the Galápagos as an international wildlife sanctuary (quoted by Larson 2001, 176). A directive for GIs prohibiting them from shooting animals was sent.

18. Some years later, MacArthur and Wilson (2001[1967]: 152–180) further posited oceanic islands and archipelagos as "excellent theaters" not only to observe

evolution but also to perform "natural experiments" by which evolutionary theses could be tested (Simberloff 1974, 161–182). These served as valid samples to make inferences about dispersal, competition, adaptation and extinction processes and apply them, in a lesser or greater degree, to continents, and all natural habitats. The scientists further suggested to manipulate their insular biotas—by adding or removing elements (or by removing the entire biota), manually or by poisoning, so that processes of natural extinction could be assessed (see, for examples, Chernela 2012: 26). After decades of research, such experiments allowed island biogeography to move from a descriptive activity to a quantitatively supported, theoretical phase, while also providing the guiding principles by which nature reserves were designed in an effort to maximize their ability to increase habitat diversity (Diamond 1975, Losos and Ricklefs 2009).

19. For a long time, "wilderness" was deemed as the site of satanic temptation—where Jesus was tested by the devil (Matthew 4); a "horrendous place full of decaying trees, rotting leaves, parasitic plants and venomous insects" (as per 1749 Buffon's Histoire Naturelle, Wulf 2015, 60); as unnatural places where "beasts ran wild" (Olwig 1996, 382); and later as the desolate, the hostile, the waste; the counterpoint of humanity; the "zone of free land," a frontier filled with "primitive savagery" (Cronon 1992). But, in 1864, Yellowstone—the first 'modern' natural park—launched a new model with the enclosure of a wilderness that combined images of the 'pristine' with the pastoral, thus setting a principle on the aesthetic (untamed) appearance of the new "natural scenery" (Whiston 1996).

20. It took a lot for "wilderness" to become "Nature." From the doctrines of Enlightenment thinkers who introduced Cartesian mind/body, human/animal, and culture/nature divides in the Age of Reason, to the travel accounts of naturalists from the eighteenth century through the Victorian era (Pratt 2008 [1992]), and finally, the undertakings of Romantics who learned from pastoral poets to place the sublime in the countryside (Cronon 1992, 1996) and then in the wild, at the edge of the "expanding cultural landscape" (Proctor 1996). Such reinvention had to be built with the progressive removal of "nature" farther away from Europe's countryside and into the regions "which were not dominated by Europeans" (Pratt 2008 [1992], 37). Such spaces were imagined "unclaimed and timeless . . . occupied by plants and creatures (some of them human)" (ibid., 123). That was precisely the kind of nature that Humboldt claimed to discover in America, "a primeval world where man did not disturb the course of nature" as the naturalist recorded some decades before Darwin's voyage (Wulf 2015, 66).

21. In accordance with evolutionary humanism, the philosophy of the newly created UNESCO, "man is seen as fighting, consciously or unconsciously, to create more opportunities to transcend the material world and open up intellectual activities which, in an urgent and painful manner, seek a richer development" (Huxley 1992 [1964], 92).

22. In the 1890s, Lewis H. Morgan recast classificatory systems and evolutionary ideas to do comparative kinship studies, further developing a cultural evolutionary ladder that could speak to the views of Herbert Spencer (1864), Edward B. Tylor (1871), and James S. Maine (1861) on the progress of societies. From the nineteenth

century to the middle of the twentieth, Social Darwinism was the dominant theory among social scientists (see Stocking 1991).

The concept of struggle in Darwin's theories was largely based on Malthus' work. He realized that: "the organisms must die if they multiply beyond the carrying capacity of their environments," as Livingstone (1992, 182–3) explains. It was a question of being better adapted in terms of leaving more descendants. "It was a struggle to reproduce, that is to say, it was a theory of relative reproductive success" (ibid.).

23. In fact, both disciplines—ecology and anthropology—had emerged simultaneously from the same scientific framework at which evolution theories were at the core. The concept, however, worked differently for ecology and anthropology (Diener 1974, Bowler 1988). For ecologists, evolution was understood in functional terms through the classification of species as any directional or cumulative change in the characteristics of organisms over time (Endler 1986, 5). Anthropologists, on the other hand, tended to link it to the idea of civilization, constructing a scientific theory of race to deal with the deep-seated anxiety about the survival, hybridity, or decline of individuals and the larger (Western) society after the encounter with colonial subjects. Nonetheless, founding figures of both disciplines, like Haeckel and Spencer, were involved as leading proponents of racial theories, scientific racism, and Social Darwinism (Wulf 2015, 352–71).

24. Ecologists thought they could uncover the equilibrium points at which nature could maximize its output. In such framework, nature is regarded as an entity with a discernible goal; that of constantly increasing diversity until attaining "the most diverse, stable, well-balanced self perpetuating society" (Worster 1994: 202). Nature is thus depicted as a mechanical factory that, like the female body (Martin 1987), is defined by her ability to succeed in the productive enterprise. The role of the ecologist is consequently to guard nature's purity for the sake of her own reproduction.

25. Around twelve European families lived in the island at the time (as per Lundh, *Noticias de Galápagos* 2006). Some other attendees on that day were the soldiers of the Ecuadorian Navy. On the other hand, some of the descendants of "natives" and "old migrants" in the archipelago (from San Cristóbal and Isabela Islands) gradually moved to Santa Cruz, attracted by the opportunities there. By 1964, they were, however, not the majority of the first settlers of this island nor the attendees of the inaugural event.

26. According to the census, there were 651 "new migrants" in the islands by 1962 (Grenier 2007, 190). Most of them became the first settlers of Santa Cruz Island.

27. The 1975 Master Plan for the islands also stated that 12,000 tourists a year would not cause any serious damage to the park's resources (*Noticias de Galápagos* 1975). Yet in 1978, 14,000 tourists visited, and forty years later, 275,000 in one year.

Chapter Three

From the Andean Highlands
to the Galápagos Islands

According to the 1932 census, most of the early settlers of the Galápagos were Indigenous laborers who had come from the Ecuadorian highlands, mainly from the Tungurahua Region. Before arriving to the islands, the majority had lived locked in *haciendas* and textile mills (*obrajes*) in the central highlands.[1] After buying their debts from their previous bosses, Manuel J. Cobos and Antonio Gil ascribed them to work as *conciertos* in the *haciendas* they established in San Cristóbal and Isabela Islands. Some others were instead enlisted in the streets of Guayaquil. Being imprisoned for debt was, nevertheless, a common condition for Indigenous peoples across the Ecuadorian highlands.[2] It was an inherent part of the *concertaje* system by which Spaniards—and later the creole elite—held Indigenous peoples bound to a life of serfdom under threat of prison. So why was the Tungurahua region specifically the main source of *colonos* (first settlers) of the Galápagos?

   In particular, the Salasaca people (from the Tungurahua) were part of the earliest groups of settlers of the archipelago and later became central players in the late colonization of Santa Cruz Island, which occurred from the 1960s onwards. Today more than fifteen thousand people live on this island. At least one in every five has Salasaca origins. Despite their large presence, most had to opt for a silent strategy of ethnic declassification after reaching the Galápagos.[3] As soon as they arrive, the Salasacas leave behind their traditional dress of handwoven, colorful fabrics and their mother tongue, Kichwa, while affirming every time they are asked that they come from the *mestizo* city of Ambato.[4] By doing this, they aim to "pass" as *mestizos* (of mixed race) in the islands. It was thus surprising to find that in the highlands, the Salasaca people proudly identify themselves as a homogenous, pure-blood, Indigenous group that have historically refused state making projects, notably *mestizaje*.[5] This can result from a racial mixture and/or cultural whitening. Why then do they make

83

themselves invisible as soon as they reach the archipelago? Who are the *Salasacas* and in what context did they move from the central highlands of Tungurahua to establish a secondary settlement on Santa Cruz Island?

To answer these questions, I start by following the journey of the Salasacas from Bolivia, in the central Andes, to Tungurahua in the Ecuadorian highlands, and later to the Galápagos Islands.[6]

As I will show, their presence in the archipelago can be traced back to the 1878 list of *"pagadores"* (literally "payers," previously known as "tributaries"), who formed part of Manuel J. Cobos's *hacienda* at the parish of San Cristóbal Island. However, I found more significant evidence in the history behind the name "Salasaca" given to the old district of Santa Cruz (the same that the teacher in Puerto Ayora and other *mestizo galapagueños* want to erase).

Understanding the history of the Salasaca people further allows examining how race works at the local level, and the ways Indigenous settlers navigate through categories in order to migrate and remain in the Galápagos archipelago. The current racial dynamics gradually emerged after the inception of the Republic of Ecuador and the annexation of the archipelago. On the mainland, the local Euro-descended, creole elites had to reinvent new categories of race in order to sort out the growing population of hybrid peoples (a mix between Euro-"white," creole-Indian, and sometimes African). They knew that the old colonial distinctions between Spaniards and Indians (or "landlords" and "laborers") did not suit the thesis of popular sovereignty by which nation-states were founded in the republican era. More importantly, they needed to ensure their monopoly of rents, profits, and privilege after independence from Spain. At the same time, the new racial order offered new mechanisms for Indigenous peoples to "whiten" themselves in order to incorporate into the state-sponsored homogeneous ideal of the "Ecuadorian [*mestizo*] citizen." These mechanisms still come into play in the Galápagos Islands.

SALASACAS OF THE HIGHLANDS

On the mainland, the Salasaca people consider themselves—and are considered by others—to be a pure-blood, homogeneous, Indigenous group with Bolivian origins. Indeed, as I will show, the cultural background of the Salasacas of both Tungurahua and the Galápagos Islands is firmly rooted in the culture of the Colla-Aymaras, whose center was the Tiwanaku at the southeast edge of Lake Titicaca (present-day Bolivia). Nevertheless, it seems that in Ecuador, the *Salasacas* emerged as a distinct ethnic group from their union with other groups of natives of different origins, which between the eighteenth and nineteenth centuries decided to maintain their Indigenous identity despite increasing pressures towards *mestizaje* (racial mixing).

The Origins of the Salasaca People

The origins of the *Salasacas* have been the subject of long-standing debates between historians and anthropologists. However, in the collective memory of the community there is a growing consensus of an origin story that holds that they came from a group of pure *mitimaes* (or *mitmajkunas*, a conquered people forced by the Incan Empire to resettle in a remote area) who ended up on the slopes of the Tungurahua Volcano in the mid-1400s after the Incas invaded their lands in what is now Bolivia.[7] The Inca did so because they say they were "a warlike nation which did not submit to his supreme will," as stated by the Salasaca Parochial Government.

According to this version, the original *Salasacas* must have belonged to one of the Colla-Ayamara lords of the great Tiwanaku-Wari civilization, the oldest in pre-Incan America and "the mother culture of all the American civilizations."[8] Their center was located close to the ancient city of Tiwanaku, which lies four thousand meters above sea level in the basin of Lake Titicaca, as was recently acknowledged by a group of Salasaca *yachak* (local historians and wise men) who visited the area.[9]

The influence of the ancient culture of the Colla-Ayamaras, in fact, prevails over the beliefs later imposed by the Incas as evidenced in the current ritual practices of the *Salasacas* (of the highlands and the Galápagos).[10] While the spirituality of the Incas was based on worshipping the Sun, that of the Colla-Ayamaras, like that of the *Salasacas,* is based on the relationship the *ayllus* (sub-town units of Indigenous organization) have with their deceased and their worship of the *urcus* (snow-covered peaks and summits).[11] It seems that the first peoples of Salasaca (Tungurahua) were able to conserve their traditions after they were uprooted by the Incas because, even though the Inca sovereigns imposed the Kichwa language and worship of *Inti* (the Sun) and his direct son (the sovereign), they nevertheless allowed their subjected nations to continue to adore their own deities after domination.

Above *Inti Raimy* (the Inca ceremony to honor the Inca and the Sun), for the *Salasacas*, the "Day of the Dead" is the most important celebration in their ritual calendar. It is the moment they visit and pray to the sacred places (*w'akas* and *urcus*), which embody the protective spirits of their *taytas* (fathers) and *mamas*. In contrast with the Catholic creed, which separates the body from the soul after death, the pre-Hispanic religions did not make this division, nor did they deny non-humans the possibility of having a spirit. Henceforth, to this day, the creatures of Nature are able to capture and hold onto the spirits of their ancestors after their bodies are buried in the sacred mountain of Cruzpamba in Salasaca, next to the Tungurahua Volcano—also called "*la mama.*"

The dead can therefore always be present and transcend by first incarnating into the landscape of the ancestral territory; then by participating, after death, in rituals through the offerings of food, such as *cuyes* (guinea pigs), rabbits, potatoes, and *choclo* (corn), and the libations of *chicha* (*corn beer*) that the living pour over their graves. *Chicha* drinks are accompanied by the words of one of the elders of the community (be it a man or woman) that celebrate the life of ancestors and gods in the midst of a ceremony which, nowadays, combines Christian symbols with ancestral Andean rites (Masaquiza, in Vinueza 1995, 230–36). In that way, the ritual life of the *Salasacas* is linked with that of some modern Aymara communities of the Bolivian Andes and also of the ancient culture of Colla-Aymaras, which left traces of their devotion to their dead in the burials of the Tiwanaku. These beliefs remained rooted in that first group that left for the north, settled on the slopes of the Tungurahua Volcano, and then turned into the founders of the "Salasacas."[12] Six centuries later in the Galápagos, the death of a member of the Salasaca community on Santa Cruz Island, followed by the urgent need to honor him after death in the appropriate way, marked the start of the link between Salasaca settlers on the islands and those who live in their ancestral home in the highlands of Tungurahua, as I will describe in the following chapter.

Until today, the *Salasacas* of the Galápagos Islands still feel obliged to return to their homeland every November in order to attend the ceremonies

Figure 3.1. Day of the Dead, Salasaca, Tungurahua, November 2016. Source: Photo: Tania Macera.

Figure 3.2.   Food for the living and the dead, Salasaca, Tungurahua, November 2016. *Source*: Photo: Tania Macera.

Figure 3.3.   Day of the Dead, Salasaca. Vicente Masaquiza (left) and Rufino (right) Masaquiza. Vicente is one of the first settlers of Santa Cruz Island, and Rufino, one of the most respected local yachak in Salasaca, Tungurahua. They were both crucial to my research. *Source*: Photograph: F. Masaquiza, Salasaca, Tungurahua, November 2017.

of the Day of the Dead there, amidst both the living and the dead. They also insist to their children that when they die, they should be buried alongside their *ayllu* on the sacred mountain because "who is going to visit if they toss you into the ground here on the islands?" as a Salasaca woman told me, even though she arrived at the archipelago forty years ago and lives there, in Puerto Ayora, with her children and grandchildren who were born and raised in the Galápagos. On the other hand, like the Aymaras, the ritual calendar of *fiestas* and the *fiesta*-sponsorship careers continue to be essential devices in the construction of prestige and authority among the Salasaca people.[13] To work in the Galápagos has allowed many *Salasacas* to sponsor the ritual *fiestas* in their native Salasaca.

Nevertheless, despite the fact that their cultural roots can be traced back up to the ancient culture of the Colla-Aymaras of Bolivia, the idea that they are the descendants of a homogenous Indigenous group is unlikely. Furthermore, to have *mitimae* ancestors (a conquered people forced by the Incan Empire to resettle in a remote area) would hardly make the *Salasacas* unique in the Ecuadorian highlands. Even so, their origin story is specifically used by *mestizos* to label Salasaca people as "outsiders" of the Galápagos and the Ecuadorian nation. For the *Salasacas* of the Galápagos, this label overlaps with the conservationist framework that classified all natives and first settlers of the archipelago as 'aliens' in their homeland.

Labor Migrations

The forced displacement of whole groups of natives was the crucial mechanism by which the Inca sovereign (1432–1535) and later the Spanish Crown (1535–1830) asserted their dominion over the Andes. The scheme of exploitation was based on the payment of tribute and the temporary or permanent displacement of large masses of people from their homelands. The local *caciques* (or "natural" Indigenous lords) were responsible for collecting tribute and for orchestrating a series of planned migrations of people who were recruited to work on public projects, food production in different ecological niches, and the control of newly conquered territories.

To do so, the Inca ordered groups who were regarded as bellicose—but loyal—to move to newly conquered lands and exile rebellious groups from their homelands in order to occupy their territories. Sometimes these warlike groups, who were inclined to lead a nomadic life, were relocated near groups of modest craftsmen and small farmers who were attached to the soil. The Inca also distributed groups in accordance with their talents. Groups who were experts in this or that calling were expatriated, so that they could teach their skills to the local inhabitants of other regions of his empire. All these colonies came to be known as *mitimaes*. During the reign of the Incas, the contiguous western slopes of the northern Andes (Latacunga, Riobamba, Sigchos, Angamarca, and Chimbo) and districts near Salasaca (like Quero, Pelileo, and Ambato) in the central highlands all received different groups of *mitimaes*.[14] Therefore, a single place might become inhabited by natives of multiple ethnic origins.

The transfers of people continued during the colonial period. After the conquest, subjects were classified by labor categories such as *mitayos, camayos,* or *forasteros*, paying tribute there by working for their *cacique* (hereditary lords), and through him, for the Spanish sovereign.[15] The *mitayos* had to work ten months of the year on public works such as the construction of temples, roads, bridges, and aqueducts. The *camayos*, for their part, were responsible for specific jobs in other ecological zones, like, for example, growing coca leaves in the lands of the Tungurahua and other parts of the central highlands. Neither the *mitayos* nor the *camayos* lost their ethnic affiliations and usually maintained two homes—one in the place where they worked and the other in their homeland—although they spent most of their productive life outside of their communities. Meanwhile, the *forasteros* ("stranger Indians" listed as "*sueltos*" or vagabonds) were those who, after fleeing to distant lands far from their communities (to avoid having to work for the *m'ita* there), turned into "*indios sueltos*" ("loose" or unattached "Indians") with no ethnic affiliation or access to communal lands.[16] Since 1601, in rural Ecuador under the *concertaje* system, they were all ascribed to landlords in *haciendas* and textile mills.

When they reached the Tungurahua region in the mid-1440s, the earliest *Salasacas* encountered native groups of the central highlands as well as other groups of *mitimaes* (Moreno Yañez 1988, Oberem 1981). In the following centuries, other Indigenous peoples from different places throughout the Andean region, continued to arrive to work there as *camayos*, *mitayos*, *forasteros*.[17] They were all later called *conciertos*, who were classified by their occupation and by the *hacienda* or landlord to whom they work for. Eventually, these laborers became natives of their host regions. Therefore, the label of "outsiders" which was assigned to the *Salasacas* could be applied to a large part of the Indigenous peoples of Ecuador.

So, why is this category only applied to label the Salasaca people? It seems that by identifying themselves as a pure *mitimae* group of Bolivian origins, the Salasaca people justify their traditional isolation, their distinctive refusal to assimilate the dominant culture (in contrast with other Kichwa groups of the nation), and the extraordinary determination of their ancestors when they decided to hold onto their Indigenous identity in the face of the intimidation and violence from the state and *mestizo* society. They however do not consider themselves as outsiders of Ecuador. This is a category that is rather imposed on them by *mestizos*. In so doing, mainstream society seem to punish the Indigenous group's refusal to incorporate into the hegemonic racial project of Spanish America and the Ecuadorian nation, while also justifying their removal from the Galápagos archipelago.

The Inhabitants of Salasaca

During the colonial period, "Salasaca" was to authorities only the place-name of the district located at the slopes of the Tungurahua Volcano. It was not used to identify an Indigenous community. Moreover, colonial archives confirm that for nearly two centuries the inhabitants of this area did not call themselves "*Salasacas*."

A large portion of the population reached the region between the 1600s and 1800s as *forasteros* or *camayos*, either to work or because they had intermarried with one of the first inhabitants of Salasaca (Corr 2013). Under such conditions, the majority had no access to communal lands and were thus not subject to the *m'ita*. However, they eventually became attached in one way or another to the textile mill of San Ildefonso and its adjoining *haciendas*.

San Ildefonso was an important mill which—for over three centuries—demanded thousands of Indigenous laborers in order to fulfill the mission to supply the textile industry of the Real Audiencia of Quito from the Tungurahua region. Founded in 1594, in Pelileo (three miles away from Salasaca), the mill operated on the basis of a royal decree by which the Spanish Crown had allowed the recruitment of African slaves and Indigenous 'volunteers.' And so *cacique* Francisco Hati became the lord in charge of supplying the labor force by sending the natives under his orders. Most were part of the Tacungas and Sigchos Collanas who were at the time peons at the *encomienda* (labor grant) of the Bernardine Nuns of Madrid. They initially settled in Salasaca in order to grow agave (*cabuya blanca*, or century plant) and extract wood lice from the fleshy leaves of the prickly pear cactus (*opuntia*) for the production of cochineal dye.[18] These two plants, natives of the Andes, prospered in arid terrains like those of the Salasaca, as documented in 1771 by a Jesuit named Cicala.

Some of the inhabitants of Salasaca were attached to work directly as *conciertos* of the textile mill. Once there, they rapidly turned into debt slaves due to their inability to pay back the foodstuffs they had obtained on credit at exorbitant prices, among other sanctions. In San Ildefonso, they were always short of food and sleep, were cruelly punished, and worked without a salary or rest. Their only payment was a garment at the end of each year (Costales 1975).[19] Most of the workers who survived owed it to the help of their families, who provided them with food or offered to replace the children working at the *obraje* (textile mill) when they were to be chastised (Corr 2018, 3–4).

Elders in Salasaca recall how their *taytas* (fathers) had to flee from San Ildefonso in order to survive (Interviews, Salasaca, August 2016).[20] They sometimes fled to other regions or hid at their *chacras* (small plots of subsistence farming land) in Salasaca where they started to build enormous wooden looms, tied with *cabuya* (century plant) cord, in order to establish their own workshops at their houses. Eventually, the production of textiles consolidated in Salasaca until it defined gendered divisions of labor, with men working as skillful weavers who taught their skills to their male children, and women taking on the responsibility of spinning, raising sheep, and producing threads and wools.[21] However, the textile production at Salasaca remained marginal until the first decades of the 1900s.

Before that happened, labor exploitation and debts to the landlords was what marked the precarious lives of the inhabitants of Salasaca (Tungurahua). After the cochineal dye production had declined, the dwellers of this region started to produce fiber sacks which the San Ildefonso textile plant needed in order to transport its textiles from the highlands to the Ecuadorian coast. Early in the 1800s, in one of the revolts against the imposed tribute (*diezmo*), they complained about barely being able to survive with the *cabuya* sacks, since their lands were arid and their domestic animals weak and sickly (Reino 2004). Nevertheless, parallel, crucial political processes were taking place in Salasaca, transforming the entire community in the course of a century.

It was around this time, between the 1860s and the early 1900s, that Manuel J. Cobos was actively recruiting squads of Indigenous *conciertos* to work for him on the Galápagos Islands. A large part of his *hacienda* workers had previously been imprisoned for debts (locked in *haciendas* and *obrajes*) in the Tungurahua region. He forcibly enlisted them by buying their debts from their previous bosses. Then he took them to the Galápagos where they became *conciertos*, but for his *hacienda* El Progreso at San Cristóbal Island. As the *hacienda's* lists of tributaries show, some of them had Salasaca origins.

José Valdizán and Antonio Gil, the two other landlords of the Galápagos, did likewise: they forcibly recruited debt prisoners of the Ecuadorian central highlands for their *haciendas* at Floreana and Isabela Islands. They enlisted some more by recruiting 'vagabonds' on the streets of Guayaquil, which were mainly Indigenous peoples who had fled their home provinces to escape *m'ita* (forced labor) obligations or other catastrophes that hit the central highlands.

All in all, the exile of Indigenous peoples in the Andes was for centuries a customary practice. It was the crucial mechanism by which Inca and Spanish sovereigns expropriated Indigenous lands and labor over the Andes and gained control over new subject territories. The colonization of the Galápagos thus followed the same model which, updated under the *hacienda* system, also met the objective of exerting sovereignty for Ecuador over the newly annexed oceanic islands.

TO BECOME A SALASACA: RACE AND *MESTIZAJE* IN THE ANDEAN REGION

During the 1820s, most of the nation-states in the region emerged, founded upon the republican values of equality, freedom, and discourses of popular sovereignty. Ironically, at the same time, full-fledged racial categories emerged to replace the old colonial categories in a way these could ensure that the post-colonial elite maintained their privilege, based on their "superior whiteness" (Abercrombie 1996, 96). Over the course of those decades, modifications in strategies for symbolic distinction were at work in the region to build a sort of citizenship that was not constitutive of universal equality but rather perceived as the privilege of social and racial hierarchy (Guerrero 2003, 283).

From then on, the "Indians" in the Andes had two options: turn themselves into *mestizos* or hold onto an Indigenous identity at the expense of being treated as marginal, "barbarian," or "uncivilized" by the state and mainstream society. *Mestizaje* further became a state project by which the *creole* elite sought to whiten native populations by erasing nonwhite identities—to the point that, in 1857, the word "Indian" had vanished from official registers. From there on for the Ecuadorian state, there were only two categories of people: some were "citizens," (or *vecinos,* people of Spanish descent) and the rest were "subjects" (Indigenous peoples and people of ambiguous origins) (according to the 1842 census).[22] Accordingly, the earliest censuses of the Galápagos did not specify ethnicity or race but rather occupation. All Indigenous laborers-settlers were thus labeled as *"conciertos,"* either as day laborers, farm workers, or artisans (Guevara 2015).

On the mainland, most of the natives had to "whiten" themselves in order to survive. One way to become a *mestizo,* was to become an "urban Indian" (or *"cholo"*). By fleeing from their communities and moving into a city, the Indigenous migrant or his (or her) children could eventually blend in with the urban population. In so doing, he could aspire to be free of tributes still imposed on the natives, resorting to his recently acquired racial status. Yet in the city, the Indigenous newcomer first had to learn some long-established cultural forms to turn from being a *"cholo"* into becoming part of the working class (or *"la clase popular"*).[23] If he was not rapidly employed or attached to a landlord, he could face punishment through laws against "vagabonds" and joblessness. One example of this was the 1870 decree that allowed Manuel J. Cobos and Antonio Gil to forcibly recruit vagabonds in Guayaquil to work for their *haciendas* as *conciertos* in the Galápagos.

In contrast, those who remained in their rural/Indigenous communities and/or maintained their Indigenous customs (notably dress and language) were automatically categorized as tributaries, mainly a *concierto* enclosed and exploited in a *hacienda*, mine, or textile mill. Beyond just forced labor, such status entailed punishments, debts, impoverishment, the constant loss of children, and the denial of rights to citizenship, property, lands, and sometimes water.

Although they were in the minority, some natives of the Tungurahua region chose to move to Salasaca to join the merging Indigenous community. Certain conditions were required for an Indigenous person to become a Salasaca. Alternatively, natives of the region could choose to pursue their own "whitening." By studying both paths, I am interested in examining how the local concept of race operates and the mechanisms that allow for the production of *mestizos* in Ecuador to this day. These paths still apply to the *Salasacas* who reach the Galápagos.

To Become a Salasaca

It was not until the 1850s that the word "Salasaca" was used to identify an "Indigenous community," according to the accounting books of Ambato (Corr and Powers, 2012, 57). However, for at least a century before this happened, the district of Salasaca was already recognized as a safe haven for those natives who rejected *mestizaje* (racial mixing) and cultural "whitening."

The re-creation of the Salasaca ethnic group occurred somewhere between the eighteenth and nineteenth centuries. The group of natives that inhabited the area achieved this by going from being landless to becoming owners of a territory, and then by establishing their own norms to guarantee the exclusiveness of the community. This type of process, by which an ethnic identity is created as a distinctive and separate unit from its parent populations, is usually seen as the result of a political strategy (see, for example, Hirschkind 1995) or as the product of colonialism.[24] However, in the case of the Salasaca nation, following Corr and Powers (2013), it seems that their decision was rooted in a sense of Indigenous pride, which was not only based on political resistance but also on "cultural refusal" (Scott 2009). This could happen even in the absence of economic and sociopolitical advantages vis-à-vis dominant society (Stutzman 1981).

The Salasaca identity consolidated in the course of a century. At the same time, the Ecuadorian state was founded (in 1832) and established. Yet only until the 1950s were the Salasaca people incorporated into the nation-state. Most were registered under the "Masaquiza" name. The history of this surname not only reveals the oppressive forms of racism that forever marked the *Salasacas* and their relation to the Ecuadorian State. It will also help to understand some of the strategies that the Salasaca migrants use to migrate and remain in the Galápagos Islands.

Territory

The creation of the ethnic territory began in the 1740s when a handful of natives of Salasaca began to buy lands in their district and its surroundings from the impoverished descendants of the conquistador Hernando de la Parra.[25] In a matter of only two or three generations, many of de la Parra's descendants—like other Spanish *vecinos*—had lost their lands and fortunes after squandering their wealth on luxuries and ostentatious lives; and due to their contempt for work, absentee landlordism, and failure to till the lands they had been deeded. Some of the heirs of de la Parra could not even afford funerals for their own parents (Corr 2018, 162).Nearly two centuries after colonial land dispossessions of Indigenous peoples in the region, first records of purchases of properties in Salasaca by Indigenous inhabitants appeared. The initial purchase was usually possible only after several generations of an Indigenous family leased, worked, and lived on a property, and gradually accumulated the required capital (from growing *cabuya* (agave) plants and raising cattle and sheep) to buy the land from its owner. In other cases, acquisition of such properties was facilitated by local priests, who offered to sell Indigenous tenants the lands they had worked on in exchange for paying the funeral expenses of the properties' legal owners (ibid., 139–53). Thus, in exchange for sponsoring Masses to save the souls of the dead, Indigenous people became small land holders while Catholic priests swelled their coffers. Lastly, other families could acquire their properties by purchasing *chacras* from other natives of the region—mainly, Pilalatas, Chumaquís and Guambalós who were more frequently recruited to work at the textile mill than the *Salasacas*, thus wounding up indebted, impoverished, and tied to San Ildefonso for life. To sell their *chacras* was for some the only way to pay off their debts and prevent them from being inherited by their descendants, even if it meant depriving them of those lands.

Once a property was bought, the *ayllu* began to enlarge it by getting their relatives to acquire adjoining lands. What began as an individual or family survival strategy turned into a group strategy until an ethnic territory of fourteen square kilometers was formed. This communal land was held not by *comuneros* (Indigenous commoners who had communal rights to a land, like most of the Kichwa communities of Ecuador), but by smallholders of private property.[26] This process consolidated in spite of the precarious conditions of most of the inhabitants of Salasaca.

Things started to improve from the 1890s onwards after the decline of San Ildefonso. From then on, Salasaca increasingly became an economically and politically autonomous community. *Salasacas* developed their textile production, moving from one oriented towards self-consumption to the manufacture of a fabric called *lliglla* (of lower quality than those used in their traditional garments yet good enough to compete with the best European fabrics), that was sold in the Ambato market (Choque 1992). The *lliglla* was sent to Guayaquil via rail to Manta and motorboat to the port, so that it could be exported to the international market (Ibarra 1987). During the early decades of the twentieth century, with the *lliglla,* the *Salasacas* were even able to control the market niche that had formerly been covered by the San Ildefonso mill.

In less than two centuries, the Salasacas thus changed their status of landless *indios sueltos* ("loose" or unattached Indians)—since most of them had arrived as *forasteros* (strangers with no land or ethnic affiliation) or *camayos* (affiliated to communities in other provinces) who gradually lost their access to communal lands—into smallholders of lands of an economically and politically autonomous community. Their properties in the central highlands further started to operate more like an autarkic state, despite being located on the arid lands of the slopes of a volcano, and despite being surrounded by *mestizo* parishes at the very center of the Ecuadorian state.

Exclusiveness

Once the Salasaca ethnic territory was created, the making of a unified and exclusively Indigenous group began with an agreement on norms and their implementation through specific measures. First, endogamy was imposed as a fundamental norm for the members of the community (Choque 1992). The marriage register of Pelileo in that period (1869–1895) confirms this fact, showing that in contrast with other native communities, Salasaca was the only one with exclusively Indigenous marriages (Corr and Powers 2012, 56).

The next step towards their exclusivity was to resist the appointment of white-*mestizo* authorities by the Ecuadorian state. In 1872, acting as a group for the first time, the *Salasacas* demanded the right to elect their own officials. In addition, they forbade all sales, purchases, or the inheritance of lands in Salasaca to individuals who were not members of the community. They further rejected the *catastro* (land registry regulations), which allowed individuals to sell properties to third parties. Finally, all plots as well as the territorial borders were enclosed with natural fences of *cabuya* (agave) plants or prickly pear cactus plants and guarded by nightly patrols. Salasaca thus could became a safe enclave for Indigenous people who actively resisted cultural whitening and chose, instead, to remain on the margins of the Ecuadorian state.

Even so, the racial frontiers of the Salasaca people were still permeable. The presence of Salasaca men and women with "white" (or light) skin or surnames of Hispanic origin (like Jiménez or Ramírez which are recognized as Salasaca ones) suggests possible cases of racial mixing that *Salasacas* no longer remember (Interviews, Salasaca (Tungurahua) 2016). On the other hand, the circulation of children was common for centuries, by means of such practices as adoption and godparent relationships (*compadrazgo*). For example, there is a documented case in Salasaca in the mid eighteenth century of a woman, Juana Comasanta, who raised a Spanish baby that had been abandoned by his mother as a genuine Salasaca. She later won the custody of her adopted child in the courts despite custody claims on the part of the child's Spanish father (Corr 2018, 144–46). More recently, many Salasaca families had to resort to the practice of "consigning" their daughters to homes in the city so that they could learn to read and write, and obtain food and clothing.[27] In exchange, the girls from an early age worked as domestic servants, sweeping, laundering, and helping with other household tasks. This arrangement, which continues to the present day—and of which some of the Salasaca women who colonized Santa Cruz Island have memories—secured their subsistence and their learning of Spanish language and *mestizo* culture (Kingman 2006, 240).

Nevertheless, the porousness of racial boundaries among the *Salasacas* was more limited than those of other Kichwa nations. This can be explained in part by the desire of its members to belong to an exclusively Indigenous community and their compliance to the practice of endogamy. In contrast, their neighbors moved to the opposite direction. And so, where early colonial reports mentioned the Chumaquís (whose lands were once part of the Salasaca district) and the Guambahalós (now Huambalós) as Indigenous communities while Salasaca was not, today it is the reverse: Salasaca is considered a distinct Indigenous nationality while Chumaquí and Huambaló are recognized as *mestizo* parishes (Corr and Powers 2012, 21).

The Masaquizas: The Salasaca People and the Ecuadorian State

To become a Salasaca also meant, in Scott's words (2009), to be labeled as a "barbarian." The *Salasacas* objected against state projects, for example, to the building of a state school and their inclusion on the land registry in 1911, and later to the building of a road that would cross their territory in order to link Ambato and Baños in 1929. The press described the already "famous *Salasacas*" as follows:

> Along the way, there is an Indigenous tribe of savages, the famous *Salasacas,* who have *long hair and bronzed skin, are tall, invincibly opposed to civilization.* They show a fierce hostility to any enterprise to build roads through their territories . . .
> (*El Día* newspaper, 1928. Poeschel 2001, 77).

300 of them, armed with shovels and axes and waving flags, stopped the work . . .
How is it possible that at the gates of a civilized city [Ambato], there is *a horde
of savages* who now, as in the past and with strange capriciousness, oppose the
opening of roads that bring progress.
   (In the *Crónicas de Saturno* newspaper, Feb. 4, 1928. Poeschel 2001, 77).

The highway would have split up their lands, threatening the community's
social and cultural continuity. However, after some time, the *Salasacas* abandoned the protest and even helped out in the public works projects. Their
opposition to the land registry and official education, however, continued. It
was only in 1946 that a religious order, the Laurita nuns, was able to establish
itself in the community to teach Spanish and Catholic doctrine to the *Salasacas*. The presence of the nuns was, nevertheless, regarded as an "intrusion"
(Masaquiza 1995, 236). They recall that the missionaries often mistreated the
Indigenous students, both physically and morally. For example, the students
were all forced to cut their long hair for reasons of "hygiene." The nuns
would also confiscate and burn the native *ponchos* (a traditional, exclusively
Indigenous, male garment) of some in order to make them wear the school
uniform (ibid., 224–25).
   A decade later, the state registry offices followed apropos of the first
national census. The civil registry had recently begun campaigns to count
all nationals and to issue identification cards (*cédulas*) to them. However,
the racism of state bureaucrats was left forever inscribed in the names and
surnames assigned to the members of the community. Over and over again,
mestizo state bureaucrats vehemently refused to register their original Kichwa
(or Aymara) names and surnames, and despite complaints, they registered
most of them under the same surname: "Masaquiza." Moreover, they recur-
rently changed their first names because they said they were not appropriate,
and they even made fun of them. For example, a girl named Vicenta was
registered as Vicente (a male name); someone else named Curichumbi was
registered as Curichumbo; and another person named Llucacho was registered as Ricacho (meaning "the rich guy"). They further refused to accept
"Rumiñahui" because "it is the name of a rebellious Indian who opposed us,
did not accept civilization, and died without being a Christian," according to
José Masaquiza, who is also now known as "Rumiñahui" (Masaquiza 1995,
222–23).[28] Public officials ended up choosing their names: Rosa for many
women and Mariano, or Manuel, for most of the men.
   The registry practice was continued to the point where there are many
with the double surname "Masaquiza Masaquiza" (even though their parents
are not directly related), and there are many homonyms within the Salasaca
population today. In addition, a large number of their traditional surnames,
which were accurately registered by the priests in previous centuries, began

to disappear (for example: Pampashu, Cuñya, Curichumbi, Patiac, Guaruga, Chimbo, Huasinga, etc.) (Poeschel 2001, 67).[29] For the following generations, the assigning of such names led to serious problems when it came to claiming their legal right to inherit or share of the inheritances of their parents, as some of my interlocutors told me (Interviews, Puerto Ayora, Galápagos and Salasaca, Tungurahua).

The history of the surname Masaquiza thus reveals the way the state regarded the Salasaca people. Under the republican regime, natives were supposed to become members of the nation-state. Yet, those who opted to remain Indigenous were still considered "uncivilized" populations and therefore "not apt for the quotidian forms of exchange inherent to the relationship of equality among citizens" (Guerrero 2003, 272). By assigning the surname "Masaquiza," which is a distinctively Salasaca surname, the state bureaucrats incorporated a large part of the community in a way that they could be permanently marked as Indigenous subjects (from Salasaca) and not white or *mestizo* individuals. They further denied them their right to affirm their actual genealogical roots through their identity. Moreover, even though the *Salasacas* were private property owners and had actively engaged for almost two centuries in numerous lawsuits to defend the lands they purchased, to the Ecuadorian state of the 1950s, they were mere Indians—collective agents who lacked autonomous judgment needed to sign contracts, hold private property, or become full citizens of the state. These events would take an unexpected turn some decades later after population controls were enforced in the Galápagos Islands, as I will describe in the chapters that follow.

Meanwhile in the highlands, the stigmas and the fight for rights continued. The most notorious protest in recent times arose in the 1960s after one of the irrigation channels the *Salasacas* had built was seized and rerouted by a landlord in the region (Poeschel 2001). The uprising ended in the massacre of nearly fifty Salasaca demonstrators and led a group of Salasaca leaders to travel to Quito where, for the first time, they negotiated their rights in the Ecuadorian Congress. It was not a favorable outcome. However, the incident strengthened the political organization of the community.[30] Some years later, the *Salasacas* would also participate in the protests of the broader Indigenous Movement, which led to the removal of two presidents of Ecuador in the 1990s and the drafting of a new constitution in 2008. From then on, Ecuador was declared to be a "plurinational" and "multicultural" state made up of fourteen Indigenous nationalities. For its part, the Salasaca nation was acknowledged as part of the biggest Indigenous nationality in the country, the Kichwas of Ecuador.

Yet the stigma of being "barbarians" is still used to label the Salasaca people. For example, after four decades of attempted indoctrination, the Laurita nuns admitted, "they had not achieved their purpose" in Salasaca (Tungura-hua), further depicting the community as uncivilized peoples:

> Salasaca is a community with very peculiar characteristics. Clinging to their customs and traditions, they have remained on the margin of civilization for a long time despite being close to [the *mestizo* cities of] Ambato and Pelileo (Masaquiza 1995, 236).

This also resonates with the way that many *mestizos* regard *Salasacas* in the Galápagos. On the other hand, the label of "savage" or "barbarian" can be examined as a category imposed to all those who leave the state space in order to escape taxes, conscription, disease, poverty, or prison. For Scott (2009), the label Barbarism is:

> A political location vis-à-vis stateness—a positionality. Nonbarbarians are fully incorporated into the taxpaying population . . . All those who had reason to flee state power are, in a sense, tribalizing themselves. Ethnicity, once again, began where sovereignty and taxes ended (Scott 2009, 121–22).

The *Salasacas* fit in this category as they historically opposed the registry of their lands. It not only meant starting to pay real estate taxes. More importantly, this would be a recognition that the lands of their ancestors (starting with those who arrived in the mid-1400s to the Salasaca region) belong to the relatively recently created Ecuadorian state. Yet in 2006, this changed thanks to an initiative by a Salasaca man (a medical doctor) who, after being elected as the mayor of Pelileo, convinced the members of his community of the benefits of having title deeds to their properties, since these would act as a warranty whenever they needed to ask for loans from savings and credit cooperatives. This "would never have been allowed if the mayor hadn't been Indigenous" (Many 2006, 96). In so doing, the *Salasacas* in theory moved away from the "barbarian" category, in Scott's (2009) terms, by incorporating themselves as taxpayers of the state and potential debtors of the financial system.

To Become a Mestizo

Most of the natives across the Andean region chose instead to "whiten" themselves. To achieve this, one possible way was racial mixing. The colonial system of work and property had placed Indigenous men and women alongside the Spanish conquistadors and their families in *haciendas*, farms, mills, and households, where both Spaniards and "Indians" shared the most intimate spheres. At that time, the family was not only composed of children, grandchildren, and relatives by blood but also servants—all of whom lived together under the same roof—although subjected to clear demarcations in the use of the household space. As a result, concubinage and *mestizaje* were recurrent practices, due to a system that combined intimacy and exploitation on a daily basis. This can be seen in the high rates of illegitimate children among families, who could be raised by the customs of the Spanish or *creole* father or, more frequently, by those of their own mother—usually an Indigenous maid.[31] The mixed children therefore frequently became servants of their half siblings and father's spouse in *haciendas* and households.

Alternatively, natives could opt for a silent strategy of ethnic de-classification based on a series of vital decisions like: migrating to a city, speaking Spanish and not their Indigenous mother tongue, wearing European clothes instead of their traditional ethnic dress, becoming a practicing Catholic, abandoning or hiding the use of ancestral medicine, learning the Spanish customs, marrying a Spanish *don* or a *mestizo* of a higher status, and/or adopting a Spanish surname. These were all cumulative in the path to racial whitening. The price paid by "the Indians," as described by Peruvian writer Vargas Llosa was:

> The renunciation of their culture, their language, their beliefs, their traditions, and customs, and the adoption of the culture of their ancient masters. After one generation, they become *mestizos.* They are no longer Indians (de la Cadena 2000, 1).

Yet this path also enabled Indigenous peoples and recently made *mestizos* to move through various identities (*mestizo* or "Indian") at different times (by changing their dress, social circle, or place of residence) and carrying themselves in different ways depending on their audience. A single person could therefore belong to and then vanish from a certain category. *Mestizos* thus "formed not so much a category as a challenge to categorization itself" (Schwartz and Salomon 1999, 478).

To this day across the Andean region, racial categories are not necessarily evident in skin color or may not be related to descent. It is telling, for example, that subjects could appeal their racial classification to the colonial courts in order to avoid the payment of tribute.[32] To do so, they could present materials, witnesses, and evidence to the judges of the Royal Court (*Real Audiencia)* (Minchom 1994, Rappaport 2014). Evidence had to be of a genealogical and cultural nature like: their workplace, occupation, tax category, spouse, or place of residence, among others. And while certain traits began to be associated with Indigenous phenotypes (brown, hairless skin; black, long, lank hair; slanted eyes [*achinados*]; and a short stature), the physical appearance of the claimant was not conclusive evidence of his or her race. The only definite visible marker of "Indianness" was to wear ethnic dress.[33]

And so when colonial officials inspected the territory in their periodic surveys, they found the distinction between "Indians" and *mestizos* problematic, so that in the end they classified many *mestizos* living in Indigenous communities as "Indians" (*indios*) (Rappaport 2014, 217). At the same time in the cities, those who escaped the *m'ita* and the tribute could pass as or eventually become classified as *mestizos* (even if they were full-blooded Indigenous).

1857 was a turning point in Ecuador in that respect. From the inception of the Republic in 1832, the principle of equality among citizens made the tributary system and old criteria of difference obsolete. After the abolition of tribute, the native population could choose to avoid identifying themselves as members of a specific community. Instead, a new lexicon of race developed which turned Spaniard creoles into "whites" (*blancos*) or *white-mestizos*—and therefore superior—while creating new labels for the rest, particularly, for all the varieties of mixture (Euro-Indian and sometimes African people).[34]

Racial categorization was thus related to the ability of the increasingly hybrid population to move up or down the social ladder. Upward social mobility could then produce *mestizos* or even *blancos* (whites) or to the contrary, when *blancos* or *mestizos* became impoverished, remained in the countryside, or married Indians produced Indigenous persons (or *"longos"*). In such context, the more prosperous *mestizos* began to identify themselves as *blancos* while those who had recently become *mestizos* were called *"cholos"* (a derogatory term to all those whose cultural hybridity is manifest), since they are "people who are by nature Indigenous, although dressing as *cholos* in the city" (Minchom 1994).

Yet in order to qualify as "white" and a full citizen of the state, it was also necessary to have property with peons and servants included. Because "he who has nothing is of no importance, since he does not have a *"patria,"* that is, patrimony and property" (Kingman 2006, 158). The "white" person thus had to accumulate symbolic and economic capital which included *haciendas*, servants, or "people in his charge" (*"gente a cargo"*), horses, elegant clothes, and objects of art (ibid., 158–59), while also behaving in accordance with his *habitus*, which was defined by criteria of honor, decency, and privilege.[35] In such context, "Indians" and servants were sometimes treated as members of "white" families, yet always considered part of their property. This is evident in the way families in Quito speak of their possessions when colloquially referring to "our own *indios*" (*indios propios*), "our own servant" (*sirvienta propia*) or someone who "belongs to the house" (*de la casa*).

For its part, the word *"mestizo"* was originally interchangeable with the term "natural child" (or illegitimate child), thus used to designate all children who were not recognized by their fathers. Under this logic, the term *mestizo* also encompassed all those who were born out of wedlock (even for the offspring of two Spaniards) or the child born from a union between an Indigenous *cacique* (native lord) and a *mitaya* Indian woman (since they crossed the dividing lines of class among the natives) (Rappaport 2014, 16–17).[36] As such, the idea of *mestizaje* embraced the offspring of unions that transgressed social class, even if their parents were of the same race. The local language of race thus indexed a racial order that was built on social status more than skin color or descent. Moreover, racial classification was closely linked to the local property regime, in which some were owners (of both lands and natives) and others—the tributaries and the dispossessed.

Cultural whitening gradually advanced in accordance with the consolidation of a mostly urban society in Ecuador.[37] This did not occur until 1990, the year in which the census reported that the majority (55 percent) of the population of Ecuador lived in cities (compared with 28 percent in 1950). The organization of the city itself (as well as of households) reflected a model of integration where whites lived at the center (around the city's main square or plaza), while *mestizos, cholos,* and *"Indians"*—the urban servant class—lived on the margins of the city at the intersection between rural and urban space.

The vast majority of the urban population of *"mestizo* cities" today (like Ambato, Pelileo and Quito itself) are, in fact, made up of Indigenous migrants.[38] Nevertheless, the racial logic took care to erase any contaminating trace that could unveil Indigenous heritage or descent in the memories of families, cities, and of society in general. This remains true to the point that when an Ecuadorian in the Galápagos Islands says he or she "is from Ambato," the person inevitably asserts that he or she is *mestizo* and therefore radically different from the Indigenous person who comes from Salasaca, its neighboring district.

Among Cousins

Relations between *mestizos* and *"Indians"* have always been tense. Conflict between races was present in *haciendas* and textile mills in which labor was organized under an interethnic network of domination consisting of a "white" *hacienda* owner who was in charge of hundreds of Indigenous laborers managed by overseers who were sometimes a slave (for example, in San Ildefonso in Pelileo, [Tardieu 2012]) and other times, a *mestizo* from a neighboring town. In the cities, the tensions exploded every time that the government announced new tax rates based on racial classifications (Moreno Yañez 1976). For centuries, the registration of "Indians" for the purpose of charging taxes led to riots and clashes between the various castes, which were extinguished by local authorities by hanging those who were found guilty or by whipping them, exiling them, and cutting their hair.

More recently, problems of inheritance of communal lands have led to clashes between first-generation *mestizos* (with an Indigenous father or mother) and their Indigenous cousins. For example, property boundaries between Salasaca and its neighboring parishes are frequently disputed between the two parties: the *Salasacas* and their relatives, members of the self-identified peasant communities of *"mestizos"* in the parishes of Benitez, Rosario, and Teligote (Choque 1992, 88–92).

During the first half of the twentieth century, the word *"primo"* (cousin) acquired two additional meanings at the local level. The first appeared in the context of an emerging *indigenismo* in the region: an ideology that was characterized by its romantic and humanitarian impulses but that was actually a form of Spencerian Positivism by which elite intellectual *mestizos* aimed to incorporate surviving Indigenous peoples in the Americas into the mainstream (Hispanic-*mestizo*) national culture (Becker 1995, 2).[39] In Ecuador, the Salasaca people became particularly interesting for local *indigenistas,* anthropologists, and folklorists. They valued their ethnic authenticity and specificity in maintaining their Indigenous customs and identifying themselves as a pure *mitimae* group of Bolivian origins (Choque 1992, 81). Local intellectuals in Ambato then started to refer to the *Salasacas* as *"primos"* (cousins). In so doing, they tried to emphasize they had found their own links to this group in their ancestry.

Yet in colloquial language, the word acquired a racist overtone, indexing the unequal status of *mestizos* and *indios*. This version of *"primo"* is often heard on the streets of Puerto Ayora, Galápagos. When a *mestizo* on the islands calls a person *"¡primo!"*, they are usually mocking the other by signaling his or her Indigenous (usually Salasaca) origin or the fact that he or she is closer to the Indigenous world. In other words, the self-identified *mestizo* is calling the other "Indian." Although used as a racist joke, *"primo"* actually connotes the tensions and closeness between *mestizos* and *Salasacas* on the archipelago.

Being identified as an "Indian" still entails a threat of violence. This is usually emphasized in the context of urban life and among the newly made *mestizos*. All sorts of strategies and compulsive practices of denying or hiding an Indigenous past can be observed. Worse yet, in the Galápagos, certain relations with Indigenous people are violently censured because these may jeopardize or reverse the other party's own "whitening." While there, I often heard stories about the beatings dealt to men of Salasaca origin by the fathers or brothers of the *mestizo* women they were courting, cases in which paternity rights were denied (along with the right of their children to bear the Indigenous forename of their father or have any relationship with him), and where children who resulted from such relationships were obscured. Yet in one of the accounts, a native *galapagueño* whose parents are *Salasacas*, first settlers of Santa Cruz, noted what his in-laws' rejection unveils:

> Her parents and uncles treated me badly because of my surname [Masaquiza]. When I went to visit her in Riobamba [in the central highlands], her parents made up this story that I was a thief and they got me imprisoned . . . they sent me to jail. There, they hired someone to beat me up . . .
> All this to [later] find out that her grandparents wore a *poncho* [a male garment that is exclusively used by Indians in Ecuador]
> (Interview, Puerto Ayora, December 2018).

In many ways, society on the Galápagos Islands reflects Ecuadorian society on the mainland. Not only in the diverse origins of many of its inhabitants but also because the settler society was largely made up of Indigenous people. On the islands, however, *mestizos* had to create their own class and racial distinctions in the framework of two overlapping civilizing processes. One which understands decency, honor, and culture as related to the adoption of the Hispanic, or "white" customs. The other aims to forge a good resident in the Galápagos: obedient of conservation law; aware of the value of endemic fauna and the threats of invasive species; and playing an active role in the protection of nature, for example, by being willing to denounce those who transgress the rules or remain illegally in the archipelago. The issue of race, however, determines the initial location of each subject in the process of becoming civilized in the territory of conservation.

FROM THE ANDEAN HIGHLANDS
TO THE GALÁPAGOS ISLANDS

The Tungurahua region is peculiar in two ways. It is, first, located right at the center of the Ecuadorian highlands between the coast and the Amazon. Since pre-Columbian times, its capital city, Ambato (Hambato before), was an obligatory stop on the road between Guayaquil and Quito. It became a meeting point for merchants, products, and different cultures, and the axis of commercial exchanges. For some time, it was also the seat of the most important market fair in the whole highlands (Ibarra 1992). Flows of people and goods between the highlands and the coast constantly crisscrossed the Tungurahua region. These would further intensify at the height of the textile production in the colonial period, during the cacao boom on the coast (between 1760–1820 and 1880–1920) and with the building of the trans-Andean railway (1872–1908).[40]

At the same time, the Tungurahua region is located in the middle of a chain of big, conical volcanoes. They are especially clustered in what is known as the "Avenue of the Volcanoes," with the Tungurahua, Chimborazo, and Cotopaxi Volcanoes dominating the landscape. For Andean societies, these high peaks were objects of devotion and worship. However, constant volcanic eruptions, along with earthquakes, marked the life of its inhabitants, forcing them to rebuild and relocate city centers and towns (like Ambato, Riobamba, Pelileo, Píllaro, and Salasaca itself) several times in recent history.

It is said that in 1534, it was due to a sudden eruption of the Tungurahua Volcano that the Spanish were able to defeat the Indigenous army of Rumiñahui, who feared it meant a divine punishment. Strong earthquakes, whose epicenter was the central highlands, were also documented in 1687, 1698, 1703, 1736, and 1757. After a five-year period of constant eruptions of the Tungurahua Volcano, the region was hit again in 1797 by an earthquake, which was the longest and most devastating in the history of Ecuador (with more than four months of aftershocks). Its epicenter was the city of Riobamba, thirty-one miles away from Salasaca. The activity of the Tungurahua resumed in the next century, with downfalls of ash and lava flows (1886), explosions (1888), and emanations of gases and ashes (between 1911 and 1918).[41] And whether the volcanic eruptions caused human fatalities or not, they always brought serious damages to housing, crops, grasslands, rivers, and livestock in the affected areas. More of this would come in the twentieth century, notably, the so-called Ambato earthquake in 1949.

Seismic and volcanic activity of the central highlands led to an entire redistribution of the population of Ecuador throughout this period.[42] Between 1780 and 1909, the number of inhabitants who lived in the central highlands sharply fell from being 41.5 percent of the total population of the country to 24.9 percent. During the same period, the population of the coast, particularly in el Guayas and the southern littoral, increased fourfold (from 5.3 percent to 21.2 percent) (Bromley 1979, 288). Natural disasters thus accounted for a large number of displaced persons, many of them fleeing from the highlands to the Pacific Coast.

When Cobos, Valdizán, and Gil were recruiting for their *haciendas* (roughly between the 1860s and the early 1900s), they recruited a large part of their laborers by buying their debts from other landlords in the central highlands. Yet another part was made up of "vagabonds" or "unemployed" who were wandering the streets of Guayaquil. Some of them could have been the recently displaced from the Tungurahua. Natural disasters in Tungurahua and the central highlands, therefore, partly explain the rising population of the Ecuadorian coast as well as the early arrival of *Tungurahuenses* to the Galápagos.

The Earliest Salasacas in the Galápagos

Some of the eldest Salasaca settlers recognize Pedro Chango as one of the first Salasaca to reach the Galápagos. Gaspar Masaquiza, who lived with him in San Cristóbal Island, recalls how often Chango talked about the way workers were treated back in those days in hacienda El Progreso. "They worked for a time, got paid, and when they were about to return [to the mainland], right behind them, the boss, Cobos, sent his thugs to kill them. There, it all ended." (Interview, Puerto Ayora, July 2017). [43] At the time Chango arrived, he instead chose to work close at the port. There he was hired to clean the streets of Puerto Baquerizo Moreno. Chango also rejoiced when he remembered the time when he became the *prioste* (sponsor) for over a year of the ritual *fiestas* in his native Salasaca. Chango could afford this by spending the savings he made with his work on the island.

Despite these and other memories, it is not clear, among the first Salasaca settlers with whom I talked, who were the first to arrive in the Galápagos. On the other hand, there is very limited information available about the earliest inhabitants of the archipelago.[44] The isolation, the weak presence of the state, and the low esteem in which the first permanent colony was held on the mainland explain this.[45] Most of the existing data comes from the field notes of travelers to the islands and from the surveys and statistics gathered in the National Archives in Quito.[46] The Territorial Chief (*Jefe Territorial*) who lived in San Cristóbal Island provided these numbers. The first surveys, however, do not mention the place of origin of the inhabitants. For its part, the surnames of the *conciertos* who were listed are not conclusive of their origins. In that period, there was much more flexibility in the norms for assigning or adopting surnames, particularly after being exiled or attached to a different landlord. In many cases, peons were named after their masters, the place they had been recruited, or the occupation they held.[47] It is also well known that there is a lack of information about the archipelago from the time that Cobo's *hacienda* declined (1920s) and up to the arrival of conservationism to the archipelago (1960s). This historical void reflects the abandonment in which the Ecuadorian government left first settlers of the Galápagos.

Yet according to the 1878 list of taxpayers (former tributaries) of the parish of San Cristóbal Island, some of the earliest permanent settlers of the Galápagos had surnames that are distinctively Salasaca.[48] For example, Gregorio Guamán, Segundo and Manuel Piña, and Fructuoso Guaranga lived in San Cristóbal Island. They must have arrived with the first squads of Indigenous laborers that Cobos brought to the island—later, a José Lindo Chicaiza who appears in the correspondence between the parish of Puerto Baquerizo (San Cristóbal) and the municipality of Pelileo (Tungurahua).[49] Later in 1934, a Juan Chango is one of the signers of a petition by the "inhabitants of this land" who petitioned the governor of Tungurahua for the ousting of the Territorial Chief of San Cristóbal Island. In the letter, the signatories claimed that the official was drunk all the time, was very abusive, and did not fulfill the responsibilities of his post. The *colonos* (first settlers) thus asked for a delegate who would set a good example for the "moral and intellectual progress of the children" of the parish in order to form "honorable and hardworking citizens and good parents of families" (ANE). Meanwhile in Isabela, Gregorio Caiza, one of the eldest *colonos*, recalled two midwives who lived on the island in the 1940s, one of them also of the surname Chango (Rodas and Vivanco 2012, 290–92), who were probably, like himself, also Salasaca.

Although these documents provide evidence of the early presence of *Salasacas* in the Galápagos, I argue that the most significant proof is to be found in the history of the name of the old district, "Salasaca," on Santa Cruz Island (the same that some *mestizos* on the islands want to change) as well as in the *cabuya* (agave) plants that were introduced in the Galápagos beginning in the 1890s.

"Salasaca" on Santa Cruz Island

I learned of the existence of a district called "Salasaca" in the upper part of Santa Cruz on my first day I arrived to the Galápagos Islands. At the same time, that day, I heard of the campaign to change its name. Later after visiting the area, I realized very few people currently lived there. The history of this place was furthermore unknown to every Salasaca I talked to. None of my interlocutors knew why that district bore the Indigenous name of their birthplace (and ethnic group) in Tungurahua. Yet all of them mentioned how happy they were when they arrived at the Galápagos and found that there was a place called: "Salasaca." Someone told me that *cabuya* (agave) plants had been grown there.

By that time, I already knew of the strong link between the *cabuya* and the *Salasacas*. On the mainland, the agave plant runs through the entire history of the Salasaca people and had turned into a symbol by which others identify their lands and the members of the community. A Spanish Jesuit who was also a naturalist, José de Acosta, described the plant in 1572 as follows:

I have identified a tree, sacred for the natives, which they worship as much as a god, since it provides them with food, a roof and a drink. . . . From its heart, buried in the highlands, they extract a white blood which they drink, and with it, they drink life itself.
(de Acosta, 1590, in *La Hora* newspaper, 2019).

The agave plant plays a central role in the lives and history of the *Salasacas*. From the 1600s onwards, to cultivate agave on the slopes of the Tungurahua Volcano, don Francisco Hati sent groups of Indigenous *camayos* (including some Masaquizas, originally Matza Kitza) to Salasaca. They had used this plant since ancient times to prepare the *tzawar mishki*, a ritual drink with energy-giving and curative properties, which protected their ancestors through their long journeys across the peaks and snow-covered summits of the cordillera de los Andes. When they drink it today, the Salasaca elders still recite their genealogy and ancestry while exalting their *mitimae* roots.

The agave plant became a symbol of the Salasaca lands because it was used to demarcate the boundaries between properties and delimit their ethnic territory as a whole. The plants grew so well that, in 1908, the *Salasacas* were accused of "having allowed the agave leaves grow too much" so that they could prevent *mestizos* and other intruders from crossing their lands (Choque 1996, 88). Moreover, the fibers of this plant were always found in homes and in traditional Salasaca clothing. They were used for building the roofs of their houses and to make the cords that held together the enormous looms located at the center of every home. It was likewise used for making *shigras* (bags), footwear, fabrics, and sacks. Finally, agave was a symbol of progress for the *Salasacas* since it was associated with the manufacturing of textiles, which allowed many of them to survive or save money to buy lands in the colonial period, and later, to attain the economic and political autonomy that was needed to be recognized as a unified Indigenous nation in Ecuador.

Agave further became one of the three signs, which combined are used to represent the Salasaca people to the present day: the first is "*la mama*" (mother) Tunguraha Volcano; the second, the *cabuya* (agave) plants; and third, their traditional dress made of fine cloths from Salasaca. These are depicted here:

Figure 3.4.   Salasaca people. *Source:* Nations and Ethnic Groups of Ecuador. *Source:* (Nacionalidades y grupos étnicos del Ecuador, 2013)

Agave plants were also the link I found between the Salasaca people of the highlands and one of the earliest human settlements on Santa Cruz Island. In 1846, French captain Henri Louns reported the presence of a small group of laborers living in Whale Bay, as well as a path that linked the bay with the upper part of the island (Lundh 2001). In 1852, Captain Andersson confirmed this. It was the same place where, later, Heyerdahl (1956) found archaeological remains that he and others argued were the fishing camps of the Manteño-Huancavilcas of the Tiwanaku, Chimú, and Incan empires. The trail connected, possibly since pre-Hispanic times, one of the most important

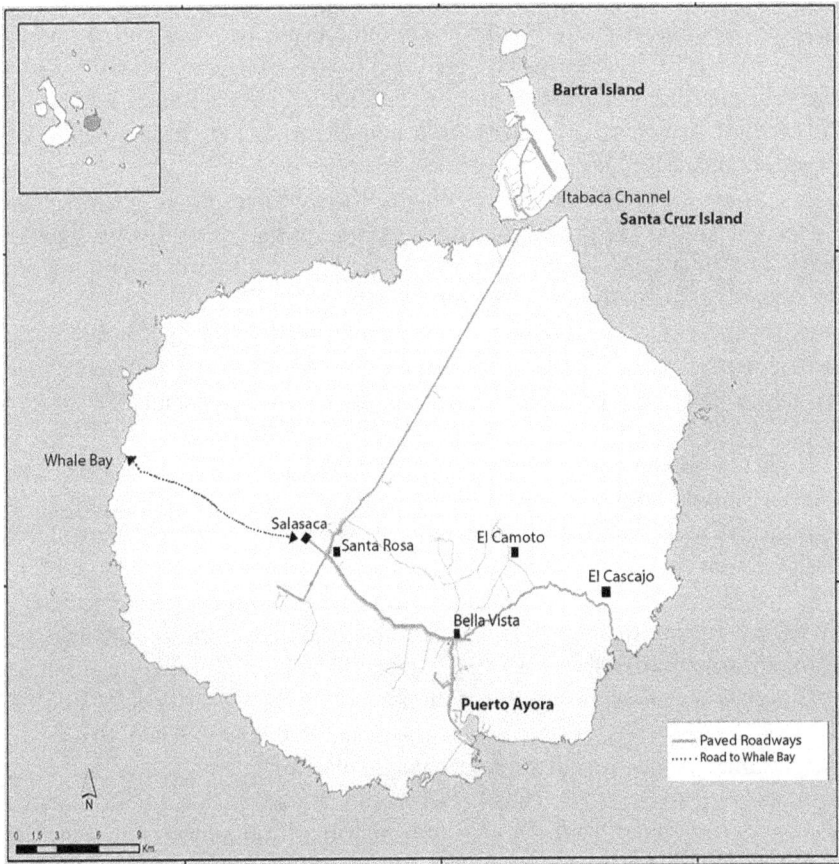

Figure 3.5. Salasaca in Santa Cruz Island. The ancient trail connects Whale Bay (or *puerto de las chacras*) with Salasaca and Santa Rosa (*sierra de las chacras*). There is a paved road that links Puerto Ayora and Santa Rosa with Canal Itabaca (where a motorboat takes people to the airport on Baltra Island). *Source:* Map created by Mauricio Salinas.

places for whale hunting on the archipelago with the only source of fresh water on Santa Cruz (located close to what is now known as "Salasaca" in the Galápagos).

Lundh (2001) argues that the group of laborers that Captains Louns (in 1846) and Andersson (in 1852) reported were *conciertos* of General Villamil, who had arrived to the islands in the 1830s. These laborers were later shifted to Santa Cruz Island in order to collect orchil linen there. Some decades later, inland from the port, Manuel J. Cobos also sent a group of workers to establish gardens and grow food that would supply the squads of hunters he periodically sent to that island in order to bring tortoises to his *hacienda* on San Cristóbal. Since the time of Cobos, the bay began to be called *"puerto de las chacras"* (harbor of the food plots), while the upper part was called *"sierra de las chacras."* The latter was divided into two districts, each with their own *chacras*: the first, in the lower part of the humid region is "Salasaca," while the second—which was further inland and closer to the spring—is "Santa Rosa" (Lundh 1995).[50]

According to an 1891 report by the Territorial Chief of the archipelago, Cobos introduced the growing of agave plants in the lower district, that is, Salasaca (Santa Cruz Island) (Latorre 1991, 53). It seems that the landlord was planning to replace all of the internal fences of his *hacienda* with natural boundaries of agave plants, just as was done in Salasaca (Tungurahua) on the mainland. When Nicolás Martínez visited the island in 1906–1907, he considered it a "very valuable investment" for Cobos's hacienda El Progreso (ibid.).[51]

A scientist first recorded the presence of agave on the islands in 1906. The Charles Darwin Foundation soon included these plants in its survey of invasive species in the archipelago. The agave is described as follows: the plant's fleshy leaves can grow to a height of up to six meters (twenty feet) and turn into "dense and impenetrable thickets which keep out most plant species."[52] Those planted in Salasaca (Galápagos) "were already forming thickets" in 1911, according to Stewart (1911), a botanist from the California Academy of Sciences who came across them when he was surveying the species of cacti in the Galápagos Islands (*Noticias Galápagos* 2006, 64). Stewart also documented small-scale plots of manioc, papaya, plantains, taro roots, sugar cane, oranges, *camote* (sweet potatoes), and lemon in the *chacras* of Santa Rosa. However, throughout those decades, scientists made no records regarding the human settlers who lived or farmed in this area.

In the late 1920s, when Norwegians tried to settle in Santa Cruz, they did note that some "mountain farmers from Ambato" were already living on the island, farming the *chacras* of the higher elevated area, as Hoff (1985) later noted. When the Norwegians left the island, the old *chacras* continued to survive in their original form for at least two more decades (as the Darwin station also documented it).

Colonos (first settlers) of this area only arrived until 1959. Segundo Chapi was the first to know of this place after being sent to the island as a soldier of the Ecuadorian Army. He arrived in 1941, soon after the US military base had been installed in Baltra (the neighboring island). Once in Santa Cruz, Segundo and his peers went to the upperpart in search of fresh water and wild cattle they could hunt in order to survive. They found the only spring in the island in Santa Rosa. They also learned that some *Salasacas* had farmed and lived by the agave crops in the lower part of the highland. In 1944, Chapi went back to the Ecuadorian mainland.

A decade passed and Segundo Chapi decided to return to the desolate Santa Cruz. This time he had in mind to establish an agricultural colony with fifteen partners in the very same district he had found fresh water. They started by requesting titles of these lands to the Ecuadorian Institute of Agrarian Reform and Colonization (IERAC), which was interested in encouraging the colonization of the Amazon and the Galápagos archipelago.[53] Soon after in 1959—on a very short notice—the IERAC demanded the new settlers to move to Santa Cruz. According to Segundo's surviving wife, they had to arrive "before the new institution was created," by which she meant the Galápagos National Park and the Charles Darwin Station (Interview in "Tribute to pioneers of Santa Cruz Island").[54]

I was able to talk to Chapi's son Oswaldo, the first park ranger hired by the Galápagos National Park. The vivid memories of his late father better clarified the origins of the name "Salasaca" in the Galápagos. When he was alive, Segundo told his son about the *Salasacas* who had lived in Santa Rosa's neighboring district. They were responsible for the agave crops, probably through the years that Cobos introduced and cultivated them in the archipelago (1890s to early 1900s). This was the reason why, when Chapi and his partners founded the parish of Santa Rosa in the highland, they decided to call the *chacra*, in the lower part, by the pioneers' birthplace: "Salasaca." It is however uncertain when these first *Salasacas* left the agave crops as well as this area. Yet, the Indigenous name, along with the emblematic plants, native of the highlands of the central Andes (Bolivia and Perú), remain in the inland area of Santa Cruz until today.

Why is so little known of these first *Salasacas* of Santa Cruz Island? And, why are some *mestizo* (more recent) settlers trying to erase the name of the "Salasaca" district in Santa Cruz Island? I argue that what the current campaign to change the name of this district actually reveals is the marked racism, the "anti-Indigenous" sentiment of *Santacruceños* (Grenier 2007 [2002], 397), which grows as more and more *Salasacas* settle in the archipelago.

Furthermore, this initiative is part of a series of long-established practices aimed at erasing Indigenous pasts in order to become more white (and 'civilized') as families, towns, and cities do when making their own history.

At the same time, to erase the Indigenous name from Santa Cruz Island fits into the set of practices that have been used to create "natural parks," following the Yellowstone model in the U.S. (West et al. 2006, 258). These included: the violent eviction of thousands of Native American people, the appropriation and destruction of farms, the revocation of rights to use the lands as common hunting grounds, and the removal of all archaeological traces of existing villages, along with the systematic erasure of history (Olwig 1996, West et al. 2006, 258). It further materialized Western imaginaries that divide nature and culture (Strathern 1980). In line with this, the creation of Galápagos National Park has likewise implied the silencing of human pasts—starting with the memories kept by the archaeological remains found in Whale Bay and followed by other human accounts, such as the *Salasacas'* history in the archipelago. Other devices inherent to conservation work will be discussed throughout the following chapters.

Meanwhile, today, in Salasaca (Santa Cruz Island), one can only find a "natural," nearly uninhabited landscape, except for a luxury boutique hotel that is there, owned by a European family. On the heights of Salasaca, elite tourists arrive to contemplate the views of Whale Bay, which embraces the rest of the islands and islets of the Galápagos, that is, the natural patrimony of mankind. From Salasaca (Santa Cruz Island), following Williams (1975: 124–6), the eco-tourist of the Galápagos (the "self-conscious observer") can look to the natural landscape, as that landlord who cares for his lands from a "separated vantage-point."[55] Meanwhile, most *galapagueños* do not have access to this area, that is now a private property, or to the emblematic sites of the Galápagos National Park. Access to these sites is only possible by boat, launch, or cruise. The average *galapagueño* cannot afford the cost of such voyages.

Colonization of Santa Cruz Island

The first wave of permanent settlers arrived in the Galápagos through the *haciendas* established in San Cristóbal and Isabela Islands. Most of them had been recruited in the Tungurahua. By the end of the 1930s, after the decline of the *hacienda galapagueña,* the archipelago's population reached 800 people (Naveda 1952). One decade later, 1,346 lived on the islands with most living on San Cristóbal and only 215 living on Santa Cruz Island. Some of these early settlers were the "Ambato mountain farmers" (probably some were Salasacas) who were living in the highland when the Norwegians tried to settle by the bay. However, they are never mentioned in the lists of *colonos* of Santa Cruz, which rather highlight the names of a handful of European families who stayed or arrived in the following decades.

A second wave of settlers arrived to the Galápagos from the 1950s onwards, particularly after the 1949 devastating earthquake that shook the Tungurahua Province and the 1959 creation of the Galápagos National Park and the Charles Darwin Station. Many came after the 1949 catastrophe, which gutted thirty communities, causing around five thousand deaths, and leaving more than one hundred thousand homeless. Its epicenter was only five miles away from Salasaca. Chilcapamba (or Capillapamba), the old ceremonial center of Salasaca, as well as other surrounding cities and towns were completely destroyed.[56] In response, the government offered *"tierras baldías"* (lands which were not yet privatized) to displaced families while also launching a campaign that sought to populate the Amazon and the Galápagos. Apart from Chapi and his partners, most of the beneficiaries were from the Tungurahua Province.[57]

By the late 1950s, Galápagos landowners actively started to recruit workers to farm their lands. Many of the newcomers were *Salasacas*. However, after arriving to Santa Cruz, they preferred to take on different jobs, settling by the pier (rather than inland) nearby Academy Bay where the Charles Darwin Station had started to build its offices. They also chose not to take lands from the government's offer for the reasons I will describe in the next chapter. Some years later, in 1964, the population of Santa Cruz alone had increased fourfold, reaching more than 700 inhabitants. Until the passing of the 1998 law, these first settlers, along with those that arrived in the next two decades, were all legally identified as *"colonos"* (first permanent settlers) of Santa Cruz Island.

From another angle, the origins of both the first and the second wave of migrants in the Galápagos can be observed in the important presence of plants and animal species native to the Ecuadorian highlands. In 1965, scientists of the Charles Darwin Station reported that *cuyes* (guinea pigs) as well as rabbits and sheep were there in the higher elevated part of Santa Cruz.[58] All these animals are an essential part of the traditional Andean (*"serrano,"* highland Indigenous) diet. Particularly, the guinea pigs play an important role in a great number of social, ceremonial, medicinal, and culinary practices for many Indigenous groups throughout the Andes. This is also evidence that proves wrong the local dominant discourse that claims that *mestizo* people from the Ecuadorian coast (and not from the highlands) were the first to settle in Santa Cruz and the Galápagos.

114 Chapter Three

NOTES

1. The *hacienda* system thrived in the sierra—particularly, in the central high-lands. This region includes the provinces of Tungurahua, Cotopaxi, Chimborazo, and Bolívar.

2. The provinces of Azuay, Bolívar, Carchi, Cañar, Chimborazo, Cotopaxi, Imba-bura, Loja, Pichincha, and Tungurahua make up the Ecuadorian highlands.

3. While the local notion of "race" embraces all Indigenous peoples, ethnicity alludes to a community or village: a group that identifies under a singular culture, history, and customs.

4. Ambato, located seven miles away from Salasaca, is the capital city of the Tungurahua Province.

5. *Mestizaje* was also an "ideology of inclusion" (through acculturation) of native peoples embedded in nation-building processes throughout Latin America (Whitten 1981,13). Since the wars of independence, the *creole* elite promoted it because they believed progress and modernization was represented by *mestizaje*.

6. The central Andes encompass southern Ecuador, Perú, western Bolivia and northern and central Argentina and Chile. The Tungurahua region lies in the northern Andes.

7. In 1432, Pachaqutig, the ninth Inca, seized Tiwanaku, the center of the Colla-Aymaras. Once the Tawantinsuyu (the Incan State) was consolidated, the Incas im-posed the Runa Shimi or Kichwa language in the region along with the tribute (tax paid in kind) and a theocratic centralist rule based in Cuzco.

8. According to UNESCO, the history of this civilization goes back to at least 1200 BC. Its fall has been attributed to a severe climatic change in the region and constant internal wars between native lords that preceded the Inca invasion.

9. During the preliminary research I did in Salasaca, Tungurahua, Rufino Masa-quiza told me about the investigation he and other *yachaks* made of the roots of the Salasaca people in Tungurahua (with the aid of the elders of the community) and in Bolivia (also see: Rumiñahui Masaquiza in Vinueza 1995). The elders recall the story of a *mitimae* group that reached the Tungurahua area from a district now known as Ladrillo. There was a general there who ruled over the whole region, from Pelileo to Panzaleo, Mocha, and Tisaleo. When they arrived, the *mitimaes* found no place where they could live. They continued to the north but the Panzaleos stopped them continuing along that route and they had to return. Towards the south, the Purúhaes also stopped them from crossing their borders. The general then granted them a terri-tory and assigned a mission: they would have to guard the region crossed by the river Pachanlica, from Quero to Patate, including Guambaló (on the slopes of the Tungura-hua Volcano). Those districts turned into the borders of the territory of the *Salasacas* during the Inca empire and up to the Spanish Conquest.

10. To understand the ritual practices of social memory in an Aymara community and their interaction with European traditions, see Abercrombie (1998).

11. The *ayllu* was an institution which formed broad networks united by blood re-lationships, communal production, ritual practices, reciprocity, and the sharing out of

resources. Today the *ayllu* refers to the extended family, which at times may include godfathers, godmothers, godchildren, or adoptive children.

12. The group of Salasaca *yachak* who investigated their origins in Bolivia in 1989 likewise acknowledged their cultural affinity with the Aymaras in terms of their shared dress, names, and customs (Interview, Salasaca, 2016).

13. *Fiestas* were a rite of passage associated with agricultural and herding tasks, warfare, healing, and other forms of shamanism, with marriage and funerary rights. (Abercrombie 1998).

14. The town of Quero, for example, joined together three different groups of *miti-maes*, among them the *ayllu* of the "Inca Carpenters" (*Incas Carpinteros*), natives of what is now Perú. Another group of "Carpenter" *mitimaes* settled in Pelileo.

15. The *m'ita* was an ancient Inca institution of obligatory labor on public works, which the Spanish Crown took over.

16. In their new homes, the *forasteros* were forced to work but with a lesser burden of work in the mills and *haciendas*. *Forasterismo* served the caciques as a strategy to evade part of the tributes they had to collect by claiming that certain of their subjects had fled.

17. A number of authors have rightly argued that the *Salasacas* resulted from the fusion of different Indigenous groups. Peñaherrera and Costales (1959), for example, suggested that the *Salasacas* were descendants of the Pachanlicas, Panzaleos and Puruhayes; Peréz (1962) and Reino Garcés (2004) held that they were a fusion of the Quitu-Pantsaleos, Pillajo-Nazcas of Perú and Colla-Aymaras Kichwas of Bolivia; Corr and Powers (2012) instead argued that they came from the Sigchos-Collanas, Tacungas, Pilalatas and Puruhayes.

18. After gold and silver, cochineal dye became one of the most valuable American products and main export items in the colonial period.

19. Escaping, aborting their unborn children, and hiding their newborn ones became recurrent practices the natives resorted to in order to resist the cruelty of these textile mills in Ecuador (Ortiz de la Tabla 1977). Costales (1975) further speculates on the possible psychological effects that centuries of abuse and ill-treatment had on the Indigenous population of the region.

20. According to the archives of tribute accounts for 1619 and 1699, several Sigcho Collana men with the surname Masaquiza worked as *conciertos* in San Ildefonso (Corr and Powers 2012, 44)

21. Up to a short time ago, you could still find one or two looms in the center of each home, where they took up a large part of a family's private space.

22. The word "*vecino*" [neighbor] was used to refer first to beneficiaries of Crown grants (government posts, rights to property, lands, and servants in villages and cities). The word continued to be used to designate urban dwellers.

23. "*Cholo*" in Ecuador (as in Peru and Bolivia, see Abercrombie 1996), is not a category of self-identification but rather a derogatory label given by others to recently made *mestizos*. "*Cholo*" differs from "*longo*"—an insult that is rather used to punish Indigenous peoples that seem to refuse to acculturate or adopt a *mestizo* identity.

24. Patricia Albers (1996) points out that for a process of ethnogenesis—the creation of an ethnic group—to be completed, the union and solidarity of its members must prevail over any differences from their ethnic pasts.

25. In 1576, the Spanish Crown had granted conquistador Hernando de la Parra the lands of the region, along with the labor of an *encomienda* of the Indigenous Chumaquí group, as recognition of his services as a subaltern to Sebastián de Belálcazar.

26. To defend their properties, the *Salasacas* resorted to colonial law, not only for the legal purchase of lands but also to bring lawsuits before the *Real Audiencia* (the Spanish Royal Court) and later to judges in the courts of Quito, whenever they had to defend their property rights (Corr 2018).

27. In the case of the Salasaca girls, this usually occurred in Quito or Ambato.

28. The official referred to the famous warrior Rumiñahui (1490–1535), son of the eleventh Inca, Huayna Capac, and Nari, the princess of Pillaro. He won several battles against the Spanish until he was defeated by the conquistador Sebastián de Belálcazar and his army.

29. The priests at the parish in Pelileo had previously been responsible for counting the number of "Indians" in the region by registering births, deaths, and baptisms.

30. In 1964, the new *cabildo* (governing council) was founded, along with the *Junta de Defensa del Campesinado* (Board for the Defense of Peasant Communities). In 1972, the status of Salasaca was raised from community to a parish, which meant that it could then have a *teniente politico* (a local political authority). In 1983, the Union of Salasaca Indigenous People (Unión de Indígenas Salasacas) was founded; it later became affiliated with the Tungurahua Indigenous Movement and after that with the Ecuadorian Confederation of Indigenous Nationalities (CONAIE).

31. During the seventeenth century in Mexico, for example, 50 percent of the children there were born out of wedlock and only in a few cases their fathers formally or informally recognized them. In Nueva Granada (Santafé, Colombia), although concubinage was regarded as wrong, it was widely practiced. Many homes were made up of a Spanish couple, their children and servants, and the illegitimate children that the head of the family had with one or several of the female servants (Rappaport 2014, 127–29). In the homes of Quito as well, a large number of illegitimate children were recorded at that time (Kingman 2006, 176).

32. If a person was labeled as a "tributary," even if he was *mestizo* (of mixed race), he was an Indian to the state.

33. This of course was not permanent, since the same individual could change his or her dress in a single day (de la Cadena 2000). Ethnic dress signified being "Indian," while accessories and fabrics of their garments indicated the status of such person within the native community.

34. For example: *cholos* (urban Indians), *longos* (Indians or closer to Indians), *blancos* (whites, usually of Spanish descent), *mestizos* (mixed race but raised under Hispanic tradition), *trigueños* (*mestizos* with lighter skin), *montañes* or *serranos* (highlanders), *morenos* (dark skin), *zambos* (with African and Indigenous ancestry), *mulatos* (European with African ancestry), etc. (See also Minchom 1994).

35. To maintain one's whiteness also depends on life decisions, like choosing the right partner, occupation, and conduct. Honor and decency are thus permanently at stake; they are easy to lose and difficult to gain.

36. The *caciques* had a privileged position: they did not have to pay tribute, they wore European clothes and enjoyed the title of "*don*," or if they were women, "*doña.*" In addition, they assumed the role of intermediaries who administered Indigenous manpower and collected the tribute owed by their communities.

37. By the end of the colonial period (1830s), 46 percent of the Indigenous population belonged to and worked for the *hacienda* system (Oberem 1981, 315). Up to 1964, when the *hacienda* regime was abolished, most of the Ecuadorian population continued to be bound to *haciendas*. They thus lived in rural areas and their private and public lives were organized around the *hacienda* and its landlord.

38. Pelileo, close to Salasaca, congregated native Pilalatas, Chimaquís, Guambalós, Puruhayes and Tacungas, as well as a large number of "*forasteros*" and the "Inca Carpenter" *mitimae* group. Ambato, the capital of the Tungurahua, reduced natives from Quisapincha, Izamba, Santa Rosa, Píllaro, and other communities. Its initial population was made up of 150 "families" (Spanish landlords, conquistadors, and soldiers), 4,000 self-declared "*mestizos*," and 6,000 "Indians"—most of them *camayos*, as documented in the archives of Tungurahua (Fondo de Documentación). Meanwhile, the population of Quito registered 500 nobles out of a total of 24,000 inhabitants in 1789, according to the reports of the *cabildo* (city council) (Buschges 1997, 47).

39. *Indigenistas* ascribed to themselves the right to speak for Indians about the "Indian problem" (taking the role of "ventriloquists" in the words of Guerrero 2003). While they appreciated the cultural heritage of Indigenous peoples, they often "wished to leave it at the level of archaeology." They thus tended "to triumph the past accomplishments of past civilizations while leaving the current descendants of the Inca and Aztec empires languishing in an impoverished and disempowered state" (ibid., 1). In such a context, present-day Indigenous peoples were constructed as passive recipients of government policies (Martinez 2014), whereas the term "*mestizaje*" was increasingly used to invoke an ideology that affirmed the unity of the people (Whitten 1981). Recently, a type of *indigenismo* reemerged, but in the context of the declaration of Ecuador as a diverse, "plurinational" and "multicultural" country (2008). The word "ancestral" was used throughout the new laws, for example, in the Organic Law of Intercultural Education, relegating Indigenous knowledge to the past in a classical *indigenista* fashion (Martinez 2014, 116).

40. The project to enlarge the railway network also included schemes to establish a link with the Amazon from Ambato. The *Salasacas'* opposition to the building of any road or railway line through their territory is thought to be the reason why the route of the railway line was changed.

41. Between 1856 and 1868, three earthquakes hit Ecuador (in the north and south highlands), the epicenters of which were Cuenca, Quito, and Imbabura.

42. At the beginning of the nineteenth century, the population of Ambato alone had fallen by half from 4,000 to 2,000 inhabitants. In Riobamba, it was more drastic: from 8,500 to only 2,500 inhabitants (Kingman 2006, 61).

43. The dates are not clear. When Pedro Chango talked about "the boss, Cobos," he may be referring to the founder (Manuel J.) or to one of his descendants who took charge in the period between his death (1904) and the sale of the *hacienda* to Tous (1928). Other Salasaca *colonos* (first settlers) confirmed this story.

44. Mainly, the work of Octavio Latorre 1991, 1996, 2011, and J.P. Lundh 1995, 2001.

45. At the time, the only representatives of the Ecuadorian State in the Galápagos were: the Territorial Chief (*Jefe Territorial*) and two groups of seven people (a secretary and six policemen), each on a different island—San Cristóbal and Isabela (Bognoly and Espinosa 1905, 198–99).

46. Like French captain Henri Louns in 1846, Swedish Professor Nils Johan Andersson in 1852, and Alexander Mann in 1909, and local visitors such as José Bognoly, José M. Espinoza in 1905, and Nicolás Martinez in 1906–1907.

47. For example, in the 1878 list, there were many peons named after places (like Quito, Carchi, Campoverde, Sangolquí and Seminario), by their occupation or by another feature (such as Servant—*Sirviente*, Steer—*Novillo*, Blow—*Sopla*, Spirit Blows—*Espiritu Sopla*).

48. I went through the lists of names in the archives with people from Salasaca. For a list of distinctive Salasaca surnames, see Corr and Powers (2012).

49. Chicaiza, along with Andrés Guachamboza, petitioned for a reduction of their sentences which had condemned them to forced labor on the islands for the theft of two donkeys in Patate, a neighboring town of Salasaca, Tungurahua.

50. For a short time (in the late 1920s), Norwegians who visited the island called this district the "*chacras de los piratas*" (pirates' food plots) because they incorrectly believed these were established by buccaneers (Lundh 2001, 95).

51. In fact, agave plants were used to delimit the boundaries of lands from pre-conquest times throughout the Andean highlands (de Acosta 1590, in Magan 2002, 212).

52. The Darwin Scientific Station classified agave, or *cabuya* (*furcraea cubensis* or *agave hexapetala*) as an invasive species that was intentionally introduced, whose status of aggressiveness was classified as "transformer." Today it is found on three islands: Santa Cruz, Isabela, and San Cristóbal. The "transformer'" species are a subset of invasive plants that change the character, condition, form, or nature of ecosystems.

53. A good part of the fertile lands had already been distributed among sixteen settlers, twelve of them Europeans (as illustrated by Villacís (1937) in Lundh 1995). However, for the next decades, the IERAC continued to grant titles in the rest of the island until all the lands were privatized.

54. In an interview with doña Anita Farfán de Chapi.

55. The term "landscape," which originally denoted a painting whose primary object was natural scenery (Olwig 1996), was later coined to evoke a certain "way of seeing" that emerged with the rise of capitalism (Berger 1980). Anthropologists examining non-Western societies also remarked that landscapes are not "nature" but forms of dwelling experienced and also infused "in people's pragmatic engagements with its constituents" (Ingold 2011 [2000], 154); temporal and subjective (Bender 2002); and an integral part of how people make social memory (Abercrombie 1998) and their own biographies (Raffles 2004).

56. It also destroyed towns and cities such as Pelileo, Ambato, Píllaro, and Guano. Yet despite the widespread media coverage, there was no mention of the damages, the number of displaced, or the victims it claimed in Salasaca. Latorre (2011, 223) attributes population growth in the Galápagos during these decades to the 1949 earthquake.

57. There is no record of a Salasaca settler who benefited from this campaign.

58. Scientists particularly feared that the invasive rodents could multiply and run free on the island, joining the other prolific feral species, like dogs, goats, hens, cattle, and pigs. This never happened because the *cuyes* (guinea pigs) were too domesticated to survive outside the farmhouse, as the station later reported (ibid.). In the end, neither the *cuyes* nor the other species prospered due to the restrictions of conservation law and their predation by feral dogs.

Chapter Four

Salasaca Colonos

In April 2017, I arrived in Puerto Ayora on Santa Cruz Island—the most populated town in the islands—where Galápagos National Park and the Charles Darwin Research Station are headquartered and tourism is centered. At the time, I did not know anyone of Salasaca origin on the archipelago. But I knew of the existence of the Salasaca Association and had been told about the soccer stadium in the Miraflores neighborhood, which was the place most frequented by Salasaca people on Santa Cruz.

Thus on my first Sunday there, I went to Miraflores stadium. A lot of people were there, dressed in casual clothes and cheering on their teams who were

Figure 4.1.   Salasaca Sports League fans. *Source*: Photo: P. Sánchez, Puerto Ayora, Galápagos, December 2017.

competing for the "Salasaca Cup." I climbed up into the stands and, after watching part of the game, I asked one of the spectators if she knew the members of the Salasaca Association. She first asked the reasons why I was looking for them, and then recommended that I go to the Darwin Research Station and look for a woman who worked there, Margarita Masaquiza, who was the president of the Salasaca Association. She then took the opportunity to tell me, "we are all *Salasacas* in the stadium here. There isn't a single *mestizo*." Yet contrary to the practice in Salasaca (in the Ecuadorian highlands), in Miraflores, none of them were wearing their ethnic dress. Some, however, were cheering on the players or shouting at them (or the referee) in Kichwa rather than in Spanish.

It felt like we were in the highlands of Ecuador. The stands around the field were selling *cevichocho, choclos,* beer, and regional food from the Ecuadorian highlands (like *guatita* and *fritada*).[1] Next to the stadium in the heart of Miraflores, there was an outdoor market that was held every Sunday on the neighborhood's "*ecuavoley*" court.[2] As on the mainland, most of the vendors in the market were women, who sat beside the farm produce they sold. However, this marketplace was peculiar. Most of the food on sale had been shipped by boat from the mainland in one of the freighters, which supplies the islands (tourists, cruise ship passengers, and locals) every three or four weeks. The prices of the produce are therefore exorbitant, more than seven times what they cost on mainland Ecuador. And they frequently run out. The vendors blame the high prices on the fact that the freighters periodically sink or are shipwrecked when they approach the coasts of the Galápagos.[3]

Figure 4.2.   Miraflores market. *Source*: Photo: P. Sánchez, Puerto Ayora, Galápagos, April 2017.

The next day, at the entrance to the offices of the Park and the Research Station in Academy Bay (*Bahía Academia*) I met Margarita Masaquiza. She and her sister did work at the Darwin Station as cleaners. I introduced myself and told her about my project. She seemed very receptive. It was the first time they had someone interested in volunteering with the Salasaca Association to conduct research among the Indigenous collective in the Galápagos.

A few days later, Margarita invited me to her home in Miraflores, where she introduced me to some of the fellow members of the Association who, like her, were Salasaca *colonos* (first settlers) of Santa Cruz. She told them I had come to undertake a research project with them and then she clarified their expectations. "We want this to result in a document," was the first thing she said, and continued:

A text. All of the books talk about the fauna of the Galápagos Islands. That has nothing to do with the reality of the children in the Galápagos. We want people to learn about their history.

In the Association, we come here to get together, speak Kichwa, and joke around . . . We feel as if we were *"outside" (afuera)*. We would like you to get to know us, to share our lives, go to our *fiestas* dressed as a Salasaca.

(Puerto Ayora, June 2017)

When Margarita said that the members of the Association felt as if they were "outside" at the community center, Margarita used a term that is often heard in the archipelago. Among the *Galapagueños*, "outside" (*afuera*) means to be off the islands—on the mainland. Both the *mestizo* and Indigenous inhabitants of the islands use this expression to convey the feelings of enclosure and isolation that mark their memories and everyday lives on the Galápagos. According to Grenier (2007, 270), they feel they are trapped in the heart of an archipelago to which they do not have access. There are no trails to walk through the National Park and they cannot afford to pay for a cruise in the ships that sail around with tourists visiting the islands. If the mainland is the "outside" (where the "*afuereños*," or outsiders, come from), they thus live on the "inside," enclosed within the designated settlement areas. The park borders thus seem to enclose not the natural property but human settlers on the islands. Grenier (2007) calls this the "syndrome of the island-dweller" (*síndrome del insular*).

You suffer from a feeling of limitation, due to the difficulty of leaving the island when there is an emergency, and your fear of a hospital that does not provide good medical care.

The symptoms of this syndrome are somatization and anxiety [*"problemas nerviosos"*]: many *Galapagueños* often imagine health problems they do not

have . . . They consider a trip to the mainland every year as something which is
indispensable to their health, not only physical but mental.

(F. Uribe, a woman *colona* (first settler) in Santa Cruz, cited by Grenier 2007,
270).

Indeed, the lack of sound medical services and the "syndrome of the island-
dweller" affect all *galapagueños*. Even the young working adults travel to the
mainland (usually to Guayaquil or Quito) every year and pay for expensive
health examinations in order to prevent a medical emergency when they return to the islands.[4]

For the Salasaca *colonos* (first settlers) of the Galápagos (those who hold
residency permits and are able to leave), this yearly journey takes place every
November—but they travel instead to Salasaca, Tungurahua.[5] In doing so,
they comply with their ritual duty to meet up with their ancestors and their
ayllus on the sacred mountain of Cruzpamba for the "Day of the Dead" (All
Saints Day). Throughout the rest of the year on the islands, they often use
ancestral treatments for illnesses: cleansing with herbs, massages from mas-
seurs known as *sobanderos*, and treatment with *cuyes* (guinea pigs).[6] From
time to time, they also make use of the minimal health services offered by
the municipality.

Salasacas, too, feel the "syndrome of the island-dweller." They told me
they only feel "free"—as if they were "outside" (in their native village in the
Ecuadorian highlands)—when at the headquarters of the association and some
other places where they gather together (like Margarita's home) in Miraflores.
"We can spend time with one another here without racism," ("*podemos com-
partir sin racism*") one of the Salasaca *colonos* told me. They do not have to
hide in these places. Moreover, in the community center, they can speak in
Kichwa and can wear their traditional Indigenous dress for *fiestas* and meetings. On the contrary, in their everyday life on the islands, they must speak in
Spanish and dress as "*cholos*"; that is, they wear *mestizo* clothing which, in the
opinion of the Salasaca people, are in poor taste and of low quality.

After that first meeting, I began to accompany Margarita two or three times
per week to meetings with members and non-members of the Salasaca Association and also with politicians from the island and the mainland. For these
meetings, Margarita always used and asked me to wear Salasaca traditional
clothing. She was one of the very few who could claim her Indigenous identity outside the Salasaca Association. She was the second Salasaca woman
who had arrived on Santa Cruz Island, and because she was Indigenous, she
had to remain "hidden" ("*estabamos ocultándonos,*" as she told me) for more
than thirty years—from her arrival in 1980 to 2010. Although she became,
like the rest of the *colonos* (first settlers), a legal "resident" of the Galápagos

Figure 4.3. Celebration at the Salasaca Association. Margarita, another Salasaca woman, and I cooked chicken for a special gathering of the Salasaca Association. *Source*: Photo: P. Sánchez, Puerto Ayora, Galápagos, October 2017.

as per the 1998 law, Margarita still needed to shed her ethnic identity in order to avoid both symbolic and physical violence on the archipelago.

However, in recent years after the gains of the Indigenous Movement on the region, Margarita and few other Salasaca leaders could opt for "re-indigenization" in order to gain political leverage. This was only possible after the gains of the Indigenous Movement on mainland. Between 1857 (the year in which the tribute was abolished in Ecuador) and the 1990s, Indigenous people in Ecuador became perceived as "fossil cultures" or perhaps as peasant communities who had undergone *mestizaje* processes when incorporating to the nation-state (Guerrero 2003, 272). During this period, the Salasaca people resisted these processes and continued to dress in their ethnic attire while maintaining their racial and territorial borders enclosed from the intrusion of *mestizos* and other outsiders. Additionally, from the 1910s to the 1950s, the income from the textile production allowed Salasaca (Tungurahua) to enjoy economic autonomy. Yet outside Salasaca, most Indigenous peoples in the country were making themselves invisible in order to integrate into *mestizo* society. The pressures intensified on the islands due to the way local officers translated and enforced conservation policy.

By the late 1980s, a prominent resurgence of indigeneity in politics took place across the Andean region. In this decade, the Indigenous Movement organized to protest against state policies of racism and exclusion, massive economic inequality, and the absence of political representation. They further advocated for land and education reforms on behalf of Indigenous peoples throughout the region.[7] Within this context, the Indigenous Movement in Ecuador set up an alliance with President Rafael Correa (2007–2017) at the start of his administration (de la Torre 2015). Although Correa's agenda gradually diverged from that of the Indigenous Movement, this alliance made possible the drafting of a new constitution which declared Ecuador in 2008 as a "plurinational" and a "multicultural" state.[8] Such changes explicitly made Ecuadorian state law plural and, at the same time, internally contested by Indigenous groups that, in practice, continue to be largely discriminated against by state bureaucrats and *mestizo* citizens.[9] Like the notion of "cultural citizenship" (Rosaldo 1994), the idea of a "plurinational," "multicultural" state further attests to the inherent contradiction of the liberal modern discourse, which at once envisions their subjects as equal citizens before the law while also celebrating multiculturalism (the right to be different), thus allowing exceptions to citizens due to their ethnic and religious backgrounds.[10]

The appropriation of Indigenous symbols and demands was crucial throughout the turn to multiculturalism. Indigenous women and men (who formerly identified themselves as *mestizos*) manipulated their identity (to "re-indigenize" themselves) in order to gain access as political actors (Pareja 2018). *Mestizo* political leaders did the same but to gain popular support. For example, in Ecuador, Correa received his investiture as president of the nation in the high páramo of Zumbahua on a rural parish inhabited only by Kichwa inhabitants. Moreover, during his presidency (2007–2017), in official state visits and national events Correa always used a tailored, elaborately embroidered shirt (typical of some Indigenous highland villages), elevating it as a symbol of his alliance to Indigenous movements in Ecuador (Colloredo 2012). Nevertheless, during Correa's government, Indigenous inclusion proved to be, in practice, only symbolic with "Indigenous" being construed as passive recipients of governmental policies (Martinez 2014).[11]

Nonetheless, legal and symbolic inclusion of Indigenous peoples in state law and Ecuadorian politics on the mainland gave a way for Salasaca leaders, like Margarita Masaquiza, to find a voice in the Galápagos. She recalled the moment when she felt "able to be Indigenous" in Puerto Ayora (Galápagos) when I interviewed her:

> When Correa took over, a lot was understood. . . . We felt more free, I felt like that, freer, more able to be Indigenous . . . to drop my fear of speaking or dress-

ing in accordance with who we are . . . Now on the main holidays or festivities, I wear my own dress, I am *present*.
(Interview, Puerto Ayora, July 2017).

Around 2010, she started to wear her Salasaca attire on the islands. In asking me to dress in Salasaca, Margarita asked me to perform indigeneity in order to show in public my support to Salasaca political causes on the islands. She thus resorted to the strategies that were made available since the 1990s across the Andean countries. Yet for the majority of *Salasacas* of the Galápagos, this is not an option. Outside Salasaca (Tungurahua) and the community center (in Puerto Ayora, Galápagos), they need to shed their ethnic identity in order to be safe.

In addition to accompanying Margarita to meetings, my work at the Salasaca Association included writing *oficios* (letters or communiqués) on behalf of the association and delivering them to other organizations. Every now and then, I also walked with Margarita and other Salasaca women through the neighborhoods of Puerto Ayora to ask for help for communal causes, involving people in Salasaca (Tungurahua)—for example, accidents, a funeral, or the restoration of the church. To do that, we met at night and followed a route that Margarita knew well, by which we visited all of the homes of her *"paisanos"* (fellow *Salasacas*) on the island, almost all of them located in the neighborhoods of Miraflores, La Unión, and La Cascada. Finally, every Sunday starting at six o'clock, I helped Margarita cook dinner at her home in Miraflores, along with Panchita, her childhood friend. Some Salasaca *colonos* arrived early to Margarita's house in order to relieve their *chuchakis* (hangovers).[12] Others came later in the day to talk about different subjects, such as: the future of the association and its projects, the news of relatives or friends who lived back in their homeland, the red tape and permits needed to ensure that the Peruvian band hired for the New Year's *fiesta* could enter the Galápagos without problems, or the political candidate the association would support in the next elections.

Within a few months, I had gotten to know many Salasaca people on Santa Cruz. However, I began to notice I had been working on the side of the more privileged *Salasacas* (although still discriminated against by *mestizos*) of the archipelago. After the 1998 Special Law, there was a profound divide within the community. On the one hand, there were the *"colonos"* (legal "residents"), most of whom were members of the association who had arrived to colonize Santa Cruz from the 1960s onwards until the conservation law was ratified. On the other, there was a larger group of *Salasacas* who settled on the island after the passing of the 1998 law which prohibited further colonization, thus classifying all new migrants as "illegals" in the Galápagos.

In what follows, I study the specificities of the colonization of Santa Cruz Island and the role that Salasaca *colonos* had in building Puerto Ayora, the main city of the archipelago, and in taking a part in the *galapagueño* settler society. Through the voices of the Salasaca first settlers (*colonos*) of Santa Cruz, my aim is to acknowledge their early presence on the island, while addressing forms of Indigenous work and the strategies they had to adopt in order to ensure their permanence in the Galápagos. Their history, combined with specific ethnographic data that I collected, further illuminates how Salasaca cultural roots played a part in their joining together in the archipelago and the way ritual obligations remain solidly entrenched in the Salasaca *colonos* identity in the Galápagos. On the other hand, their everyday lives on Santa Cruz speak to the ties that Salasaca people have with conservation and tourism, and the positions they occupy on the islands, in accordance with a racialized division of labor that was established in the Galápagos a century ago through the transplantation of the *hacienda*.

INDIGENOUS LABOR AND COLONIZATION OF SANTA CRUZ ISLAND

Until the end of the 1990s, colonization of Santa Cruz Island was a state project. Early in the 1960s, few people lived on the island. Yet after the founding of the Galápagos National Park (1959) and the inauguration of the Charles Darwin Research Station (1964), the Ecuadorian state took on the task of rapidly building a city—Puerto Ayora—close to the foreign scientists' headquarters in order to reinforce its presence in the archipelago while profiting from the tourism industry. The presence of Ecuadorians, and particularly Indigenous Salasaca laborers, on Santa Cruz Island was crucial to this project.

Salasaca Pioneers in the Galápagos Islands (the 1960s)

Among the Salasaca *colonos* whom I interviewed, the first to reach Santa Cruz did so during the 1960s. At that time, it took four days and four nights to get to the Galápagos Islands. They had to take a ship that embarked from Guayaquil only once every six months, whose mission was to supply the inhabitants of the archipelago with food and drinking water. Later on Salasacas migrated in greater numbers, traveling in the Hercules airplanes of the Ecuadorian Army, which landed at the airport built by the US Marines during World War II on Baltra Island (close to Santa Cruz).

Up until the 1980s, the *Salasacas* who went to the Galápagos were only men, assembled in work gangs of eight or ten. They were initially recruited to work on farms in the upperpart of Santa Cruz and San Cristóbal Islands.[13] Agricultural work was, however, not their strong point. The only crop in which they had specialized was the cultivation of agave. At the same time, since at least the heyday of the textile factory of San Ildefonso in the 1600s, Salasaca men became skillful weavers and, later, owners of workshops. From the early 1900s, they gained a reputation for the high quality of their weaving and their original designs.[14]

José Pilla Masaquiza (also called "don Mullimba"), for instance, was one of the pioneers of the Galápagos and had been known in Salasaca (Tungura-hua) as a prosperous man. He had six looms in his house; all worked every day by him and his sons. They themselves sold their products or traded them through Indigenous Otavalo merchants in and beyond Ecuador. However, little by little, the textile production of the *Salasacas* was displaced by that of the *Otavaleños* (those from Otovalo), who first hired Salasaca weavers to manufacture from their own town in Ibarra (in the northern highlands of Ecuador), and later installed big electric looms in Otavalo to better compete in the textile industry.[15] Eventually, the Mullimba family workshop, like most of those in the homes in Salasaca, went out of business.

Concerned with the declining sales of their industry, don José, four of his brothers, three of his cousins, and some other Salasaca men decided to travel in the mid 1960s to the Galápagos. They were "hooked" (recruited) by an "engineer" from Benites (a *mestizo* town near Salasaca in Tungurahua),

Figure 4.4.   Salasaca *colono* of Santa Cruz Island. "Don Mullimba" on the day I inter-viewed him, at his house in Salasaca, Tungurahua. *Source*: Photo: P. Sánchez, Salasaca, December 2016.

who promised them jobs on a farm on San Cristóbal Island.[16] Soon after they reached the island, the engineer took them inland and abandoned them there. He promised to return the next day to inform them of their job duties.

The group waited in the thicket, living off wild fruit and learning how to use a *machete*, so they could exchange their work for food with the farm owners in the area. "So we were clearing land every day with a *machete* to get our food . . . that's what we did, with blisters on our hands. Ay, my God! I had never used a *machete*!" recalled Andrés Pilla, who is not a relative of don José but was also a member of that group (Interview, Salasaca, Tungurahua, November, 2016). After some weeks, the group came to accept that the engineer would never return. They thus decided to move down to the port—to Puerto Baquerizo Moreno. There they found work with the municipality, which hired them as construction workers to build the first stadium on San Cristóbal. Every day near the building site, they would encounter a big herd of sea lions. "They wallowed around there like pigs," don Andrés added.

What those Salasaca pioneers most remember about that time is the arrival of the ship from the mainland. It was undoubtedly the most important social event in the archipelago. From afar, people born in the Galápagos—old and new migrants in the island—all heard the sound of the ship's horn, which signaled the arrival of rice, sugar, and other products, as well as news from the mainland. They all gathered at the port and celebrated the ship's visit with a feast that often lasted several days. The inhabitants of the inland region also took advantage of the occasion to barter plantains, coffee, fruits, and beef or goat meat for salt and fish. All kinds of "interesting exchanges" took place at those celebrations, as documented by foreign seamen in that period (Grenier 2007, 90, citing Toumelin 1953). In broken Spanish mixed with words in Kichwa, don Mullimba recalled this over and over again:

> Ship, you knew [it was] coming . . . It was already honking, you knew, from afar, [everyone was] happy, dancing. Daddy is coming! Mommy is on the way!
> That period, there was no food, rice, it was like that. That time! Fuck! Food, nothing. We went around hungry.
> (Interview, Salasaca, Tungurahua, December 2016).

A while later, the group left San Cristóbal for Santa Cruz Island, where they were told there was lots of work. They arrived at the end of the 1960s to lay the foundation for the construction of a new city: Puerto Ayora.[17]

Arrival on Santa Cruz Island (1960s–1980s)

When the Salasaca pioneers got to Santa Cruz, there were only three or four wooden houses which were built with wood left by the US Marines after they had evacuated the military base on Baltra. These houses were close to the dock, made by the Norwegians during the late 1920s. There they also found a church, "The Immaculate Conception of Mary" (*La Inmaculada Concepción de María),* which had been built in 1955 by the Franciscans. Behind that first line of beachfront, there were only stones, large cracks in the ground, cacti, and small woods of carob trees.[18] The landscape was desolate: "there were no people, there were no streets . . . it was only rough ground, full of stones" (Interview, Salasaca, December, 2016).

At the time, the recently arrived Salasaca pioneers also heard about the government's offer of lands in Santa Cruz. They were the last of the *"tierras baldías"* (lands that were not yet privatized), which the IERAC (the Ecuadorian Institute of Agrarian Reform and Colonization) gave away on the upper-part of the island, along with some other terrains in what is now downtown Puerto Ayora. "Go grab them, they told us," one of them related. "But why grab them, if they were only rocks and thorns?" Others explained that they never thought of staying in the Galápagos for good; they just wanted to save money and return to Salasaca to be with their wives and families. Another man reflected that, "if we grabbed hold of [the lands], they wouldn't let us leave the islands." In general, the remarks of the pioneers wavered between a longing for Salasaca of the mainland and a distrust of the *cholos* (*mestizos*) and the Ecuadorian state, perhaps based on their recollections of the way they were incorporated into the nation-state or their longstanding memory of the *hacienda* system, which in exchange for a *chacra* (food plot), forced Indigenous people and their families to work for the *hacienda* landlord for the remainder of their lives. In the end, none of the Salasaca pioneers accepted the state's offer.

The Problem of "Fresh" Water

Year after year, following the inauguration of the Darwin Scientific Station in 1964, the job market in Santa Cruz grew. New settlers, however, had to face a serious problem when moving to the island: it had no sources of drinking water.[19] The earliest inhabitants made do by collecting rainwater in tanks on the roofs of their houses, as noted by the foreign scientists when they visited the island. The tanks gathered water during the months of rain and *garúa* (drizzle).[20]

However, the earliest groups of *Salasacas* did not have access to houses of their own or to the water tanks that were used in that period. After their arrival, they all lived together in the municipal warehouse. It resembled "a chicken coop," one of them said. There, they gathered to cook beef, goat meat, and the lobsters they caught over a wood fire. Then they would salt and dry the meat to eat it, little by little, in small portions. For them, the only source of fresh water was the well built in Pelican Bay, which is now known as "Fishermen's Dock." The well stored rainwater, which accumulated in the basin that runs down the top of Crocker Hill (on the upperpart of the island) and drains into the sea at Pelican Bay.[21]

For decades, "the wash station" of Pelican Bay was the center of the social life on Santa Cruz. It was the place where the inhabitants drew water from the well. It also marked the end of the old road that linked Puerto Ayora to Itabaca (where people cross by boat to the airport on Baltra Island). It was also where people met up to wash their clothes while their children played on the seashore. From there too, they watched thousands of live animals, especially goats and calves, pulled by their necks from the pier to the ships that embarked with them to their final destination: the port of Guayaquil. "They were pulled through the water, nearly swimming," somebody told me. In particular, the meat of the *chivo galapagueño* (Galápagos goat) was said to be of excellent quality for preparing *"seco de chivo,"* a characteristic dish of the Ecuadorian coast. Meanwhile, the water in the well was so esteemed it became legendary. Up to the present day, the first settlers of the island say "the person who drinks the water of Pelican Bay always returns to the Galápagos" (Interviews, Puerto Ayora, 2017–2018).

But the "fresh" water of Pelican Bay was, in fact, salt water. "Very salty! Our coffee, juice, broth . . . we drank it like that. We lived off that water," a *Salasaca* woman who arrived on the island in the mid-1980s told me (Interview, Salasaca, November, 2016). Another *Salasaca colona* recalled her first impression when she reached Puerto Ayora in 1980:

> I arrived in the hot season. What thirst! So, when I got to the port, I bought a *bolo* (an ice lollipop of water). And it turned out to be a salty lollipop! Wow! I said, I don't want it. 'Why do they put salt in it?' I asked. That's how I found out that the water was salty.
> (Interview, Puerto Ayora, July 2017).

She stressed that the only fresh, potable water on the island was the water that was brought by ship from the continent in bottles and containers, as still happens today.[22]

Building Puerto Ayora (from 1974 onwards)

In 1973, the state of Ecuador declared the archipelago a province independent of Guayaquil (of the Guayas Province on the Pacific coast), establishing the Autonomous Government of Santa Cruz (also known as "the municipality"). This would be the direct employer of almost all of the Salasaca pioneers of Santa Cruz and those who arrived during the following decades. The municipality hired the Salasaca men as "laborers," assigning them the work to fill in the enormous cracks in the ground, which began behind the waterfront. Later they became responsible for building Puerto Ayora and for the collection and disposal of waste on the island.During the first decades, no machinery was available on the island. Jobs had to be completed "with sheer muscle power" as one of the Salasaca *colonos* recalled it. José Manuel Masaquiza, known since his childhood as "Tractor," remembered how four or five men had to join in to haul each rock. The holes were so big it seemed that they would never be filled in:

> With a pry bar, we had nothing else . . . And, boom! There were these big rocks and we had to break them up, by hand. Or we carried them and threw them into the holes and that is how we filled them.
> The holes were so big; we wondered when they would ever be filled. They refused to get filled! And that's what we had to do: throw the rocks in, break them up, and carry the rocks, every day.
> (Interview, Salasaca, Tungurahua, August 2018).

Don Vicente Masaquiza, founder of the Salasaca Association in the mid-1990s, arrived on the island in 1979, brought by Segundo Pilla. He also described his work in those years:

> Everything was rock. The whole town, from what is now Megaprimavera [near the dock] to the marketplace over there [in the Miraflores district]. Everything is built of rocks dug up by us, with our own hands, with sheer muscle power . . .
> We were the ones responsible for building the streets, first clearing the terrain by hand. Rufico, from Otavalo, was the expert in breaking up rocks, they sought him out.[23] Every rock was bigger than this table [a dining room table]. Boom! We broke them up . . .
> Hauling stones every day during those years. That is why I have a problem with my spine.
> (Interview, Puerto Ayora, January 2019).

It was a very hard job. The good thing was that the minimum wage was higher on the islands than on the mainland. In addition, life was more peaceful than on the Ecuadorian coast. No one stole anything. The bad part was that the municipality always took a long time to pay them. Until 1991, there were no banks on the islands and due to the shortage of cash, the municipality could take up to eight months to pay them their wages.[24]

> You thought that the money that came [from the mainland], was moving around over there... Money came from Quito, from Guayaquil, I don't know . . . It didn't arrive. They said, 'keep working, money will come!'
> I had never handled such big banknotes as I did then. There in the Galápagos, I found out about the one of 100 *sucres*. Here [on the mainland], we had

banknotes of 50 or 20 *sucres*. "Whoa, you guys have so much you'd think you sold a whole herd of cattle," they used to say to us.

Now, this money, what could you do with it, how could you send it back here [to Salasaca on the mainland]? There were no banks or anything at that time. So everyone tucked it under his shirt, flattening it out with some little thing. Some wrapped it in a piece of cloth, covered it with plastic and squashed it under a rock and that was our safe, so that it would be well guarded. Anyone could have lifted that rock and taken it, stolen it that way, but no one stole anything.

(Interview of "Tractor," Salasaca, Tungurahua, August 2018).

In 1983, the first tractor finally reached Santa Cruz. The municipality then ordered the *Salasacas* to build roads and tracks, including the new road from Itabaca to Puerto Ayora. With increasing frequency, "white" men arrived along the groups of Indigenous men there to work; they were employed to run the tipper trucks, tractors, and excavators (Interview, Salasaca, August 2018).[25] Meanwhile on top of the landfills, the Salasaca men also began to build the first buildings that the state bureaucracy needed in the province as well as offices, schools, the slaughterhouse, the stadium, hotels, and houses.

Parallel to this work, authorities on the island assigned the collection and disposal of garbage to Salasaca men. As the population grew, they had more work collecting waste after every *fiesta*, periodically cleaning the streets, and collecting the garbage of the new city and the increasing advent of tourists in the recently arrived dump trucks.[26] At present most of the workers whom the municipality employs to collect garbage and dispose of and/or recycle solid waste are still of Salasaca descent. One of them, son of Salasaca *colonos* of Santa Cruz but born and raised in the Galápagos, explained to me: "this is a job the *cholos* [*mestizos*] won't do" (Puerto Ayora, January 2019).

Tourism Takes Off in the Galápagos Islands (1970s–1990s)

While Salasaca *colonos* were building the city of Puerto Ayora, the tourism business began to take off, organized under the model of "floating hotels" (Epler 2007). This model in which tourists were housed on cruise boats that toured the archipelago was ideal for journeys that aimed at following in Darwin's footsteps. They also worked well to maintain the idea of the Galápagos as a territory of nonhumans, only inhabited by giant tortoises and other ancestral endemic species that are to be studied and protected by science.

Most of the revenues from tourism in the Galápagos Islands have come from cruise ships. In 1968, the "floating hotel" business was launched with the schooner *Golden Cachalote* (with a 12-passenger capacity), which was jointly owned by the Metropolitan Touring (of Quito) and Lindblad Expeditions (of New York) companies. A year later, the *Lima* also began sailing, accommodating 66 more passengers on each voyage. By the end of the 1970s, the available fleet rose to forty ships, able to carry a total of 600 passengers (Epler 2007). The founding of Ecuador's first airline, TAME (which is owned by the military junta that governed the country between 1972 and 1979), the commencement of commercial flights to and from the airport on Baltra in 1974, and UNESCO's declaration of the islands as a "World Heritage Site" in 1978 all led to exponential growth in the number of tourists thereafter.[27]

In two decades, eighty vessels, owned by forty-five individuals or companies, were operating in the Galápagos.[28] And although no new licenses were further permitted, by 2016 the same eighty ships carried seventy-three thousand passengers through the islands. This was possible due to the constant updating of the vessels with models that have had a greater passenger capacity. As a result of this growth, the pioneer companies (Metropolitan Touring and Lindblad Expeditions) consolidated their business, becoming the two biggest beneficiaries of the tourism sector in the Galápagos. In a parallel manner, the majority owners of these two companies became active members of international conservation organizations (like the World Wildlife Fund and Ocean Elders) and also members of the assembly which directs the Charles Darwin Foundation on the Galápagos.[29]

Between the 1970s and the 1990s, some local families were able to gain access to tourism boats, which is the most lucrative activity of the archipelago. Among them were European families who lived on Santa Cruz in the late 1960s, taking advantage of their proximity to the port, their knowledge of different languages, and their collaborating with the scientific station for use of their boats.[30] The Darwin station hired them for positions of responsibility, like administrators and boat captains. They were responsible for ferrying the scientists around the islands, thus receiving the training needed to become the first nature guides of the Galápagos (Grenier 2007, 125). Very soon, these European settlers chose to fully devote their attention to foreign tourists who visited the archipelago, mainly coming from the United States, Great Britain and Germany.[31] For their part, some *galapagueños* who had formerly been fishermen revamped their vessels to accommodate tourists. Most of them have competed for the low-end tourist market, with smaller ships, which have fewer cabins or no cabins at all, thus specializing in day outings.[32]

To this day, most of the tourists continue to travel by boat in a kind of "ecotourism bubble" (Quiroga 2009) with itineraries that visit the uninhabited islands, trying to hide locals from the view of visitors, or at least leaving that to the end.[33] They rarely see more than two or three boats at any particular site, although eighty ships are typically traveling at the same time across the Galápagos waters. Furthermore, tourists are divided in groups of twelve to sixteen. Each group explores with a naturalist guide who controls the group's pace and behavior toward animals in order to create a sensation of being alone in the wild (Honey 2008, Hennessy 2014).

At present, eighty tourism ships generate 84 percent of tourism revenue in the archipelago. This means that only forty-five ship owners, along with the national political elite of Quito, have become the greatest beneficiaries of one of the fastest growing economies of the world: the Galápagos National Park (Taylor et.al. 2006).[34]

Salasaca Women (from 1979 onwards)

The rapid growth of tourists and state bureaucrats led to a drastic increase in the number of humans permanently living in the Galápagos, particularly on Santa Cruz Island. From the 1970s onwards, bureaucratic posts as well as the jobs created by the tourism sector began to be filled by *mestizo* migrants from the cities of Guayaquil and Quito (Grenier 2007, 205–212). Meanwhile in 1979, the first Salasaca women began to arrive on Santa Cruz in order to provide services for these two sectors. Two years later, the first Salasaca natives of the Galápagos were born.[35] Today Salasaca women and their children tend to hold the same jobs on Santa Cruz: laundry, cleaning, garbage collection, and construction.[36] In particular, Salasaca women clean the premises of institutions, hotels, and homes of whites and *mestizos*. They also take care of their children and wash and iron clothes for locals and tourists on the archipelago.

The Salasaca female pioneers recalled doing laundry as a particularly demanding job. They had to go from house to house to wash the clothes of locals. In turn, they received the laundry of tourists at a certain place and then returned it clean to the supply personnel of the ships, so they could deliver it to the next stop on the cruise itinerary.[37] Their work, like the women themselves, was thus made completely invisible to tourists visiting the Galápagos. During my interview, Rosa, a Salasaca *colona* who arrived at Santa Cruz in 1996, remembered her experience as a laundress while she was washing her family's clothes at her home:

> When I came here, I didn't adapt to Puerto Ayora, not at all . . . It was very hot, the sun was strong, the water you drank was so salty . . . I used to wash clothes in Ambato . . . I washed and ironed. And here, the first time I went to wash, there was a big pile of dirty clothes . . . It was really enormous! I didn't finish until it was nighttime . . . socks, everything. And I cried because I was worried: 'What did I come here for?' I told myself. I cried, but I finished the job.
>   (Interview, Puerto Ayora, May 2017).

Like Rosa's, the testimonies of every Salasaca *colono* is crisscrossed by memories of hard work, holding two or three jobs in the island simultaneously, and no rest. All of them had started their working life on the "outside," in Salasaca (Tungurahua) at a very early age. The Galápagos was not the first place they migrated. All of the women had left their hometown when they were young girls to work as domestic servants in homes in one city or another. For their part, most of the male *colonos* had worked somewhere on the coast of Ecuador before migrating to the Galápagos. For both, leaving Salasaca meant hiding their Indigenous identity in order to stay safe.

Migration and Concealment

Each of the Salasaca *colonos* remembered a different reason for migrating to the Galápagos. Many remarked that they migrated because, like Pedro Chango (the pioneer at San Cristóbal), they wanted to be able to sponsor the ritual *fiestas* in Salasaca (Tungurahua), performing as "captains," "*caporales*" (chiefs), or "*priostes*" of a confraternity, or to participate in them in the role, for example, of "*noños*" (transvestites). Up to the present time, that is still a common reason for migrating to the Galápagos.[38] Other *colonos* said that they traveled to Santa Cruz because "we were told that there was a gold mine on the islands."[39] Some mentioned the obligations they had, like debts owed to moneylenders (*chulqueros*) or relatives, or plans to get married and build a house in their hometown.[40] Others instead stressed that they wanted "to have an adventure" or that they were escaping from a failed romantic relationship. One man sternly told me that he left at the age of thirteen "because in Salasaca I went around without shoes or trousers. I wanted to dress like a normal boy," that is, with the clothing of a *mestizo* (Interview, Puerto Ayora, January 2019).

Beyond the various personal reasons, the economy of Salasaca (on the mainland) was a major factor. It had been profoundly affected by the decline of its textile industry and the pressure on the land of a growing population. In addition, during the 1960s, the town suffered a drought, exacerbated by the consequences of the increasing fragmentation of lands with younger generations inheriting smaller and smaller parcels within the ethnic territory (Carrasco 1982, 31).[41] Moreover, families could no longer survive off their work with agave fiber as they had done for centuries. With no jobs and no money in Salasaca, family obligations and medical emergencies forced Salasacas to migrate. Today, this is still—for most—the only way out.[42]

Yet to leave Salasaca (Tungurahua) involves an act of transvestism and ethnic concealment. In their memories, the women who left clearly recall the exact moment when they had to abandon their traditional dress. All of them spoke of it in a spontaneous way. Changing their clothing allowed them to "hide" themselves in order to be safe outside Salasaca. Margarita Masaquiza, for example, remembers her first trip to the archipelago as follows:

I first went to Guayaquil. My aunt lived there. I slept there the night I arrived. The following day, I was traveling to the Galápagos.

I had always worn our traditional dress, the one of my land, which is Salasaca. But, my aunt said: 'In Guayaquil, the *mestizos* mistreat the Indigenous people, they insult them—all of those things. You have to put on the clothing they wear here. Look, I go around with that clothing [of a *mestiza*] and no one says anything to me. They are going to criticize you; wear something else.'

What a pity it was to stop dressing like that. I felt really bad . . . only wearing those ragged clothes . . . I hadn't felt like that in the highlands. In Quito, I worked in my own clothes, in Tulcán as well. No one criticized me because there are Indigenous people all over the highlands. On the coast, on the other hand, [the contrast] is very marked . . . Here, too, in the Galápagos we spent a lot of time *hiding* ourselves ("*ocultándonos*").

(Interview, Puerto Ayora, July, 2017).

Juana, another Salasaca *colona*, who left her homeland at the age of eight, also recalled her "hiding." When she arrived in the Galápagos in the mid-1980s, she was already dressed as a *mestiza*:

We had to go around *hiding* ("*teníamos que ir así a escondidas*"), without our ethnic dress . . .

My dad and my mom lived off agave alone: they made rope from it, nothing more. But already in that period there was no more agave, there was nothing.

(Interview, Salasaca, August 2018).

For both the Salasaca men and women, it was clear that the racism targeted at Indigenous people was stronger on the coast than in the highlands. Even though the coast and the Galápagos Islands were mainly populated by people from the Ecuadorian highlands, the identity of these two regions was based on the idea of being more "white," more distant from the Andean world of the *serrano* (person from the highlands), the Indigenous person.[43]

Since the moment they arrived in the Galápagos, the *Salasacas* felt racism in the kind of work, wages, and businesses they had access to, the poorer quality of the water they drank, and the obligations they had, such as collecting the garbage of Puerto Ayora. Additionally, all of their testimonies speak of them being bullied by *mestizo* settlers, including the frequent incitement of fights, hate, insults, and discrimination against them. For example, on the streets of Puerto Ayora, when they were heard speaking Kichwa, the *mestizos* shouted at them to "speak Christian" (Spanish) or scolded them for wearing their ethnic dress (Interviews, Puerto Ayora, 2017–8). These insults were in addition to those that labeled them as "predators," "invasive," or "introduced" on the archipelago, which signal the appropriation of conservation lexicon as I will examine in Chapter Six.

All in all, the first strategy the *Salasacas* had to adopt upon migrating was to conceal their Indigenous identity, especially if they were heading to the coast or the archipelago. Even today, leaving Salasaca means for men to stop wearing their *ponchos* and to cut their long hair. For the women, it means abandoning their Indigenous *anaco* (skirt), *bayeta* (shawl), and accessories. From there on, they start to wear pants and the clothes *cholas* wear. Furthermore, they must speak in Spanish and no longer use in public their native language. Nevertheless, even after becoming ethnically invisible, most expose their origins through the combination of certain physical features associated with the Indigenous race, the social circles they ran in, and, above all, their Salasaca surnames: Masaquiza, Pilla, Caiza, or Chango.[44]

Their determination to hide their ethnic identity and pursue their own cultural "whitening" is particularly surprising considering the history of the Salasaca people, which was forged in a sense of pride about being Indigenous. Nevertheless, in spite of having to become invisible in the archipelago, even today that pride continues to appear every time the *Salasacas* of the Galápagos return to the highlands.[45] As soon as they reach their homeland in Tungurahua, the *colonos* (first settlers) take back their ethnic identity and customs, the Kichwa language, and Salasaca dress. Beyond alternating between two identities, *mestizo* on the islands and Indigenous in their homeland, what can be noted in their ongoing highlands-islands journeys is their determination to reaffirm their ethnic affiliation to the present day. They do so particularly by means of participating in the ritual *fiestas* calendar in Salasaca (Tungurahua). At least once a year, the *Salasacas* of the islands continue to comply with their obligation to take part in the rituals of the Day of the Dead. It does not stop there: the most prosperous *colonos* on the islands save money for a long time in order to sponsor such *fiestas*. In so doing, they gain prestige within their community.[46] These are not small expenses; paying for a *fiesta* of *caporales* (chiefs) in February or of *capitanes* (captains) in December may cost between thirty and forty thousand dollars. The wealthiest Salasaca families that I met in the course of my fieldwork sponsored one or two *fiestas* during the time I lived in Puerto Ayora (2017–2018).

THE SALASACA ASSOCIATION
ON THE GALÁPAGOS ISLANDS

In 1998, the death of the first Salasaca on Santa Cruz was a turning point in the history of the Indigenous collective on the island. The urgent need to give the deceased a proper burial and to have a place to hold wakes for their dead was the motive that prompted Salasaca *colonos* to unite in the Galápagos

Islands. At the same time, they needed to defend their permanence on the archipelago upon hearing growing rumors that the Darwin station had plans to expel the local population from the archipelago.

The Death of "Cali"

When Bernardo Caiza, also known as "Cali," arrived on Santa Cruz, he was only twenty. He had traveled to the Galápagos following his first love. She, Justina, had migrated to the island a few years before with the husband her parents had arranged for her. Since his arrival, Cali, like every other Salasaca, had to work for the municipality as a peon, fastening together and hauling enormous rocks every day to fill the cracks in the ground beyond the waterfront. After some time, he got involved in construction work, becoming a mason and later a foreman in Santa Cruz. His younger brother always assisted him in the work.

On the day of his death, Cali was sitting in the back of a truck, which was carrying cattle from Bellavista to Pelican Bay. It is said that one of the cattle kicked his hand and made him fall. His younger brother gave me an account of his final moments, which took place in a situation that is still inexplicable:

> It was a bit strange: no one saw how he fell . . . Someone who helped him says that when the accident happened, he and another guy helped him to stand and he walked. He was normal, except he had a headache. When they took him to the hospital, he said that he was talking alright, with my older brother and my cousin . . .
>
> I don't know how . . . because they gave him an injection, nothing else happened. And then they sent my brother and cousin to buy some medicine. But when they returned, they told him he had died. Suddenly, in the hospital . . . !
>
> The doctors weren't good. And that was the end of it.
>
> (Interview, Puerto Ayora, November 2017).

His cousin and younger brother were horrified. All they could do was to remove his corpse. But on Santa Cruz, there was no place for Cali's wake. Moreover, they had no resources to arrange for Cali to be shipped to the mainland, to Salasaca, so he could have a proper burial there. Margarita Masaquiza remembers the tragic moments surrounding his death:

> It was terrible . . . Since we were Salasacas ourselves, we felt that sorrow.
>
> We went to the hospital, but they didn't say anything, only that he was dead. So we removed the corpse and, what? What do we do now? Where are we going to mourn this man? There was no place to do it!
>
> We went to ask the authorities to help us with a place. Nothing. We were *on the street with his soul,* with the deceased. On the street.
>
> (Interview, Puerto Ayora, July 2017).

When she spoke of being on the street with "the soul" of the deceased, Margarita was indexing the pre-Hispanic belief that the soul does not leave the body after death. For the *Salasacas*, the place where the dead person is buried is important because his body (along with his soul) will reawaken every year on the Day of the Dead to drink and eat with his *ayllu* as they pour forth their libations and food onto his grave. Furthermore, the body and soul incarnate the ancestral landscape, the sacred mountain of Cruzpamba. For this reason, through this day and after more than forty or fifty years on the islands, the Salasaca *colonos* refuse to imagine being buried on the archipelago. Amable Pilla, another *colono*, continued the story of what happened next:

> We went to plead with people. To raise the money to send the deceased back home . . . At that time, the *mestizos* did have a place to mourn their dead. But they did not want to lend it to us. They pushed the *Salasacas* aside. They didn't want to acknowledge us. If we spoke in Kichwa, they criticized us. And worse when we dressed like a Salasaca.
> (Interview, Puerto Ayora, January 2018).

After asking all over for help, the island's *mestizo* beauty pageant queen agreed to ask "el Chino" Velasquez, who was from Ambato, to help them. He lent them the house he was building in Puerto Ayora for Cali's wake. After convening there, they shipped his body to Guayaquil and from there, by truck to Salasaca. Finally, in his hometown, Cali was dressed in his traditional clothes with the finest *poncho* he had and his body placed in a better coffin. Then his family began the funerary rites, which lasted for three days and included children's games, the dance of "the captains," and a feast that offered three cattle and a pig for his relatives, friends, and neighbors. In so doing, Cali's *ayllu* carried out the ancestral rites of Colla-Aymara origins.

On the Galápagos Islands, Cali´s death underlined the various beliefs and practices around death that shape the spiritual lives of different cultures. In particular, the Andean Indigenous techniques to mourn and bury their deceased (that include singing, drinking, and dancing rituals) were labeled by Spaniards as signs of idolatry and barbarity. These rituals further

> threatened to make patent the constructed and therefore conventional or arbitrary nature of *civitas* and Christianity . . . A recognizably analogous and alternative form of social memory could be nothing other than satanic mimicry, designed by the devil to conceal Truth from Andeans. Thus, Andean forms of social memory became errors and superstitions, the very memory of which it became the Spanish duty to erase.
> (Abercrombie 1998, 18).

As such, more than an act of racism, the refusal of *mestizo* settlers on the islands to help the *Salasacas* after such a tragic event was an indication of the persistence of the colonial project itself, which included erasing Indigenous ways to understanding the past in order to "colonize Andean forms of historical consciousness," as Abercrombie argues (1998, xxiv). In this way, the cultural "whitening" of the Salasaca people in the Galápagos not only required them to erase the external marks of their "Indianness" but also to obscure other forms of spiritual practice. Cali's death nevertheless became the definite moment for the *Salasacas* to start thinking about their union as a proper ethnic community in the archipelago. They needed to join together to defend themselves against racism, find a place of their own to hold wakes for their dead (before they were shipped to the mainland), and preserve their ties to their ancestral origins and homeland.

The Salasaca Association (1990–1998)

At the beginning of the 1990s, there were growing rumors about the Darwin station planning to force locals out of the Galápagos. This was a subject that was discussed every day on the streets of Puerto Ayora. In particular, for those who worked in the offices of the national park and the scientific station, the expulsion of the local people seemed to be imminent. One of them was Vicente Masaquiza, a Salasaca *colono*, who was working as a watchman at the Darwin station at the time.[47] When I interviewed him, don Vicente remembered how frightened the local people felt at the time and what he heard in the installations of the station and the park:

> At the station, I heard that the directors thought that the Galápagos Islands could no longer support so many people. Especially the people who didn't have enough money would have to leave . . . As soon as they arrived, they would have to leave.
> So, when I heard that, I told myself: 'no, I think that everywhere in the world Indigenous or aboriginal people are treated like dogs! Or they actually think they are! As if they were not able to think, as if they were not able to understand.
> I said to myself: 'no, that's not right. If we don't organize ourselves, they will throw us out. We have to organize; we have to be organized people, be politicians, so that no one will treat us like a dog.'
> (Interview, Puerto Ayora, January 2019).

Some other *colonos* I interviewed, along with some lawyers and ecologists, all mentioned the plan that the scientists had to expel the local people from the archipelago. They spoke, for example, of a report by the CIA which referred to "a big plot, where what the discourse of ecological defense really conceals is an interest in ensuring that the Galápagos Islands are uninhabited ... to get rid of the Ecuadorian population on the islands," as a lawyer of the province told me (Interview, Puerto Ayora, June 2016). Someone else added, "they had said that they were going to buy the properties of the poorest people so that they would leave." Another person I interviewed made clear, "it was not only the station, the big tourism companies were also interested in kicking us out" (Interviews, Puerto Ayora, 2017–2018).

The rumors grew over a ten-year period while at the same time the scientists from the Darwin Station, the directors of the National Park, and representatives of the national government began to draft the Special Law for the Galápagos (passed in 1998). The new legal framework was intended to forbid further colonization, introduce new measures to control the growth of the islands' population, and establish the parameters to govern the archipelago that were to be different (or "special") from those that rule in the rest of the provinces in Ecuador.

Understandably, the islanders felt threatened. Thus the majority decided to organize themselves in groups mostly defined by occupation, such as carpenters, truck and taxi drivers, and construction workers. However, as Indigenous persons, the Salasacas did not feel fully represented by any of these organizations. They were very familiar with the racism on the archipelago and were worried that when the new norms were applied, they would be further victimized—"treated like dogs" due to their race as the founder of the Association stated. They needed, in short, an organization to protect them: "so that we would not be expelled ... we needed to act as a legal person, with statutes" (Interview, V. Masaquiza, Puerto Ayora, January 2019).

Soon after, the leaders of the community took to the streets and went from house to house, across the new neighborhood of Miraflores, to talk to the *Salasacas* on Santa Cruz. They all agreed they needed an organization. But they had different views on the agenda it should pursue. Extensive discussions were therefore held regarding the name of the association and whether it would be a nonprofit one or not.[48] Some of the members thought the organization should not only defend their rights on the islands but also develop projects to boost their incomes and allow them to participate in the island's economy. Creating a processing plant for waste on the island and a crafts center were the two main ideas they wanted to pursue. In contrast, other members thought that the association should be a nonprofit organization, mainly focused on providing a venue where the community could get together, preserve their customs, and mourn those who died on the island.

On May 1, 1996, on the International Workers' Day, the Salasaca *colonos* legalized their organization.[49] They finally settled on a name: Galapagupi Kauska Salasaka Runakunapak, Tukui Laya Llankakunapak Tantanakui (the

Figure 4.5. The Salasaca Association logo. The logo places a Salasaca man, originally native of the Andes, close to the sea between giant tortoises and native fauna of the Galápagos Islands. Source: Courtesy: Salasaca Association.

Association of Autonomous Salasaca Indigenous Workers Resident in the Galápagos—AISREG, for its acronym in Spanish). In that way, the members affirmed their identity as "autonomous workers" on the island, stressing the characteristic which distinguishes them the most from the *mestizo* population: their devotion to work as a dignified activity, no matter what the job entailed (Interviews, Puerto Ayora 2017).[50] Also, by adding the word "residents" (after the passage of the Special Law), the members reiterated that they had a legitimate right to residency in a society which, in accordance with conservation law, was no longer made up of "*colonos*" (first settlers) but "residents" of the Galápagos. Nevertheless, in claiming to be residents (and because of sanctions imposed against those who help illegals in the archipelago), they had trouble dealing with the growing number of *Salasacas* on the island who were legally categorized as "illegals."

Access to Property Rights

The founding members finally agreed on a policy of promoting projects aimed at improving their access to the island's economy. They elected Vicente Masaquiza as their first president. In line with that, in November 1997, the association members submitted a proposal for the construction of a plant for processing organic waste on the island at the municipality. They suggested that the plant should have the capacity to handle the waste of a population which, according to their estimates, would quadruple in two decades to reach twenty thousand inhabitants on Santa Cruz Island alone. These estimates were, in fact, in line with the recent projections of the Ecuadorian National Institute of Statistics and Censuses (INEC).[51] The proposal also included the establishment of recycling services, the production of organic fertilizers, and the creation of educational campaigns on waste management aimed at residents, visitors, and tourist companies. To back it, they cited their long experience in dealing with waste on the islands. Since at least the mid-1940s, *Salasacas* had been managing waste on the Galápagos. Moreover, during the time of the proposal, the *Salasacas* of Santa Cruz had already begun to process organic waste to produce compost and topsoil.

The mayor enthusiastically accepted the proposal and encouraged the members of the Association to begin work on the project. However, a year later, the park and the station decided to award the project to the recently created Galápagos Foundation, owned by the four biggest tourism operators, headed by Metropolitan Touring.[52] The loss of this opportunity as well as the unsafe conditions of his current job as a construction foreman were the events that Andrés Pilla most regretted when I interviewed him.[53] As a child, before arriving at the Galápagos, Andrés was dedicated to weaving alongside his father, don Mullimba, in Salasaca (Tungurahua):

> We had already begun the recycling center, which is now named after Fabricio Valverde . . . For a long time, we were the ones who went around collecting the garbage after each *fiesta* . . . It was ours, our initiative, the *Salasacas* . . . but we did not have the money.
> (Interview of Andrés Pilla, Puerto Ayora, June 2017).

The following year, construction began on the Fabricio Valverde Recycling Center in a rural area of Puerto Ayora.[54] Throughout the following decade, the municipality gradually took over waste management until it completely controlled the operation. Meanwhile, the *Salasacas* continued to be relegated to the position of hourly recycling workers at the Fabricio Valverde facility without any real possibility of obtaining better jobs on the payroll of the municipality.[55]

The municipality's ousting of the Salasaca *colonos* from the project for a waste disposal plant is significant because it confirms the existence of a racialized system of property and structural violence that still forces Indigenous persons to subsistence production and minimum wages, and compels them to do manual labor and servile work for white and *mestizo* bosses and newcomers to the archipelago. The legacy of the *hacienda* system further designated them as collective agents in the 1950s, identifying the majority under the surname "Masaquiza," as I described in the previous chapter.

Authorities in the Galápagos excluded Salasaca *colonos* from ownership and access to the most lucrative activities of the archipelago. Despite having been pioneers in the colonization of Santa Cruz and having played a leading role in the construction of the city of Puerto Ayora, no Salasaca on the Galápagos Islands owns a tour ship or a tourist agency.[56] Nor do they work as nature guides or hold leading positions in the institutions of tourism or conservation (like the national park, the scientific station or other agencies).[57] A few have managed to become the owners of taxis (land and aquatic ones). But the possibilities to profit from that work were also limited by a government decree that stipulated that *pangas* (as water taxis are called) should be mainly aimed at covering the low-cost routes that are usually taken by local inhabitants.[58] One day in the marketplace, Franklin, a shopkeeper in the market whose mother is a Salasaca, rightly told me:

> My mom came here before everyone. She should have been the owner of a hotel, a restaurant, all of those things . . . but she owns nothing, during all that time [more than five decades], nothing.
>
> How do you explain that she is not the owner of something like that? That she didn't become a millionaire like others who arrived much later or don't even live here, on the islands?
>
> (Puerto Ayora, July 2018).

Even though Puerto Ayora brings prosperity to most of its inhabitants, Franklin is right to point out that *Salasacas* did not benefit from the large economic gains that followed the establishment of the national park. Furthermore, in spite of being first settlers or natives of the Galápagos (and particularly of Santa Cruz Island), most *Salasacas* don't know the park and cannot afford tours to visit its emblematic sites. Lastly, they were denied access to be stakeholders of the recycling enterprise which plays a crucial role in the conservation of the islands, and is that much more linked to their everyday work since arriving in the Galápagos.[59]

Nonetheless, among the Salasaca people of the Galápagos, there is another group that became the most vulnerable in the archipelago: those who arrived after the passing of the 1998 law. To this day, they remain "illegals" in the Galápagos. During the past decade with an upsurge in repressive measures—out of all the illegal population—the new Salasaca migrants were made the main target of conservation measures that aimed to control and reduce population size through raids and deportation.

NOTES

1. *Cevichocho* uses Andean white beans (*chochos*) marinated in lime juice and mixed with diced tomatoes, onions, and cilantro. *Choclo* is corn on the cob. *Guatita* is beef stripe stew. And *fritada* is deep-fried pork meat. They are all typical foods of the Ecuadorian highlands.

2. *Ecuavoley* is a variation of volleyball invented and played in Ecuador. The net is higher and tighter. The game is played with a soccer ball, which can be held each time it is received for one second or less. It is more frequently played by men only.

3. In 2015, six thousand tons of products were brought to the Galápagos every month by six ships (Mestanza in *El Comercio* newspaper, February 2015). In 2017, four cargo ships sank off the coast.

4. In Guayaquil, *galapagueños* purchase medical checkup packages, which include all sorts of examinations. They pay between $500 and $800 dollars annually for these services.

5. People who do not have a resident's permit are regarded as "illegals" in the Galápagos. They cannot leave the archipelago. If they do, they are not allowed to return for some years.

6. The *cuye* treatment involves rubbing guinea pigs across the patient's body and then killing the animal and dissecting it to find out the patient's illness.

7. In Ecuador in 1990 and 1994, two uprisings paralyzed the country, leading to the removal of two presidents. Over the next decade, the Indigenous Movement also succeeded in blocking the Free Trade Agreement (TLC) with the United States and in appealing for a constituent revolution that could embrace the country's plurinational nature and the decolonization of its political structures.

8. Whereas Correa wanted a "citizens' revolution" based on the idea of a "universal citizen" with individual rights, Indigenous movements appealed for a constituent revolution that could embrace the country's plurinational nature. They did, however, share the desire to curtail neoliberal policies (Becker 2011).

9. The central role of the Indigenous Movement was also expressed in the writing of the new constitution, under the Kichwa principle *Sumak Kawsay* ("good living") which purportedly guides the development strategies of the country, seeking to move past the long history of an extractive economy (Acosta et al. 2011, Gudynas 2009, 2011). It further introduced the Indigenous *Pachamama* (Mother Nature) in state law as a subject of rights and legal personality. Articles 71–74 of the 2008 National Constitution grant Pachamama the right to life and regeneration, biodiversity, balance, and restoration.

10. See Salomon (2011) for the case of Sudan and Goldstein (2012) for the case of Bolivia.

11. The Indigenous Movement's political project was appropriated by state and *mestizo* society because "of the alleged inability of Indigenous professionals to fulfill [duties] efficiently" (Martinez 2014, 117). Throughout Correa´s government and thereafter, Indigenous subjects were construed as passive recipients of governmental policies. This is how representatives of the government dealt with the demands (and with leaders) of the Salasaca Association in every meeting I participated in the Galápagos.

12. *Chuchaki* is often used throughout Ecuador. The word stems from the Kichwa *chaki*, which connotes discomfort after chewing coca leaves.

13. A few years later, the arrival of emigrants from the city of Loja, Ecuador, met the demand for agricultural laborers on the farms on the upperpart of Santa Cruz Island.

14. The Salasaca textile production flourished in the early decades of the twentieth century, after the decline of the San Ildefonso factory in Pelileo, near Salasaca.

15. Today, Otavalo is famous for its market and Indigenous population, many of whom constantly travel around the world to sell their famous handicrafts, clothes, and textiles, since the 1950s.

16. In Ecuador, the term "engineer" is often used to refer to local white *mestizo* men with some professional training (but not necessarily in engineering) who usually work as the bosses of other men and unskilled workers.

17. According to the censuses, in 1950, 215 people lived on Santa Cruz Island, but nobody lived in what came to be known as Puerto Ayora. One decade later when the group arrived, most of the inhabitants of the island lived inland at higher elevations in the districts of Bellavista and Santa Rosa. By 1974, the village of Puerto Ayora had 900 inhabitants (Santa Cruz Island as a whole had 1,577), and by 1990, it had more than 4,200 (while Santa Cruz had 5,318) (Grenier 2007, 194). In 2015, more than 15,000 people lived in Puerto Ayora (with a total of 25,244 on Santa Cruz).

18. Today, the first line of beachfront is known as "Darwin Avenue." It is now paved, with stores and hotels that were built on the waterfront, blocking the sea view from the rest of the city and the local population. Most of the owners of these waterfront properties are *"afuereños"* (that is, foreigners or Ecuadorians from the mainland) (Grenier 2017, 244).

19. The water supply of San Cristóbal Island came from "Laguna del Junco," the only freshwater lake on the archipelago. Meanwhile, the only source of potable water on Santa Cruz is the small spring of Santa Rosa (on the upperpart of the island, close to the Salasaca area). Yet it lies on a private property.

20. Settlers of Santa Cruz began to uninstall their water tanks after they heard the promises of the municipality to build an aqueduct in Puerto Ayora. In 2010, the water pipeline was installed but the water it supplies is not potable.

21. The watershed of Pelican Bay covers forty-three square kilometers from the top of Cerro Crocker through the towns of Bellavista and Puerto Ayora, and ending at the sea at Pelican Bay.

22. The fresh (salty) subterranean water of Santa Cruz, which is extracted from cracks in the ground, does not receive adequate treatment to make it apt for human consumption (Reyes et al. 2017).

23. A number of other ethnic groups (like *Otavaleños*) live in the Galápagos, but compared with the *Salasacas*, they are a small minority.

24. The first bank on the islands opened in Puerto Ayora in 1991. Yet still today, the municipality often delays wage payments to its employees, alleging—as in the past—a shortage of currency circulating in the archipelago (Field notes, Puerto Ayora, December 2018).

25. The *Salasacas* sometimes use the word *"blancos"* (whites) to refer to *mestizos*. This is not necessarily related to their skin color.

26. Over the years this job was linked in the islands to a specific race and gender: Indigenous men. Recently, the municipality even took the idea and the name of the *"mingas"* (an Indigenous tradition of cooperative and voluntary work) for the periodic campaigns by which it enlisted high school students to clean the streets, shores, and parks as a civic duty.

27. During the 1970s, 12,000 tourists traveled to the archipelago every year. In the following decade, the number rose to 18,000. It doubled in the 1990s, and kept growing (40,000 in the 1990s; 72,000 in the 2000s; 122,000 in 2005) (Epler 2007). In 2018, 275,000 tourists visited the Galápagos.

28. Among the forty-five ship owners, twenty owned between two and six vessels (Epler 2007, 12). Just ten owners, mostly foreigners or persons who live on the mainland of Ecuador, control 45 percent of the beds on cruise ships (ibid.).

29. The majority shareholder of Lindblad Expeditions is the Swiss Sven-Olof Lindblad. In 2004, he formed a strategic alliance with National Geographic, which strengthened his business and the mutual alliance between conservationism and tourism at the international level. For their part, two men from Quito, Eduardo Proaño and Hernán Correa, founded Metropolitan Touring in 1953. Their company grew at a dizzying rate, mainly thanks to its profits from tours to the Galápagos. Currently, Metropolitan Touring is part of the "Grupo Futuro" holding company, made up of fifteen companies in tourism, hotels, insurance, and healthcare. Its current owner, Roque Sevilla, was also in politics, holding the position of mayor of Quito between 1998 and 2000.

30. At the time, there were about ten to twelve European families living on Santa Cruz Island. Most lived on the other side of the dock (in what is now Puerto Ayora) at the *Playa de los Alemanes* (Germans' Beach). Some others lived in the upperpart of the island, in Bellavista.

31. The most notable European settlers were the Wittmer family in Floreana Island, who are the owners of several ships, and the Angermeyer brothers who own a luxury hotel at Germans' Beach on Santa Cruz Island.

32. Thirty-nine percent of the tourist ships are owned by residents of the Galápagos (Epler 2007, 21).

33. The typical cruise itinerary includes a brief stop in Puerto Ayora (to visit the Park breeding center and the tortoise, Lonesome George). It is usually scheduled at the end of the trip.

34. The total income of the Galápagos (that is, the gross domestic product) grew by 78 percent between 1999 and 2005. The growth in the tourism industry not only propelled one of the fastest growing economies of the world but also one of the fastest growing human populations with high rates of immigration (Durham 2008, 85).

35. The new generation of *galapagueños* define their identity in a completely different way to that of their parents, as I will describe in Chapter Six.

36. Although some *Salasacas* have enjoyed a certain social mobility (such as those who service ships, sailors, or policemen), the great majority still work in construction, garbage collection, recycling, and cleaning on Santa Cruz. The most prosperous families own a taxi (land or aquatic), a grocery store, or a hardware store.

37. Nowadays, the towels and bedclothes of passengers in tourist ships are washed in industrial laundromats in Puerto Ayora.

38. The calendar of ritual celebrations in Salasaca consists of five big *fiestas* every year. A young Salasaca man who had recently arrived on Santa Cruz told me that he was there because he wanted to play the role of the ñono, the female transvestite who accompanies the steward (*prioste*) in the fiesta of Caporales (Interview, Puerto Ayora, August 2017).

39. Tales about pirates and hidden pirate treasures still circulate in the archipelago.

40. The *chulqueros* are informal moneylenders. They usually charge high interest rates, around 20 percent annually, and in US dollars.

41. In the next decades, community networks facilitated the migration of a growing number of Salasaca people to the Galápagos. Loja, Manabí and Esmeraldas were also affected by severe droughts. This resulted in an influx of migrants from these provinces to the Galápagos (Ramos 2016).

42. Nowadays, all of the families in Salasaca have at least one member who spends long periods (between two and eight years) working outside of their native village. The Galápagos Islands is not their only destination. Some migrate to the Ecuadorian coast, but many others migrate abroad (Spain, the United States, France, Italy, Brazil, Chile, and some—decades earlier—also Colombia).

43. For a more thorough historical analysis of the demographic shift from the Ecuadorian highlands to the coast, see Delaunay et al. (1990).

44. Other surnames that are distinctively Salasaca are: Jerez, Caizabanda, Chiliquinga, Anancolla, Chicaiza, Yansapanta, Comasanta, Culqui, Curichumbi, Chimbosina, and Pancha. The *Salasacas* also regard Ramírez and Jiménez as pertaining to their people, even though they are of Hispanic origin.

45. This only applies to the Salasaca *colonos* who have residency permits and not to the more recent Salasaca migrants who remain illegal on the archipelago and cannot leave—unless they don't want to return.

46. Besides the *fiestas,* the most prosperous *Salasacas* of the Galápagos also like to build modern houses in their native town, which has already transformed the landscape of Salasaca (Tungurahua).

47. Before this job, don Vicente had worked for more than a decade for the municipality as a peon and as a building laborer. At that time, in addition to his work in the Station, he started to take a course with the Ecuadorian Navy. Shortly thereafter, he became the first Salasaca seaman and later the owner of a *panga* (a water taxi).

48. In recent years, the association restructured itself. Issues like its name, the purposes of the organization, and its legal statutes were discussed again, as I observed at the meetings of the current members. Efforts to include Salasaca "illegals" into the organization, or speak politically for them, were also discussed. Nevertheless, these did not bear fruit.

49. A few months later, the General Assembly of the Association, made up of ninety-nine *Salasacas*, was legalized by the president and minister of social welfare of Ecuador.

50. Many *Salasacas* stress that dignified work and honesty are the traits that most distinguish Indigenous people from the *mestizos,* as I heard in my interviews.

51. In 1990, nearly ten thousand people lived in the archipelago—more than half of them on Santa Cruz Island. By 2015, more than fifteen thousand were living on Santa Cruz and more than twenty-five thousand in the archipelago as a whole. The INEC estimated a population growth of 20 percent between 2015 and 2020, which meant that by 2020, the population of Santa Cruz would grow to around nineteen thousand inhabitants and that of the archipelago as a whole to more than thirty thousand.

52. The Galápagos Foundation is a company made up of the top four tour operators in the Galápagos: Metropolitan Touring, Wittmer, Andando Tours, and Celebrity Expeditions (Epler 2007, 26).

53. In the interview, Andrés emphasized the poor safety conditions in his daily work. He gave me a detailed account of several accidents he had suffered and the way in which he lost an eye when he was pouring cement onto the floor of a building.

54. The center was named after a park ranger who promoted the start of recycling activities from within the Galápagos National Park.

55. Despite the seniority, experience, or knowledge that a Salasaca worker may have, the municipality regularly hires *mestizos* with a university degree for executive or technical posts. The recyclers of Salasaca origin continue to hold the same jobs they have had for decades.

56. The only exception is a young Salasaca man who, along with his European wife, owns a scuba diving shop in Puerto Ayora.

57. For decades, foreigners or Ecuadorians from the mainland have managed these institutions. In the national park, there is only one park ranger of Salasaca origin, Gaspar Masaquiza, a *colono* of the island. Meanwhile, Margarita Masaquiza and her sister work as cleaning ladies at the Darwin station. Some other Salasaca *colonos* have had temporary jobs at those two institutions but only in the service industry, logistic services, transportation, or cleaning.

58. For example, a *panga* carries tourists and local people from the dock at Puerto Ayora to Germans' beach at a cost of sixty cents. Before, *pangas* owned by the local people were allowed to offer day tours to other islands or places located in the national park. But with the recent reforms, the local government prohibited that service. Nowadays, interisland voyages and daily or weekly tours to the national park can only be handled by cruise ships and other large vessels with certified naturalist guides.

59. Although the Salasaca-owned waste plant could not be built, Salasaca *colonos* and members of the association successfully accomplished other projects in Santa Cruz Island. For example, the Salasaca soccer league (1999), the community center

(built in 2005–2006), and the Runa Kunapak Yachay School (2006). None of these projects aimed at becoming a business venture. They rather sought for the creation of spaces free of racism for Salasacas and Indigenous peoples in the Galápagos Islands. The creation of the Runa Kunapak school was particularly challenging because of the denial of local authorities that there was an Indigenous settlement in the Galápagos Province. By that time, at least two thousand *Salasacas* lived in Puerto Ayora. Salasaca leaders (like Daniel Masaquiza, the principal of the school) had to resort to Indigenous political leaders on the mainland (such as the Provincial Director of Tungurahua and the National Director of Intercultural Bilingual Education) to ask for their support. These authorities were involved with the Indigenous Movement of mainland Ecuador. The Salasaca colonos further deployed the language of rights and international treaties, appealing to the Indigenous and Tribal Peoples 169 Convention of the International Labor Organization, by which Ecuador was committed to provide autonomous education for Indigenous peoples living within the national territory. As a result, in 2006 the first intercultural, bilingual (Kichwa-Spanish) school of the islands was founded in Puerto Ayora.

Chapter Five

The Disappearing "Colono"

In October 2018, the mayor of Santa Cruz Island, the directors of the Galápagos National Park, congressmen, and other politicians from the Ecuadorian
mainland were invited to talk about the management of ecosystems in the
Galápagos and new techniques of bio-agriculture in the Ecuadorian Amazon.
I accompanied Margarita Masaquiza to this meeting in which she was named
"assemblywoman for a day." Before the meeting began, a member of the
audience (dressed as a *cholo*—non indigenous) approached Margarita and
asked her to speak on behalf of all the Salasaca people, including nonlegal
residents in the Galápagos. Margarita nodded. In that moment, we all entered
the auditorium. Margarita took her seat next to the speakers. She was the only
Indigenous woman on the platform. Leopoldo Bucceli, the mayor of Santa
Cruz Island, and Lorena Tapia, the recently elected governor of the Galápagos (or director of the Galápagos Government Council) were seated in the
front row. Most of the audience were "illegals" (*mestizos* and Indigenous) all
dressed as *cholos*.

Some moments later, the speakers began to talk about their experience in
the Galápagos Islands and the Ecuadorian Amazon. After their talks, someone
in the audience suddenly shouted:

> Imagine it: forty years without public investment in the Galápagos. We still
> don't have drinking water; it is all brought from the mainland!
>
> Imagine it! You come here to talk about ecosystems when all of the sources
> of subterranean water on the island are contaminated! Even the local bottled
> water is contaminated.
>
> (Field Notes, Puerto Ayora, October 2017).

In the back of the hall, someone else followed him up: "We need to be free, to have a resident status, and not have to hide away!" Several people in the audience cheered him on. In the heat of the moment, the mayor interrupted the protests and shifted the audience's attention. He raised his arms and energetically exclaimed: "Long live the Independent Republic of Galápagos!" The people in the audience applauded. In so doing, the mayor suggested the only possible solution to such problems is to make the archipelago an independent territory, free from the state bureaucracy in Quito, conservation authorities like the Galápagos National Park (whose managers are also appointed by the central government), and the Government Council of the Galápagos, the entity responsible for enforcing the 1998 Special Law, which aims to control the population size of the Galápagos Province. Their claims, however, had no further response.

Yet outside of the hall, when the meeting was over, a group of demonstrators with placards continued to protest. They were joined together in a group called "Pro-residency," whose main purpose is to ask the local authorities to grant them permits to reside legally in the archipelago. They have rights, they argue, because they have lived and worked for more than ten years in Puerto Ayora. Furthermore, most of them have children who were born on the island. They are all Ecuadorian citizens and at the same time "illegal immigrants" in the Galápagos. However, some were more vulnerable than others. Along with most of the Salasaca people in the archipelago, these *Salasacas* live hiding their Indigenous identity, passing as *mestizos* in Puerto Ayora. But they do so not only to avoid discrimination but also to evade population controls which would lead to their deportation from the archipelago. Furthermore, due to their race and Indigenous origins, they are more likely to be denounced than other *mestizos* who also remain illegal in the Galápagos.

Figure 5.1.   Pro-residency group. Members of this group are Ecuadorian citizens but "illegals" in the archipelago. *Source*: Photo: P. Sánchez, Puerto Ayora, Galápagos, October 2018.

Margarita was fully in sympathy with that group of Salasaca protestors. For more than four decades in the Galápagos, she had helped her *paisanos* (fellow *Salasacas*) whenever they were in a dire situation or faced an emergency. She was still doing that when I met her. I had heard her and other members of the Salasaca Association ask representatives of the government to facilitate (among other things): the "human mobility" of the *Salasacas* between the islands and the mainland; the availability of jobs to Indigenous peoples; the allocation of a space for the Salasaca elementary school (the Runa Kunapak Yachay); and their inclusion in projects to establish an official cultural identity for the Galápagos. In particular, in our last meeting, she and other Salasaca *colonos* (first settlers) had asked authorities to stop hunting down *Salasacas* in every raid done by the Government Council to deport illegals from the Galápagos.[1] Although many of the illegal migrants are not *Salasacas,* law enforcement authorities deport illegal *Salasacas* at much higher rates than illegal *mestizos* on the islands.[2] Margarita had also tried—without success—to obtain funding to build a museum to commemorate Salasaca history on the archipelago. Finally, as the head of the association, she had spent the last years trying to unite the Salasaca collective on Santa Cruz Island and get them to unify their stances with regards to the politics of the Galápagos. She knew what they could achieve if they joined together.

But Margarita could not speak for the *Salasacas* who were "illegal" on the islands in front of the authorities of the park and the municipal government. Following the reforms made to the 1998 Special Law (in 2015), the local government had passed a series of measures to reinforce population control; among them were fines and sanctions to punish those residents who helped "illegals" by giving them a job or renting them a room or apartment. Since then, too, all Ecuadorian nationals who have arrived on the islands have had to show a letter of invitation from a resident of the Galápagos, which automatically makes the resident responsible for their stay in the archipelago. Meanwhile, foreigners only need a hotel reservation to enter the islands. Worse yet, local authorities encouraged residents to denounce all "illegals" as well as the residents who helped them. Often people spoke about the severest sanction for the residents, which, in theory, was the loss of the resident's "permit," even when the person was born in the Galápagos or was descendant of the pioneers or *colonos* of the archipelago.[3]

In the end, at the meeting that day, none of the speakers talked about the situation of the "illegals" that were present. Nor was there any response on the part of the politicians to the complaints about the negligence that caused the lack of potable water on the archipelago. Once more, it was shown that the Galápagos serves as an ideal venue for holding seminars and conferences that speak about conservation as a symbol for caring about nature (or "wilderness," in Haila's words 1997, 129). But protecting wilderness and endemic species was evidently not necessarily related to caring for the environment in terms of preventing water pollution, global warming, and ecological crisis. Ironically, in the Galápagos—which are touted as a global model for conservation— potable water sources are contaminated due to the lack of a wastewater treatment plant and constant polluted runoff from the cruise ships that sail through the islands.[4]

On the other hand, while there was talk of bio-agriculture, it is well known that the local production of food is restricted by conservationist measures which, in addition to prohibiting the use of pesticides, synthetic fertilizers, agro-chemicals, and heavy agricultural machinery, try to keep out all the invasive species which threaten the endemic to the archipelago. Most of the ingredients of the Ecuadorian diet are on that list. What is more, even though there is a system of control which includes quarantines at points of access to the archipelago, invasive species (including seeds, insects, and microorganisms) continue to enter with the thousands of tourists who visit the islands and the tons of foodstuffs and supplies that come every month from the mainland.[5] Finally, neither the scientific station nor the park has shown an interest in investigating the body of local knowledge of agriculture which the *galapagueños* have developed for over a century and a half in their struggles to create productive *haciendas* and, later, in partly achieving self-sufficiency in a terrain of rocky soil and little water.[6] On that day, the meeting broke up and once more the protestors left without obtaining any response to their demands.

The issues that were brought up in that meeting reflect a particular form of governance that frames invasive species as the enemy to the conservation of biodiversity and sustainable development in the archipelago. As the 1998 Special Law for the Galápagos defined it, the task to protect Galápagos' nature entails not only preventing the introduction of alien nonhuman species but also the halt of internal migration and the separation of (local) people from protected areas. To accomplish this, the 1998 law created two sorts of Ecuadorians ("legals" and "illegals") who were, in any event, all conceived as "aliens" on the archipelago. I argue that in the Galápagos, conservationist thought is translated into a legal and institutional framework that treats settlers and natives of the Galápagos as invasive species that are harmful to the archipelago's nature. The aspiration to force all locals out is materialized in the 1998 law, which disappeared them as "*colonos*" or natives of the islands, enforced their confinement to settlement areas, made them inaudible in the government of the archipelago (while being dependent on drinking water and food from the Ecuadorian mainland), and finally, imposed increasing sanctions on them for living at the margins of one of the most valuable sites of Natural World Heritage.

To prove this, I begin by studying conservation thought as it was framed in its inception in the United States in the early decades of 1900s, and the way these ideas were expressed in the Charles Darwin Research Station's mission as well as in the 1998 Special Law for the Galápagos. Then I examine the sphere of illegality created by conservation law in the islands, with extralegal subjects and practices flourishing in the aftermath of its ratification. I pay attention to the ways Ecuadorians claim their citizenship rights over the Galápagos, particularly the Salasaca people. Salasaca migrants adopted a different strategy from *mestizo* migrants to enter and stay in the Galápagos. Ironically, they benefitted from the racist practices through which the Ecuadorian state and *mestizo* bureaucrats identified and incorporated Indigenous Salasaca people (back in the 1950s) as members of the nation-state. Nonetheless, there is a widespread consent among *galapagueños* (*mestizos* and Indigenous) on the benefits of conservationism. This, however, reflects both the structures of political and economic power (above all, their dependence on food and drinking water from the mainland) and their acceptance of their subordinate position as informed by the *hacienda* order.

"BACK TO EDEN:" CONSERVATIONIST REGIME IN THE GALÁPAGOS

Nowadays, the rumors about the expulsion of the local people from the Galápagos Islands are a matter of "coffee shop chitchat" or thought of as an "urban legend" on Santa Cruz (Interviews, Puerto Ayora 2017). Nonetheless, the reality is that the hard-line conservationists of the Darwin station still envision an archipelago with no human inhabitants. In two recent studies, some of the scientists spoke of this subject, saying that: "if we had it our way there would not be people on the islands—but, Ecuador is a democracy, so what could be done," (Hennessy 2014, 613) and further concluding: "we're trying to keep people out of the Galápagos" (Constantino 2007, 207–8).

These statements divide humans of the archipelago into two main groups: one, "we" (the foreign conservationists), and the other, "the people" (the *galapagueños* and Ecuadorians who are, in turn, divided into legal and illegal subjects). In such terms, the first (the conservationists) decide over the second. Moreover, they decide who should live or not in the Galápagos. And whether it seems like a difficult or impossible quest (because "Ecuador is a democracy"), the vision is somehow realized through the different measures and policies that make everyday life challenging, uncomfortable, or less and less profitable for locals in the archipelago. The quest is further achieved in terms of the absence of written history of the Galápagos inhabitants, which creates an impression of an absence of people in the islands. Similarly, in law this goal is realized through the removal of *colonos* (first settlers) and the non-recognition of the Galápagos as the place of birth of native *galapagueños*.

The Darwin Station Mission

Until 2002, the vision of conservationist work at the Darwin station was: to restore the conditions which made the observations of Darwin possible during his visit to the islands in 1835. That year, however, the station mission on the archipelago was reformulated, stretching its goal further back—three centuries before Darwin's time. Their efforts should now seek to: "restore the populations and distributions of the whole native biodiversity which existed, and the natural ecological/evolutionary processes, to the conditions prior to the human settlement . . . which took place in 1534" (Snell et. al 2002, 48). In other words, to go back to an imagined, pre-human time before their 'discovery' by a Spanish bishop.[7]

This new vision was published in a report entitled "Back to Eden—One Last Chance," which also noted that the 128 islands of the archipelago still conserve 95 percent of the diversity of its "original, 'pre-human'" species (Bensted-Smith et al. 2002, 1). Despite this, year after year, the organizations that monitor conservation work on the Galápagos constantly describe the "state of the property" in terms of the "threats" to the ecosystem, "the danger of extinction" of its endemic species, and the "urgent need" to take immediate actions against "invasive species" and "demographic pressure."

In so doing, the Darwin station's mission and UNESCO reports reflect a set of anxieties that combine fears regarding the extinction of species, along with their wish to pay a tribute to Darwin, Western science, and evolutionary theories. They further reveal dominant views of islands as places of edenic nature (Grove 1996, Hennessy and McCleary 2011), often associated with origin stories, primitive escapes from modernity, and controllable sites that lend themselves for experimentation (as in MacArthur and Wilson 1967). They also index imperial accounts of Latin American nature as wild, edenic, and uninhabited, aimed at the appropriation of resources, territorial surveillance, and administrative control (Pratt 1992, Raffles 2002). In turn, in the Galápagos, the Darwin station mission is translated into a series of practices that guide not only conservationist work and law but also a system of sanctions and an ideology—a common sense that penalizes local people for inhabiting the islands (and sometimes for having many children). The aspirations of Western science have thus reconfigured the meaning of this territory and the management of its population.

Conservation Thought

Anxieties related to the extinction of species (particularly the Nordic race) and the growing (nonwhite) population underwrote both the conservation and the eugenics movement in the early twentieth century United States (see Spiro 2008).[8] These were linked to evolutionary ideas that posited competition (since Malthus) as central in "the struggle for existence" (as used by Darwin as the subtitle to *The Origins*) and the "survival of the fittest" (Spencer). Beliefs in racial purity and controlled breeding, along with the desire to prevent miscegenation (the mixing of races) and eliminate the unfit in nature guided not only the work of science but also government policy (for example, in regards to family planning and immigration laws).

In particular, the conservationist project emerged with the aim to save North America's wild animals at that moment in time so that white wealthy men could hunt them in the future. Through the enclosure of lands and the creation of game preserves, a small but well-connected elite endorsed the preservation of native and endangered species and the prohibition of hunting for commercial—and not recreational—purposes. Moreover, the project embraced a sense of duty and entitlement to hand down "to posterity some portion of the heritage of wild life and wild nature," thus asserting the "unorthodox premise that the resources of a region do not belong to local inhabitants but to the nation as a whole," as Madison Grant (one of the founders of the conservation movement) put it in the 1890s (ibid., 15–22).[9] Yet this group of wealthy sportsmen saw themselves as the only ones capable of being the guardians of nature and, therefore, the recipients of that natural heritage. They eventually also became the patrons of science (Haraway 1985) and the leaders of the conservation movement. Some of these families were, in fact, advocates in the project to acquire the Galápagos Islands back in the 1930s in order to turn it into a game preserve, as I described earlier.[10]

Galápagos conservation made the quest to purify populations and the preservation of evolutionary processes the centerpiece of its efforts. Furthermore, it made conservation thought the basis for drafting the 1998 Organic Law of Special Regime of the Galápagos Province and for designing an institutional framework by which the aim to protect native species by preventing the introduction of invasive ones (both human and animal) could be achieved.

The 1998 Special Law for the Galápagos

After ten years of conversations, representatives of the Ecuadorian national government, the Galápagos National Park (GNP) and scientists from the Charles Darwin Station (CDS) agreed on the text that would govern Galápagos society in the name of the conservation of nature. The law was ratified by the Ecuadorian state in March 1998. By the end of that year, scientists at the Darwin station, however, pointed that the resulting law was "no panacea" because although "it provided an excellent framework for conservation of the Marine Reserve and represented an important advance in the conservation of the terrestrial component . . . it had weaknesses in measures to curb population growth, which underlies the central threat of introduced species" (Bensted-Smith 1998, 6). They did recommend its immediate enforcement, but advocated for improvements to be made through more strict regulation and subsequent reforms.

The purpose of the 1998 Special Law for the Galápagos was to promote conservation of biodiversity and, at the same time, sustainable development—specifically, within the settlement areas of the Ecuadorian province. The law identified the problem of introduced species (non-native or alien) as the principal obstacle to achieve the harmonious coexistence between people and the unique flora and fauna of Galápagos (Ibid.). The scope of the problem was later reduced to "invasive species" only, which are the kind of introduced species that are considered harmful to the native ecosystem.

In order to deal with this problem, the 1998 law imposed a series of regulations related to the introduction and transport of alien species and the eradication of pest species in agricultural lands while establishing a quarantine inspection system and regular audit.[11] The law also required local institutions and individuals to engage in the control of introduced species while promoting the appreciation of biodiversity through environmental education and the encouragement of locally based tourism to sites located nearby.[12] It additionally redefined the distribution of the resources generated by the visitor fee at the entrance of the natural park. More importantly, it established a "residence regime" to classify humans of the Galápagos with the goal of reducing internal migration as a vital requirement for conservation of the natural park. The 1998 law, however, did not set any limits on the entry of tourists and barely mentioned the supply system of the archipelago, which are both part of the invasive species problem. In so doing, it ratified neo-Malthusian concerns about how to avoid the increase of Ecuadorians in the Galápagos, which had framed the discourse and politics surrounding the natural park since its creation.

Two institutions, the Galápagos National Park (GNP) and INGALA (the National Institute of the Galápagos), became the central authority of the Galápagos. They further expressed in the archipelago the dual aim that conservation had since its inception: protection of nature and demographic control. Since 1959, the Park was the leading environmental authority in the islands, in charge of enforcing protection measures within the natural park. Meanwhile,

INGALA was established in 1980 with the aim of controlling population size within settlement areas. The law designated most of the resources generated by admission fees to the natural park to state conservation institutions: mainly Galápagos National Park (40 percent), and other agencies that assist its work (20 percent). Another 10 percent was assigned to the INGALA.[13]

The Special Law posited the country's political elite, mainly based in Quito, as the local guardians of nature and heirs of the Galápagos Islands. It entitled the president of the republic to appoint and remove from office the managers of these two entities. They also had to report to the minister of the environment who acted as their chairman. The design of this framework thus ensured that the Ecuadorian political and economic elite could guard the protection of the islands from afar—from Quito—while retaining, with transnational networks of tourism and science, economic gains derived from the property.

Meanwhile, 30 percent of the resources of the admission fees to the Park were allocated (until the 2009 reform) to the local municipalities and the Provincial Council of Galápagos. The heads of these institutions were the only ones who could be elected locally, thus representing the voice of the *galapagueños* in their right to decide on their government within colonized zones—that is, the 3 percent of the lands that were left by foreign conservation entities to the first settlers of the Galápagos. However, this also changed—to the detriment of *galapagueños*—after the islands were included on the 2007 UNESCO list of "World Heritage Sites in Danger."

Supranational Control

The institutional framework that was established to govern nature and society in the Galápagos ceded territorial control to the national government in Quito. Apparently, the 1998 law limited the role of the Darwin station in the archipelago. The station became only a member in the Inter-institutional Management Authority that governs the Galápagos National Park, which also includes the ministers of the environment, national defense, foreign trade, and tourism, as well as a representative of the local fishermen and members of other foreign conservation agencies. A seat (with no vote) in INGALA (now known as the Governing Council of the Galápagos) was also given to the station.

Nonetheless, the Charles Darwin Station (CDS) continued to act as a crucial authority in the archipelago due to its power to define the "management strategies" of the Galápagos National Park (which includes 97 percent of the lands of the archipelago, plus the whole of the Marine Reserve) and to process requests for heritage nominations, international assistance, and budget assigned to the property with international agencies—primarily, UNESCO.[14] Maintaining the heritage status of the Galápagos further depends on the Darwin station's assessment.

The monitoring process starts every year with the state report to UNESCO in which Ecuador notes the measures and actions taken to address the threats faced on the property. Then the IUCN visits the World Heritage site in "a monitoring mission" that evaluates the progress achieved by the state party and recommends actions including issues of governance, management, and demographics. The input of advisory bodies (such as the Darwin Station in the case of the Galápagos) is key to this evaluation. It considers, in particular, criteria related to the conservation and maintenance of the OUV (Outstanding Universal Value) of the property and its integrity. Finally, the World Heritage Committee issues a "Decision Report" in which it expresses its concerns and requests the state party to comply in order to maintain its heritage status. UNESCO then decides on the budget assigned to conservation requests for the property. More importantly, the number of tourists interested in visiting the heritage site tends to depend on UNESCO's valuation.

The power of foreign entities in the management of the archipelago became clear in 2007 when UNESCO included the Galápagos on its list of "World Heritage Sites in Danger." It led to the inclusion of a chapter that considers the "special system" by which the Galápagos district would be governed differently. Moreover, it led to the 2015 reform of the 1998 law, which eliminated the provincial government, embraced a policy of deportation, and worsened the system of sanctions that aims to control and discipline locals' behavior.

The Disappearing "Colono"

The most significant and immediate change proclaimed by the 1998 law was the removal of the old "*colono*" category from the legal framework, which was used for a long time to confer respect, recognition, and a bundle of rights to property and citizenship to those first settlers who sacrificed their lives in order to "*hacer patria*" (follow their patriotic duty) for the Ecuadorian state in the remote archipelago.

Their descendants and people born in the archipelago were also included in this category. Before 1998, for them, the National Navy issued "*Colonos* of the Galápagos Identity Cards" that, under the Ecuadorian citizenship number, stated that: "the cardholder is a *colono* of the Archipiélago de Colón, of the republic of Ecuador," on the back. [15] His or her place of birth was clearly stated there.

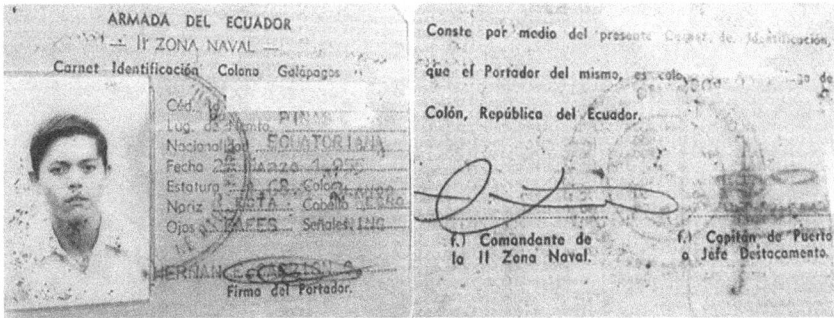

Figure 5.2. A *colono* identity card. The word colono is printed on the front and the back of the card. On the back it is written: "Through this ID, we (the Ecuadorian Navy) certify that the cardholder is a colono of the Archipélago de Colón, republic of Ecuador." To protect his identity, I erased his identity card number. *Source*: Courtesy: H. Carrión. Photograph: Sandra Ulloa.

After the 1998 law, the INGALA (which later became the Governing Council of the Galápagos (GCG)) started to issue identity cards by which *colonos* of the Galápagos became identified as "permanent residents" in the archipelago. From there on, they were identified under two numbers: the Ecuadorian citizenship number and the resident number for the Galápagos. The two numbers reflect the two main regimes that govern the archipelago: state law and conservation law. Yet the dominant rule of the conservation regime is clearly stated by Article 258 of the 2008 National Constitution, which is printed on the back of the residency permit. It declares that the Galápagos province is to be administered by a "special government," with its planning and development organized on the basis of strict adherence to the principles of conservation. The new credential does not state the place of birth of the resident of the Galápagos.

Figure 5.3. A Galápagos residency permit. Article 258 of the 2008 National Constitution is printed on the back of the card. To protect his identity, I erased his signature. To protect his identity, I erased his first name, identity card number and residency number. *Source*: Courtesy: F. Masaquiza.

For example, F. Masaquiza (pictured above) is the descendant of two Salasaca *colonos* (first settlers) of Santa Cruz Island. He is native of the Galápagos and was born in 1983 in Puerto Ayora (Santa Cruz). Before the law, he was identified, too, as Mr. Carrión (first picture)—as a *colono* of the Galápagos. Nevertheless, as of today, he needs to hold two different IDs: the Ecuadorian citizenship card and the residence permit in the archipelago. The Galápagos credential states the motive by which the Governing Council (INGALA) grants him permission to reside in the archipelago: Article 26–1 of the Special Law. This article recognizes he was born in the province and is the child of a permanent resident in the Galápagos. However, it does not state his place of birth, avoiding recognition of him as a native of the archipelago. Furthermore, this is no longer a (*colono*) identity card, but a "residency credential" by which he is granted a "permit" to live on his homeland.

The new category made *colonos* of the Galápagos disappear from the legal framework. Through the Special Law, the Ecuadorian state therefore allowed for a change in *galapagueños* identity, while negating full citizenship rights in their birthplace. As if they were "aliens," state law treated them as "introduced" on their land, granting them only a permit to live and work there. Moreover, it established an institutional framework by which the power to govern the islands is given to the national government. It further designates most of the profits gained from this property to an elite made up of the political elite and forty-five shipowners and tourism operators.

At the same time, such legal framework infringes on the rights of all Ecuadorians from the mainland. As per the Special Law, Ecuadorians visiting the islands were given the legal status of "tourist" while in the archipelago. Moreover, under the 2015 reform to the 1998 law, Ecuadorians must bring an invitation letter from a resident of the Galápagos in order to gain entry.[16] In addition to this, they are only allowed to stay in the islands for sixty days per year—as is any foreigner who comes and visits. Those who exceed this time limit immediately become "illegals" in their own country and could moreover be deported by INGALA (now the Government Council) to the mainland. In such a context, law enforcement authorities made Salasaca migrants the targets of population controls, as I will show in the next chapter.

AFTER THE 1998 SPECIAL LAW: THE SPHERE OF ILLEGALITY

In theory, the years that followed the ratification of the "Special Law for the Galápagos" (between 1998 and 2001) were a period of legalization of the human population of the archipelago. All of its inhabitants were obliged to fulfill the bureaucratic requisites required to change their legal status (from being *colonos* to "residents") in compliance with the new categories imposed by the conservation regime. Under the new status assigned, their permanence on the islands seemed conditional and temporary, as if they were "aliens" or, as the Charles Darwin Foundation often puts it, "guests" on the islands. On the other hand, the 1998 law prohibited further colonization by turning all new settlers into transgressors, thus making them subjects of persecution and deportation.

In practice, the period of legalization of the Special Law was, nonetheless, marked by the proliferation of illegal subjects and practices and an upsurge in immigration. Interestingly, many of my interviewees claimed that the 1998 law is to blame for furthering migration while trying to prevent it. A Salasaca *colona* (first settler) explained it this way: "the people on the mainland were concerned they would not be able to live here anymore after the law . . . It was like if they were about to push them towards an abyss. A lot of people came to the islands and have remained hidden since then" (Interview, Puerto Ayora, July 2015). Another Salasaca *colono* reflected: "everything got out of hand after the law, more laws less control" (Interview, Puerto Ayora, September 2015). These remarks coincide with the observations of legal pluralists who have addressed the messy contradictions and the unexpected effects that emerge, at the local level, with the introduction of foreign bodies of law and the mixing of legal frameworks.

This framework allows for an investigation of the diverse ways in which individuals interact with the law, the multiple systems of law locally available to them, and the strategies by which both dominant and marginalized groups reshape alternate orderings in a given field.

As state law, conservation law, and transnational normative instruments related to the protection of UNESCO World Heritage sites interact in the Galápagos, they provide different sets of cultural meanings, or in Geertz's words, "distinctive way(s) of imagining the real" (1983, 184). In this context, multiple notions of law, nature, citizenship, and property overlap. Through a pluralist approach (Merry 1988), I examine the Galápagos legal framework while paying attention to the sphere of illegality that it also created. As individuals interact with the multiple systems of law available, they encounter a mixing of codes of rules and counter-rules that incite "both to obedience and disobedience, legal and illegal action" (Santos 2002, 437).

Legal and Illegal Action

From 1998 to 2001, INGALA required those applying for permanent residency to submit proof that they had lived for longer than five consecutive years in the archipelago. *Colonos* of the Galápagos could clearly distinguish

families who were pioneers, their descendants, and the newly arrived. The latter had to seek the help of a "resident" (relatives, acquaintances, employers,
or friends) to come up with evidence (even if it was fictitious) to meet residency requirements. Local organizations also engaged in helping the people
they knew to obtain the status of permanent residents. This was only the beginning of a boom in illegal practices by which Ecuadorian citizens claimed
their right to live and work on the Galápagos.

The Black Market of Residency Permits

When the period of legalization ended in 2001, the Special Law only allowed
new residency permits to be issued to those born on the islands or to the
spouses of permanent residents. After 2001, new migrants thus resorted to
the flourishing underground market of residency permits. The most important
was the black market run by the very government officials of Santa Cruz who
were responsible for law enforcement at the Galápagos Government Council
(then known as INGALA). A lawyer from the province explained how it
worked to me:

> People have the permanent residence card but the folder with the supporting
> documentation shows that they didn't fulfill for the requirements for proving
> how long they had been on the islands. These are residence permits, which were
> bought for two or three thousand dollars each . . .
> A lot of people made a great deal of money that way. Imagine: at two or three
> thousand dollars each! Now, there have been audits, three audits of the proce-
> dure for granting residencies in the Galápagos, and the three have resulted in
> lists of residency folders that do not have supporting documentation. The three
> agree on the overall number, which is 2,790 or something like that. Nearly 3,000
> permits which were illegally granted, bought in fact.
> No one ever knew. No one has any idea, no one knows what went on. At one
> point, they were told to keep quiet . . .
> (Interview, Puerto Ayora, June 2015).

According to those calculations, more than six million dollars changed
hands during the issuance of those residence ID cards. "Those officials of
INGALA now own stores, restaurants, all kinds of businesses in the Galápagos," as one *colono* told me (Interview, Puerto Ayora, June 2018). Such
permits, although illegally obtained from the apparatus of the state in the
Galápagos, are still valid today.

In addition, private arrangements for fraudulent marriages with a man
or woman resident of the Galápagos began to be used to obtain permanent
residence cards. On the streets of Puerto Ayora, they say that obtaining a residence permit through marriage can currently cost some five thousand dollars.

And while formerly, marriage to a resident automatically resulted in a permit to permanently live on the archipelago, the law currently in force (that passed in 2015 to reform the law of 1998) requires a minimum stay on the islands of ten years before someone can change the status of his or her spouse from a "temporary" to a "permanent" resident of the archipelago.

From a pluralist perspective, the resistance of the Ecuadorians who evaded measures to control population size on the archipelago is, at one and the same time, an act of obedience and disobedience. The National Constitution states that its citizens have the right to work (Article 33) and the right to freely move through the territory (Articles 40–42). Article 40, in particular, recognizes the right to migrate and states "no human being will be regarded as illegal because of his migratory condition." The migrants to the Galápagos Islands who are Ecuadorian citizens thus follow and adhere to this principle when they move to the archipelago in order to work. At the same time, they disobey conservation law and enter the sphere of illegality when they exceed the sixty-day time limit allowed for both foreign tourists and Ecuadorians on the Galápagos. The contradiction is further incorporated into the very constitution by Article 258, which states that the Galápagos province will be governed by a "special regime," whose aim is to ensure "a strict adherence to the principles of conservation of the Natural Park." It therefore ceded the administration of this territory to the Government Council (headed by the president of Ecuador), with the warning that this body will limit the rights of Ecuadorian citizens to work and migrate to the Galápagos.

The "Masaquizas"

The *Salasacas* took another path to assert their right to migrate to, work, and live in the Galápagos Islands. In the years following the ratification of the Special Law, to facilitate the entrance of relatives, friends, or acquaintances, some Salasaca *colonos* lent them their ID cards and permanent residence permits. Although not all of them engaged in this ploy or were in agreement with it, entire groups of *paisanos* (fellow *Salasacas*) benefited from it and were able to enter the islands with a single ID card. Once they reached Santa Cruz, some of them illegally acquired their residence cards, resorting to the black market run by local officials at the Government Council (INGALA). Others obtained their residence papers in a legal way, but using the name of the person who had lent them his or her card. As a result, nowadays, many *Salasacas* on the island are known by the same name to the local authorities as Stella, the *mestiza galapagueña* noted on my first day on the islands. Furthermore, the Government Council cannot identify kinship ties among the Salasaca people on Santa Cruz. "They don't know if the person is an uncle, cousin, or relative," as an official of the government told me (Puerto Ayora, October 2017).At first sight, the collective use of ID cards by *Salasacas* may be understood as an act both of civil disobedience and ethnic solidarity. However, the practice also reveals the flexibility of the Salasaca people in the face of the norms imposed by the Republic of Ecuador in regards to the registry of surnames, which follow the Spanish patriarchal system of transmission (from the father to his children). In contemporary Salasaca, in addition to the large presence of the surname Masaquiza among members of the community, there are also many cases where the civil surname of a person (the one recorded on his or her ID card) is not the same as that of the person's father, mother, or siblings (even if they are children of the same parents). There are also cases where the person is registered under his or her nickname.

For example, I noticed several cases like that of a young man whose surname is Masaquiza, while that of his father is Caiza and that of his mother, Chango. Likewise, there are several instances where the person's civil surname is actually his nickname, like "Acosta" because he once lived on the coast, or "Pediche" because that is what people called her. Moreover, many of the people I interviewed are known by their nicknames rather than their true ones. In addition, recent studies found that at least seven female surnames still survive, which were transmitted in accordance with the pre-Hispanic custom of parallel descent where fathers bequeathed their surnames to their sons; and mothers, their own surnames to their daughters (Corr and Powers 2012, 21).[17] All of these cases point, on the one hand, to a greater flexibility in the use and registry of surnames, and on the other, to a way of resisting the Ecuadorian state domination and its norms to identify, register, and integrate Salasaca people to the nation.

Yet from a different angle, the collective use of identities and ID cards to migrate to the Galápagos might also be seen as an extension of the same practice by which *mestizo* state bureaucrats identified Salasaca people in the 1950s, when registering them as citizens of Ecuador. At that time, officials refused to recognize the surnames and genealogies of the Salasaca Indigenous people and, instead, assigned them a collective identity by registering most under the surname "Masaquiza," as I previously described. From that point of view, when *Salasacas* lent their ID cards to other members of their community to migrate to the Galápagos Islands, the new Salasaca migrants replicated the state norm by which they were integrated—as a collective and not as individuals—to the nation-state. In so doing, they benefitted from the long-standing racism of the Ecuadorian state as well as from the prejudices of *mestizos* at the migratory posts, who still think that Indigenous people "all look the same" and are radically different from them. "When they read the person is a Masaquiza, they don't even look at the photo in the ID because to them we all look the same," a Salasaca once told me (Interview, Puerto Ayora, December 2017). By sharing their names, photos, and residency permits, *Salasacas* were thus able to migrate en masse to the Galápagos after 2001, and able to establish their second largest settlement in Puerto Ayora (Santa Cruz Island).

Displaced Ecuadorians and Potential Voters

In addition to the dynamics unleashed by the passing of the 1998 law, there were other pressing reasons for Ecuadorians on the mainland to flee their homelands. Between 1999 and 2006, natural and economic disasters hit the country, leading to the exile of thousands and thousands of citizens from the country. On one hand, in 1999 the bank crisis, known as the "bank holiday" (*feriado bancario*), resulted in the loss of the bank savings of many Ecuadorians, the bankruptcy of small producers, and the dollarization of the economy in 2000.[18] Those years were also marked by Tungurahua's volcanic eruptions (in 1999, 2000, and 2006), which also contributed to the displacement of more people. In the Galápagos, there was greater promise of access to better-paid jobs, particularly in the growing tourism sector.

Local politicians on the islands seized the moment to offer building lots to low-income migrants in exchange for their votes. They further promised them the eventual issuance of residence cards. The plots of land offered were located on the outskirts of the city, alongside the Miraflores neighborhood. At the time, the terrain belonged to the Galápagos National Park. In 2000, after the newly elected mayor of Santa Cruz assumed office, he exchanged some lands in the upperpart of the island (which had formerly pertained to the 3 percent of the territory designated for *colonos* as settlement areas) with the terrain adjacent to Miraflores. There, in the following years, new migrants who stayed illegally in Puerto Ayora received small lots (49 ft. long by × 32 ft. wide). The new district was called La Cascada. Although today these newcomers are not yet holders of residency permits, they do represent a large mass of voters in the archipelago, capable of moving the landscape of the elections of the mayor of Santa Cruz and municipal councilors. In this sense, the presence of thousands of illegal subjects on Santa Cruz helps to affirm Ecuadorian sovereignty, through democracy, over the Galápagos. With their votes, they can counter conservation rule by choosing those candidates who promise legal residency or at least an improved access to rights for Ecuadorian new migrants in the archipelago.

During the decade that followed the ratification of the Special Law, the population of the Galápagos grew by nearly eight thousand persons (+50 percent rise vs. 1998). Around five thousand of the additional inhabitants

Figure 5.4.   La Cascada neighborhood. Only one vehicle is at a time is able to transit through the narrow streets of La Cascada neighborhood. *Source*: Photo: P. Sánchez, Puerto Ayora, February 2018.

settled on Santa Cruz.[19] The density within the settlement areas of this island (particularly, in the neighborhood of La Cascada) rose to the point where, according to a Charles Darwin Foundation report, it exceeded the rate of cities like Hong Kong (China) or Mumbai (India).[20] Today, including *colonos*, legal, and illegal residents, there are around three thousand *Salasacas* on Santa Cruz Island. Many of the newcomers who remained illegally are therefore non-*Salasacas*. However, local authorities and *mestizo* inhabitants tend to mark the Salasacas as the transgressors of conservation law. The interaction of conservation ideas and practices with local views of racial order that led to the making of Salasaca people as the primary target of law enforcement authorities in the Galápagos is the subject of the next chapter.

CONSERVATION RULE: COERCION, CONSENT, AND HEGEMONY

In 2007, UNESCO placed the Galápagos on its 2007 list of "World Heritage Sites in Danger." The official committee listed as the problems that needed "urgent solution": "lack of effective governance;" "risk from alien invasive species;" "haphazard," "unsustainable," and "inequitable" growth of the tourism sector; inability to control illegal immigration; lack of capacity and stability of national park and Marine Reserve staff; and a poor education system that "does not incorporate elements of environmental management and heritage preservation, and natural resource development, further delaying the critical need to develop an insular culture focused on sustainable development" (UNESCO 2007, 9–10). As a result of UNESCO's evaluation, the Ecuadorian state introduced changes to the new national constitution in 2008, eliminated the provincial government in the archipelago in 2009, drafted a reform to the 1998 law to make sanctions more severe in 2015, and called for more raids to deport illegals from the Galápagos.

Coercion: the 2015 Reform to the 1998 Law

In 2008, the government and the constitutional assembly approved Article 258 (now printed on the back of the residency permit of every *galapagueño*) in order to enshrine more clearly the "special" status of the Galápagos province and the need to have a "special governance structure." This paved the way for the issuing of a presidential decree which, in 2009, eliminated the Provincial Government (*la Prefectura*) on the islands, thus turning the Galápagos into the only province in Ecuador with no autonomous government. The decree additionally gave the former resources of the Provincial Government to the INGALA, which from then on became known as the Governing Council of the Galápagos (GCG).[21] In so doing, the national government transferred the responsibility for building public infrastructure for the local population in the islands to the same entity that was created to control population size. Achieving these seemingly contradicting goals was further set up to depend on the decisions of the ministry of environment and the president of Ecuador, who presided over the chairman of the GCG. The elimination of the Provincial Government thus led *galapagueños* to become even more disempowered by the political elite of the country. Ironically, the head of the GCG is often called "the governor of the Galápagos," in spite of being selected by the president in Quito. At the same time, the Ecuadorian government made additional commitments to UNESCO to maintain the heritage status of the Galápagos. In 2010, Ecuador committed to a "zero growth" policy, which entailed halting migration (in order to maintain the same number of permanent residents—that is, at the 2010 levels) while also indicating, at last, an upper limit of the number of tourists who should be allowed to visit the islands every year. After all these changes were made, the property was withdrawn from UNESCO's list of heritage sites in danger.[22]

Ecuador's commitments to UNESCO were expressed in the 2015 reform of the 1998 law, which not only worsened penalties for locals living in the archipelago but also declared that job posts at public offices in the Galápagos did not need to be filled by *galapagueños*. As such, between 2009 and 2015, locals lost preferential access to jobs on the islands, and also autonomy and democratic representation within the state entities that govern, manage, and profit from the archipelago. It was in the context of the debate that surrounded the 2015 reform that Marcela Aguiñaga, an assemblywoman in Quito (who had been minister of the environment and thus chairman of Galápagos National Park and the Gálapagos Government Council) referred to *galapagueños* as the "descendants of convicts," as Stella poignantly noted on the day I arrived in the archipelago.

At present, most of the resources generated by visitor entrance fees to Galápagos Park is given to entities that work for conservation, yet under the rule of Quito. Taking into account that, throughout Ecuador, provincial councils are the entities responsible for agricultural, public health, and public works at the regional level, then the elimination of this entity in the Galápagos leaves no autonomy for locals to respond to their necessities. The fact that *galapagueños* haven't had—since 2009—a locally elected governor (or *prefecto*) and that the majority of the money that enters the Galápagos economy is directed to conservation explains the lack of basic services in the province—particularly, potable water, wastewater, and sanitation services on the islands.[23] Access to good health services and college education is further limited to those who can afford to travel to the mainland. Meanwhile on the islands, the seven thousand school students in the Galápagos have no universities, public libraries, or textbooks available.[24] An environmental lawyer of the province reflected on this, suggesting this is part of the politics of conservation:

> There are a few things that are woven around the stories about the interest the *gringos*, scientists, and ecologists have in removing the population from the islands . . . maybe they are things which are now regarded as urban legends in the Galápagos.
>
> But why don't they provide us with potable water, for example? Why don't we have good hospitals or good doctors? Why don't the scientists solve that?
>
> What they think is that if life in the Galápagos is made more pleasant, more people are going to want to live here . . . that is their reasoning.
>
> (Interview, Puerto Ayora, June 2014).

Seen in this way, which is how most *galapagueños* perceive it, the institutional framework and the neglect to provide basic services to locals is yet another way to deter demographic growth in the archipelago. Furthermore, to put two seemingly conflicting goals (to control population size and promote local development) under the same institution (the GCG), then appears as a coherent policy within the conservation regime of the archipelago.

In addition, there are the measures that restrict the local production of food and make the islands dependent on a system of supply, based on importing foodstuffs (and drinking water) from the mainland. This leads to high prices, arbitrary increases in the monthly grocery expenses, and a constant loss of purchasing power for *galapagueños*. Finally, there are the growing number of fines and sanctions that restrict everyday life within settlement areas of the archipelago.

In this light, conservationist policy does express Malthusian concerns when drafting legal measures and public policies that aim to control population size by targeting poor Ecuadorians that are the most affected with all these measures. In particular, the deportation of Salasaca people points to the local visions of race that are historically informed by the *hacienda* order and now interact with the enforcement of conservation law on the Galápagos.

Hegemony: Conservation Rule in the Galápagos

During the term of my fieldwork, I heard some comments, on the part of *colonos* who said there was no longer respect for the sacrifice that first settlers of the Galápagos gave, nor any privilege that recognizes their efforts over a very long period of time, in which they lived isolated and abandoned in the archipelago. Old and new migrants alike also complain about the lack of public services and comment about the bizarre "illegal" status that was given to Ecuadorians from the continent, should they exceed the time limit on the archipelago. Yet, the majority agree on population controls and on having a "special" regime for the Galápagos. Furthermore, among *galapagueños,* there is a generalized consent on the benefits that conservation and tourism bring to the archipelago. Moreover, locals value their homeland for being the patrimony of humankind. From this perspective, the removal of local categories can be seen as yet another sacrifice for the wealth of nature, the nation, and the 'humankind.' But it was not always like that. In the training session on conservation law that I had to take (since it is required for everyone applying to get a temporary residency permit), an official of the Government Council remembered the complaints of former *colonos* when they were required to change their legal status back in 1998. [25] He said:

> An old *colono* comes and tells me: 'No, I don't fit, I don't like it, I don't want to be called that [permanent resident].'
> And I told him: 'Sir, if you don't like it, have the kindness to leave, there is the door. I am telling you what the paper [the law] says . . . here, we have a "Special Law" and we have to obey' . . .

> It is not true that in the Galápagos, we are regionalists, but unfortunately, we
> have a special province. In other words, we have the hen with the golden eggs
> for Ecuador. We have to take care of it.
> (Field Notes, Puerto Ayora, September 2017).

After saying this, he argued that *colonos* do deserve the respect of all
newcomers because "they cried and died for all Ecuadorians! . . . Thanks to
them we are here," he added. Yet he was very clear to state that to complain
about the loss of "*colono*" status was an unacceptable claim because this
is a "special province." In saying this, the GGC official explicitly used the
language of (conservation) law to justify the need for a unique governance to
administer this property. He argued these islands are "special" because they
are "a paradise" due to their natural beauty and endemic fauna, and because
of their relative lack of crime compared to the mainland. He also talked about
the need to take care of this "special place" "because it is the patrimony of
mankind" and, at the same time, the "hen with the golden eggs for Ecuador."
However, none of his arguments pointed at evolutionary theories, Darwin, or
the need to turn the Galápagos into his living memorial.

Throughout his speech, he made very clear that disobedience of the Galápagos law was punished with expulsion. This could happen in the case that the
visitor exceeds the time limit allowed or if he or she behaves in an inappropri-
ate way during the stay. "This could even happen," he said, "to people born in
the Galápagos, permanent residents, or people who had married them." Then
he started to list the sanctions and penalties for offences that only apply in
the Galápagos province, starting with the fines imposed on people who stay
illegally, the prohibition on their relatives traveling to the islands, and penalties for permanent residents who hire illegals or rent them a place on their
properties. He went on to the list of actions that would result in fines, which
included: visiting a site within the protected area without the company of a
certified naturalist guide; being at the beaches nearby Puerto Ayora (at the
Darwin station or Tortuga Bay) past the established hours; touching native
species or getting too close; not building a proper enclosure to prevent pets
from leaving private property; throwing garbage in a neighbor's container;
bringing banned products to the islands; or injuring an endemic animal, even
if unintentionally. (See, for example, figure 5.5 below.)

In spite of the controversies, there is an overall consensus among locals
on the importance of conservation and tourism for the archipelago. It thus
demonstrates the existence of a hegemonic order which, in Gramsci's terms,
is linked to the establishment of an ideology and a morality that is perceived
as necessary and becomes part of common sense. In the Galápagos, this hegemony has been established through laws, penalties, education, rumors, and
fears surrounding the possible removal of people from the Galápagos. It was

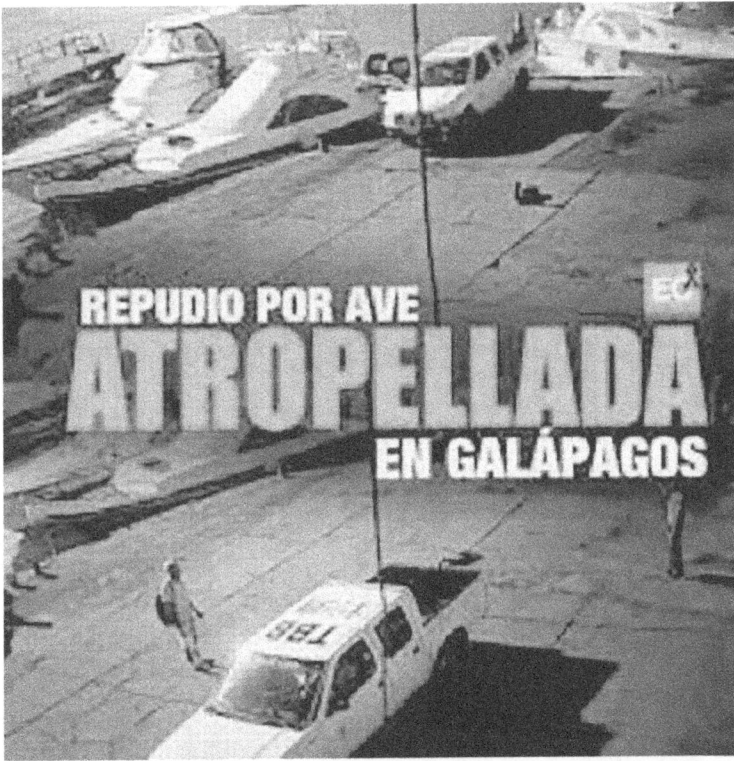

Figure 5.5.   Pelican hit by a car. A great controversy was sparked when a taxi driver ran over a pelican in Puerto Ayora. The local driver was fined US $6,382 and 100 hours of community service work. Yet on the streets, locals discussed it as an accident that could happen at any time because endemic species cohabit with people within the settlement areas. They thus point at the impossibility of drawing actual borders between humans and nonhumans in the Galápagos. *Source*: The title of this press report was "Repudiation for dead bird hit by a car in the Galápagos" (El Comercio, March 2019, elcomercio.com).

further endorsed through the deployment of extensive eradication campaigns of invasive species, as I will describe in the chapter that follows.

However, to achieve hegemony, following Merry (1986), does not necessarily mean full acceptance or a coherent process of legal reasoning. It instead reflects structures of political and economic power inflicted upon people in subordinate positions. Accordingly, *galapagueños* seem to accept their residency status not because they consider the Special Law just or reasonable, but because they think there is no realistic alternative for them. They need tourist dollars and they also appreciate and want to take care of the unique features of the natural environment in which they live. They also depend on the drinking water and the food provided by the Ecuadorian mainland. At the same time, it seems that many locals think they are actually part of the collective who owns and cares for the property even though they cannot enjoy the natural park or profit from it. Apparently, as in the earlier times of the *hacienda*, many *galapagueños* believe they are allowed to live and work on a small portion of land within a large property that is owned by a white landlord, thus being forced to accept differential access to rights, citizenship, and profits.

NOTES

1. In the Galápagos, before the passing of the 1998 "Special Law," "*colono*" was used both colloquially on the islands and officially (by the Ecuadorian state) to regard all first settlers of the archipelago and their descendants.

2. In 2007, the INGALA estimated that seven thousand people lived illegally on the Galápagos Islands. Only three thousand Salasacas (legal and illegal) live in the archipelago.

3. People often mention this sanction and threaten to use it against others. They say this may happen, for example, when the resident enters into a fake marriage with an "*afuereño*" (outsider) to give him or her legal residency in exchange for monetary compensation.

4. A recent study found that the biggest source of water contamination is the lack of a sewage system and a wastewater treatment plant as well as the discharge of waste from ships (Orbe 2019). As a result, the sources of water have a high degree of salinity and turbidity and a strong presence of coliform bacteria.

5. Making a list of introduced and invasive species is complicated by the fact that there are new species of insects and microorganisms that have still not been identified; the classification of around fifty plant species is still imprecise (insofar as it has not yet been determined whether they are native or introduced); and a gap in the data provided by the quarantine and biosecurity control system of the Galápagos Islands (Toral-Granda et al. 2017).

6. Jaramillo (et.al. 2017) suggested that learning from the body of local agricultural knowledge would be important for making the islands more self-sufficient. It is also acknowledged that more care should be taken to reduce the importation of products from the mainland, which contain invasive species (Chiriboga et.al. 2006).

7. Although no humans had permanently settled in the Galápagos before Berlanga's visit, the islands were a fishing site and a popular stopover for pre-Hispanic people, including explorers, traders, and fishermen from the coast of present-day Ecuador.

8. When the conservation movement emerged, demographic control was one of its aims. Furthermore, eugenics (the program to "improve" human race through controlled breeding) flourished simultaneously from 1890 to 1930 in the United States

and Western Europe. They were "two sides of the same coin" as Madison Grant put it when explaining it to paleontologist Henry Fairfield Osborn (Spiro 2008, xiii).

9. Grant was also the founder of the Society of Colonial Wars in the United States. He played an active role in crafting strong immigration restriction and anti-miscegenation laws in the United States, based on his book, *The Passing of the Great Race*.

10. For example, Vincent Astor, William Vanderbilt, Kermit Roosevelt, Templeton Crocker, G. Allan Hancock, Harrison Williams, Gifford Pinchot, and Franklin Delano Roosevelt.

11. The law also included controls on fishing, agriculture, cattle raising activities, and waste management.

12. In the following decades, some locals (together with foreigners and Ecuadorians from the mainland) began to build hotels for tourists who started to stay on land. Although this sector (hotels, restaurants, and stores) is growing (since 2009), it only accounts for 16 percent of tourism revenue on the archipelago (Epler 2007, 21).

13. Another 15 percent was designated to conservation institutions (the Marine Reserve, the National Protected Heritage Area, and the Quarantine System), and 5 percent to the National Navy.

14. See, for example, the Advisory Body Evaluation presented by the Charles Darwin Station (CDS) to the World Heritage Nomination committee in 2001. Through this document, the CDS requested the extension of the Galápagos National Park (GNP) to cover the marine environment. The inscription of the Marine Reserve was deferred conditional to the solution of a number of integrity problems.

15. To the state of Ecuador, since 1892, the official name of the Galápagos is: "Archipiélago de Colón" (Columbus Archipelago).

16. Currently, the governing council is trying to reduce the time allowed for tourist visits to thirty or even possibly fifteen days a year.

17. Throughout the eighteenth century in the Ambato region, Indigenous peoples continued to practice parallel descent in the transmission of surnames (Corr and Powers 2012, 21, Reino 2002, 106).

18. The crisis was the result of the government decision to freeze all bank accounts with more than $500 (USD) for a year in order to rescue the private banking industry from a crisis generated by their own failure to maintain liquidity. It led to the closing of sixteen banks (including the two largest) and the loss of the deposits of many Ecuadorians. A year after, the government announced that the US dollar would replace the *sucre* as the national currency.

19. The population of the archipelago rose from 15,311 inhabitants in 1998 to 23,046 in 2008.

20. Based on Malpezzi (2013), the Charles Darwin Foundation indicates that the population density in settlement areas of Santa Cruz Island registers values of 400 to 500 inhabitants per hectare, while in Hong Kong and Mumbai the values are 367 and 389, respectively.

21. 20 percent of the resources generated by the admission fees to the Park were then allocated to the GCG, while another 20 percent was left to the municipalities.

22. The "zero growth" policy was not implemented. In 2010, 25,124 people lived in the Galápagos. In 2018, almost 30,000 lived in the islands. The growth in tourists has been higher: while in 2010, 173,419 tourists visited; in 2018, 275,000 did. The 2017 UNESCO mission recalled the requests that were made to Ecuador in 2010 when the property was removed from the List of World Heritage in Danger. It urged the state party to comply with all its requests in order to maintain its heritage status.

23. As a result, fungal infections and intestinal parasites due to contaminated water are common illnesses in the archipelago (Walsh et al., 2010).

24. There is only one college, from a private university of Quito, that offers studies in biology, geography, and related subjects for its students on San Cristóbal Island. There are two private libraries on the islands, owned by the Darwin station and the Tomás de Berlanga School.

25. Temporary residency permits are issued for the duration of a work contract (mine was a volunteer agreement with the Tomás de Berlanga School). According to the 2015 reform, temporary residency permits can be renewed for a maximum period of five years. They are not a path to get a permanent residency permit.

Chapter Six

Translating Conservation Law

On the day Víctor arrived in the Galápagos, he felt hopeful.[1] He had left his hometown, Salasaca (Tungurahua), that dawn to take a bus that a few hours later left him at the airport in Quito, where he boarded a plane for the first time in his life. He had been thinking about leaving Salasaca for some time. For years, he had tried to pay off his debts. The most onerous was one he had acquired with a close relative to buy a truck with which he and his wife Sonia hauled gravel from a mine near Salasaca. The venture did not prosper and as the months passed, the debt only grew. There were no jobs in the town and the food he grew in his *chacra* was not enough to feed his family. To migrate to the Galápagos Islands seemed like the most feasible option, since relatives, acquaintances, and *paisanos* of his (fellow Salasacas) had found well-paying jobs there.[2] At the very least, if earning the minimum wage in the Galápagos, he would receive more than twice the dollars paid in the mainland. Borrowing money once again, he thus decided to buy a plane ticket to fly to the archipelago in May 2017. The day of his flight, he wore his Salasaca outfit: his finest *poncho*, pants, and a white linen shirt. His suitcase was nearly full with a mosquito net, a large blanket, and a sheet in which he wrapped green peas, beans, maize, and other grains.

Nearly a year before, I had met Víctor and his family during my stay in Salasaca (Tungurahua). His wife and children accompanied me when I visited and interviewed Salasaca *colonos* (first settlers) of the Galápagos Islands who had returned to spend their final years in their hometown. It was then that I learned of Víctor's intention to migrate to the islands. During that time, I also became aware of how he and his family took pride in their people and, particularly, in their distinctive ethnic dress. They told me about how they made Víctor's *poncho*, made of fine wool, which Sonia had patiently shorn from sheep they raised themselves. Some relatives who still worked with their traditional looms then wove it. On the day the cloth was ready, his extended family decided to commemorate the traditional ritual that celebrates the moment when the cloth is finished. For two days, they shared a feast of *cuyes* (guinea pigs), roasted potatoes, and chicken soup, enlivened by toasts with *chicha* (corn beer), while the cloth was soaked in boiling water. After that, a group of men dancing with small, rhythmic steps stamped on the *poncho* until it acquired the right fineness and thickness. Finally, Víctor received what became his most precious *poncho*.

One of the things that most surprised Víctor and made him laugh was the way *mestizos* had no idea of the value of the Salasaca textiles and garments. Once he told me: "the thieves who come here to rob us are *mestizos* and idiots! Imagine! They steal our television set and cell phone, but they don't steal these clothes, which are the finest things we have."

A few weeks later, I was able to confirm what he had told me when we were all called to attend an Indigenous trial organized to clear up the theft of several *ponchos* from one of the few families of traditional weavers in Salasaca (Tungurahua). The victims had to consult a local shaman to find the guilty person. They found that a youngster had stolen the *ponchos,* which were being offered for sale by some stallholders in the Ambato marketplace. They were all judged on that day. In the middle of the trial, a Salasaca man in the audience tried to defend the marketplace sellers, arguing that they might have been deceived as well. The lieutenant (*teniente politico*) then shouted at him: "I don't know what your store in the Galápagos is like. But here, we know when a theft is involved and we punish the thieves!" Then he asked the youngster to explain himself. In tears, the culprit confessed that he had stolen the *ponchos*. In front of all the inhabitants of the town, the repentant youngster swore that he would never do it again and asked to be forgiven. Martha Chango, the town councilor and my hostess in Salasaca, then climbed onto the platform. She ordered the young man to make a public apology to the community and his mother and then, in front of the audience, he reconciled with his family. The lieutenant, however, replied that it was not a minor crime, since each of the seven stolen *ponchos* might be worth one thousand dollars. He then ordered him to take off his clothes and several men, along with his mother, slowly scourged him with clusters of stinging nettle. In addition to this act of purification and reconciliation, the youngster—along with the stallholders—were ordered to clean the cemetery on the mountain of Cruzpamba in the following days.

The following May, Víctor traveled to the Galápagos. He was wearing his Salasaca clothing, expecting to meet all his acquaintances there. But as soon as he arrived on Santa Cruz, he noticed that everything was different in the islands. He saw familiar faces during the ferry and bus ride from the airport on Baltra Island to Puerto Ayora (the capital of Santa Cruz). There were even more when he got off at the first stop alongside the marketplace, and walked through the neighborhoods of Miraflores and La Cascada. But he noted that he was the only one dressed in Salasaca attire. All of his *paisanos* (fellow *Salasacas*) were instead dressed as *cholos* on the island.

Figure 6.1.   Indigenous trial at Salasaca. All of the members of the Salasaca community attended the trial. There were some mestizos present: the policeman who is sending text messages (on the left), alongside a mestizo from the coast who was also accused of theft that day. On the right, seated, there is a reporter from an Ecuadorian newspaper. *Source*: Photo: P. Sánchez, Salasaca, Tungurahua, December 2016.

Despite the heat, Víctor kept his *poncho* until he reached his cousin's home in Miraflores. When he got there, he gave her the grains he had brought from his hometown so that she would cook them for him during the following days. A few hours later, he walked to the small beach by the Darwin station. It was there that we met.

Víctor told me about his plans that day. He planned to remain on Santa Cruz for a few months and await his wife Sonia, who would follow him with the idea of working as a domestic servant in the island. Thus, they would jointly save money and return quickly to pay off the family debt and join their two children in Salasaca. I then offered Víctor a job of translating from Kichwa to Spanish some audio files and interviews I had recorded during my research while he was looking for work on the island. To accomplish that, we met up several times in the course of the following months. It was then that he told me about his impressions upon arriving in the Galápagos:

I came from Salasaca dressed like that. But, here, people aren't proud of being *Salasacas* . . . They give you a funny look! Everyone, even the members of my family, looked at me as if I was strange, as if they were thinking: "What are you doing dressed like that? Do you think you are royalty?"
(Puerto Ayora, May 2017).

He first imagined that his *paisanos* thought he was arrogant for wearing his Salasaca dress on the island. A few days later, he told me he found strange the way they looked at him, like a "weirdo." He thought it was not right that they all felt "ashamed" of being *Salasacas*. Some weeks later, however, he added that he preferred to prevent being harassed by *mestizos* and by immigration authorities. Within a short time, Víctor too decided it was better to leave his *poncho*, trousers, and white shirt in the room he was renting in La Cascada neighborhood.

Meanwhile, during that time at nights and during the weekends, I was getting together with a group of Salasaca *colonos* (legal "permanent residents" on the islands) who often wore their Salasaca ethnic dress at meetings held

Figure 6.2. Víctor (pseudonym) at the Charles Darwin Station beach. Source: Photo: P. Sánchez, Puerto Ayora (Galápagos), May 2017

in the community center of the association. By then, at a distance of a block in the Miraflores neighborhood, I could spot the difference between two spaces that are distinguished as used almost exclusively by the Salasaca people of Santa Cruz Island. The first, the Salasaca Association, is the place where Indigenous *colonos* "feel free" and affirm their ethnic affiliation on the island. The second, the soccer stadium—in which all *Salasacas* meet dressed as *cholos*—is a space devoted to their cultural "whitening." Other than Margarita Masaquiza (president of the association) and a few other Salasaca leaders within the collective, the Salasaca people in the Galápagos shed their ethnic identity in public. Víctor himself never went to the community center (of the association) during the months he spent in the Galápagos. Instead, he preferred to spend his free time with friends at the soccer stadium.[3]

It was not only how they dress. For Víctor, everything was very different in the Galápagos. He couldn't believe that he had to buy bottles and containers of potable water to drink and cook with. In addition, he was amazed by the high prices charged for rice, vegetables, and potatoes in the marketplace. It further struck him that *Salasacas* behaved in such a different manner from the way they did at home in Tungurahua. On Santa Cruz, they dressed like *mestizos*, spoke very little Kichwa, and did not celebrate their ritual *fiestas*. Within a short time, the conversations he had and the rumors he heard also confirmed what he had been told before: "there is no respect on the islands." The children of the *Salasacas* seemed more rebellious. They did not obey their parents nor respect the elders of the community. Those who had been born on the island did not speak Kichwa, didn't like to wear their ethnic dress, and had children of their own while they were still adolescents. What was more, the women on the island were "divorcees" (*divorciadoras*), which—in Salasaca—would mean that they and their children were excluded and stigmatized. In general, Víctor thought that life on the archipelago changed the moral outlook of people: "They come here to earn a bit of money . . . But later, they want more and more. It is not that they don't have any; they always want more," he told me, disillusioned.

The worst of it was that after nearly two months in Puerto Ayora, Víctor still hadn't found a steady job. Day after day, he rose early, got dressed, and went to the marketplace of Miraflores, where he'd stand on a corner and, along with a number of other Salasaca men, wait around for an offer of work. When they were lucky, a pickup truck would stop and take the men to a building site where they could earn a day's wage. One day, a truck finally picked him up as well, and took him to the house of a woman who needed some repairs done. After working at that for several hours, the woman suddenly left her home and told the men who were working: "I have some urgent business in Quito. I have to leave at once." And thus without a further word, she went to the airport without paying them.

There was also the fear of being detained in one of the raids undertaken by the Galápagos Government Council (GGC). Víctor knew of the white pickup trucks (which look like regular taxis) that prowl around the marketplace in search of illegals.[4] Every day he and other Salasaca men tried to keep a close watch on the street in case one of the GGC pickup trucks appeared.

Things became even more complicated for Víctor in those days after his wife was denied permission to visit the archipelago. When Sonia arrived at the airport in Quito, the officials there told her that the authorities of the

Government Council had prohibited her from boarding the plane to the Ga-lápagos on the grounds that one of her relatives was an "illegal immigrant." "Until he leaves, you do not enter!" they told her on the day of her flight. She therefore had to go back and remain in Salasaca. Meanwhile on Santa Cruz, Víctor learned that he was already under vigilance of conservation law enforcement authorities on the island.

During his third month in Santa Cruz, Víctor's luck finally changed. He found a job and began to adapt to island life. He worked first on a building site and later, loading cargo onto a tourist cruise ship. He also made two friends with whom he often met up near Miraflores Stadium. He especially enjoyed playing soccer on the team which represents his community in the highlands in the competition for the Salasaca Cup on the island.[5] He spent the following two months that way.

Suddenly in October, I learned that Víctor had been deported from the Galápagos. One day I met the woman who was renting him a room in La Cascada. She told me she hadn't seen Víctor for two days. "His things were left there, alongside the portable stovetop we lent him . . . He didn't even

Figure 6.3. "Illegals" in the market. This photo was taken by a *galapagueño* who denounced these men on Facebook for being outside trying to find work, in the times of Covid-19. They all come from the highlands, mainly from Salasaca. People in the Galápagos say that *mestizos* from the coast of the mainland do not like to work in construction or are not good at it. *Source*: Photo: P. Sánchez, Puerto Ayora, Santa Cruz, Galápagos, February 2019.

take the little he had brought," the woman told me. Indeed, two days before, Víctor was picked up in a raid while he was walking through the Miraflores marketplace. According to what he told me later, a group of four officials, accompanied by the same number of policemen, stopped him and asked for his residence permit. Since he didn't have papers, he was immediately taken to the airport on Baltra. Twenty people who had also been detained, almost all of Salasaca origin, were on the same flight to the mainland. None had been able to collect their clothing or personal possessions. Everything that Víctor had brought with him from the mainland, including his *poncho*, was left behind in his rented room.[6] The worst of it was that when he returned to Salasaca, Víctor did not have enough money to pay off his debt, which was the very reason he'd gone to the Galápagos Islands.

In the course of my stay in the archipelago, I never heard the conservationists speak of the Salasaca Indigenous people as transgressors of conservation law or as the target group of population controls in the archipelago. They instead proposed that demographic control should be aimed at any Ecuadorian migrants who were in the Galápagos illegally without a residence permit, regardless of his or her ethnic or racial identity. Yet law enforcement officers of the Galápagos Government Council (GGC) primarily targeted Indigenous illegal migrants in their raids, mainly *Salasacas*.

This was one of the critical issues that was discussed at a meeting that was held in July 2017 between members of the Salasaca Association (who are legal permanent residents) and representatives of the national government. On that day we were all dressed in Salasaca attire, expecting to meet Lorena Tapia, the new governor of the Galápagos (or minister of the GGC), who had been recently appointed to the position after Lenín Moreno took office as President of Ecuador (May 2017). Although Tapia didn't show up, a group of *mestizo* bureaucrats were there at the Salasaca Association to represent her. Jose María Masaquiza (JM) opened the meeting speaking to Leonardo Morena (LM) the zonal coordinator:

JM: "The Indigenous Salasaca come to the Galápagos to work. They don't come here on vacation . . . But in every raid, most of the deportees are *Salasacas*. . . . There are so many [*mestizo*] illegals on the streets, on the beach, young people, at nightclubs, everywhere. They are not working. But the Indigenous people who come to work, they are the ones who are being caught by the Government Council."

LM then replied:

LM: "I am going to explain something to you. Here we have a law, a special regime. The fewer inhabitants we have, the better . . . It is not right if they are only kicking you out. Everybody who is illegal on the islands must go."

Somebody from the audience exclaimed:

"But they detain only Indigenous people!"

LM: "It would be better if all humans were out . . . Now there is this problem with local people. You come to a place with a special regime, but then you think you are the 'special' part of it. The territory is special, not you! It is the territory that is special! . . .

People who come from the highlands and remain hidden to earn some money . . . They don't understand that this regime's goal is the conservation of nature. They are not the ones who were summoned for that purpose."

Andrés Pilla, a Salasaca *colono* in the audience, intervened:

AP: "This affects me. Even though I am a permanent resident, every time that I am there, in the street, talking to some three or four friends, these officers always stop to interrogate us . . . Can you explain why do they detain only Kichwa speakers? . . . Where are the blacks? The *mestizos* who are also illegal? Where? Not a single *mestizo* is caught in those raids! . . . The *Salasacas* who were recently detained were left there, two days, with no food, until they took them to the continent. Are the *Salasacas* the only ones who should leave?"

LM: "I will share this with other authorities . . . But think about it . . . You have to start protecting yourselves too. For example, you! You don't want those illegals to take your job in construction! . . .

"I will organize a big raid, a massive one, all sorts of people, so that everybody notices it. 500 people out of the Galápagos."
(Puerto Ayora, July 2017).

In that meeting, the Salasaca *colonos* also asked the government to give the Indigenous legal residents access to formal jobs on the archipelago. Most of these jobs are given to *mestizos* from the mainland to whom local authorities issue temporary residency permits. In so doing, both local employers and authorities promote *mestizo* migration from mainland. Often they justify this hiring because most Galápagos locals lack a college education. However, investment in education is very limited and there are no universities in the archipelago. [7]

At the same time, temporary residency permits are only available for migrants who sign work contracts, thus leaving out all those who migrate to work in the informal sector (like the *Salasacas*). Yet out of all illegals, local authorities mainly target Indigenous Salasaca migrants for deportation in compliance with population controls linked to conservation policy. How did the Salasaca people become the main target of the raids undertaken by the Galápagos Government Council?

SCIENCE AND HACIENDA MEET
IN DARWIN'S ARCHIPELAGO

Social order in the Galápagos Islands is informed by two different racialized property regimes: the *hacienda* system and the rule of conservation. The first is reflected in the occurrence of oppressive forms of racism which directly target Salasaca people. It is also informed by a system of property by which Indigenous people are supposed to have usage rights to the land (to work and pay tributes attached to a *hacienda*), but no right to profit from the landlord's property. Under this regime, ownership for Indigenous peoples is limited to the holding of *chacras* (small plots of lands) or to communal lands in the highlands. For a long time, access to property and citizenship rights in Ecuador was contingent on race and on the ability of some to climb the social ladder by undergoing a process of cultural "whitening" that allows Indigenous individuals to pass as *mestizos, cholos* (urban *Indios* or recently made *mestizos*). In this way, they can get closer to the state-sponsored homogeneous ideal of the "Ecuadorian citizen" (Whitten 1981, 12–13). For the *Salasacas* in the Galápagos, this process of whitening alternates with the re-indigenization of some, which works as a deliberate political strategy for demanding rights from the Ecuadorian state.

In turn, conservation rule is expressed in the pervasive climate of insecurity and anxiety amongst locals who feel they constantly need to affirm their right to live and belong on the Galápagos. This is because ever since conservation law transformed all *galapagueños* into aliens in their territory, membership in the archipelago became seriously challenged. Although locals constantly discuss who has more of a right to the archipelago—drawing on dominant ideology—they tend to agree with the scientists that "the only owners of the Galápagos are the giant tortoises," as I frequently heard. Such reasoning only serves to justify the rights of white conservationists, since they alone are qualified to care for the endemic tortoises after which the archipelago was named. This rationale is only the continuation of a long history of scientific imperialism based on the old maxim that scientific knowledge provides the most rational use of resources (Worster 1994, Drayton 2000), hence justifying colonial governance claims over "protected areas" in foreign territories.

Science and the *hacienda* meet in the Galápagos to govern local society. These two normative systems organized a racialized division of labor with differential access to citizenship and property rights. By tracing the practices entailed in conservation work, I will show how these frameworks are capable of transforming subjectivities, leading to cultural change at the local level, as the transplantation of law in other colonizing projects illuminates (see Merry 2000, Cohn 1996).

Racial Politics in the Ecuadorian Archipelago

Although *mestizos* today don't shout at *Salasacas* to "speak Christian [Spanish]" on the streets, in Puerto Ayora schools, new labels have become terms of insult against people with Indigenous origins in the archipelago. When I asked about the Salasaca people on the islands, a *mestiza* woman in Puerto Ayora referred to them as follows:

> The *Salasacas* are intruders, predators . . . they are not even Ecuadorians, they're from Bolivia. Here, in Puerto Ayora, it is as though they defy the law . . . . In Tungurahua, they dress as *Salasacas*. But here they wear their hair as they want, they change their clothes.
>   People don't like them, they discriminate against them, they ignore them at the hospital, they do not give them an appointment [with the doctors].
>   (Interview, Puerto Ayora, June 2016).

At the market, another *mestizo,* a native of the Galápagos, told me, "once there were only *galapagueños* here, now the place is full of those dirty people from the highlands" (Puerto Ayora, May 2017).[8] A few months later, the same person advised me to "put more of distance between yourself and those [the Salasaca] people . . . they are drunks, they wake up sprawled on the pavement . . . they beat their wives, they're savages." (Puerto Ayora, October, 2017).[9]

Every time *mestizos* speak in such terms of the *Salasacas* on the island, they assign them a lower (and less civilized) status, while also asserting that they arrived later than themselves and do not belong to the society of the Galápagos, hence, "they are intruders" on the archipelago. Moreover, they point to the origin story of the Salasaca people to argue that, as descendants of *mitimaes* from Bolivia, they are in reality outsiders not only in the archipelago but also within the Ecuadorian state.

Other *mestizos* instead acknowledge that *Salasacas* are hardworking people and united, even if they keep to themselves. Nevertheless, there is a generalized image which holds that the Indigenous people belong to and should stay in the highlands, far from a society that aims to identify itself as made up of *costeños* (coast-dwellers) who are supposed to be whiter and more civilized than Andean highlanders. They thus think that *Salasacas* should remain in their homeland, in Tungurahua, where they can live in accordance with their own "law," as whites and *mestizos* like to imagine it (tied to their land, community and ethnic dress).

In the upperpart of the local hierarchy are the wealthiest *mestizos* of Santa Cruz, who can participate in big business ventures or hold key posts in conservation agencies and state bureaucracy. This group identifies themselves as "whites" or "white-*mestizos*" ("*blanco-mestizos*"), thus locating them close to or at the same level as foreign conservationists and visitors to the archipelago. In contrast, the *Salasacas* are placed in the lowest part of the social hierarchy where they are labeled as "intruders," "savages," and "predators"; in other words, presumably harmful to Galápagos nature. Paradoxically, re-search from the Darwin station on the ecological impact of different human groups on Santa Cruz Island found that the *Salasacas* "display a behavior that is much more adjusted to the environment" compared to that of the "non-*Salasacas*" (Vervloet 2013, 15–18).[10] This is because most walk or ride on a bicycle to the places where they work, use fewer motorized vehicles, share a small living space with their whole families, usually lack air conditioning, and are more prone to save money than act as heavy consumers. Moreover, the work done by the Indigenous population is indispensable for the conser-vation of nature in the archipelago.

Salasaca Labor

Since the beginning of colonization of the Galápagos, through the *haciendas*, a racialized division of labor assigned manual labor and the harshest and least remunerative activities on the islands to Indigenous laborers. "Original" or pioneer families have come from those laborers who were forcibly recruited to work in agricultural and cattle production and artisanal work. Likewise, on present-day Santa Cruz, the Salasaca people are integrated—in a marginal position—into settler society through labor-intensive activities. Whereas most of the Salasaca men became responsible for street cleaning, garbage col-lection, and the informal construction sector, the majority of Salasaca women came to be in charge of laundering clothes and cleaning the premises of the institutions and homes of *mestizos* and the foreigners in the Galápagos.

Traditionally, according to the *hacienda* order, these jobs did not entitle nationals to citizenship in Ecuador. As it was initially conceived, citizenship required nationals of the country to be married, be at least age twenty-two, own private property, be literate, and engage in "useful" professions, thus explicitly excluding domestic servants and day laborers from acquiring full rights (Clark and Becker 2007, 9).[11] Although these are not required anymore, people engaged in such activities are perceived as second-class citizens. In turn, garbage collection is often the work of Indigenous people, displaced persons, or minority groups, which continue to be marked as isolated or mar-ginal, thus reinforcing their lower social status.

Nonetheless, the work of the Salasaca men is critical in making a "natural" landscape that must appear untouched by people to visitors. For them, the municipality of Santa Cruz continues to offer jobs in the garbage collection and recycling department. This is one of the few sources that they have to formal employment.

Figure 6.4. Municipal employees. *Source*: **Photo: Decentralized Autonomous Municipal of Santa Cruz (GADMSC).**

Day by day, the *municipales* collect the garbage of locals and tourists in the Galápagos. The garbage left by tourism ships is taken by barges to the port. On land, the municipality's garbage trucks receive the waste of tourists, and then pick up the waste of locals in the hospital, in the neighborhoods of Puerto Ayora, and in others on the upperpart of the island (like Bellavista, Santa Rosa, and El Cascajo). Finally, they collect the garbage left by the big ships on the far north of Santa Cruz. All this goes to the Fabricio Valverde plant, where the *municipales* separate it and compact it. Part of the solid waste is then deposited in the sanitary landfill of the island, while another part is recycled and put into containers, which are then loaded onto ships that transport them to the Ecuadorian mainland.[12]

On the other hand, both Salasaca men and women are engaged in activities related to food supply, transport, cargo, and logistics for the tourism sector. Their work thus allows for the generation of tourism revenues that are central to the economy of the archipelago. Furthermore, part of these profits ends up being donated to conservation agencies. In so doing, the *Salasacas* play a crucial role in the "backstage" (Goffman 1959) of conservation and tourism on the archipelago. There, the *Salasacas* and their labor are invisible to eco-tourists and naturalist guides who act, on center stage, as the people who care the most about Galápagos' nature.

A Space of Negation

After migrating to the Galápagos, Salasaca people are forced to occupy a space of negation wherein they must undergo a process of "whitening." In this process, the Salasaca *colonos* (first settlers) of Santa Cruz not only had to hide markers of indigeneity—including language, customs, traditional clothing, decoration, and grooming practices—they also had to build a community center in order to hold wakes for their dead on the island and assist their families (so they could receive the deceased in their homeland in Salasaca [Tungurahua]), as well as a separate elementary school free from racism and racial discrimination (it now also receives *mestizo* students). Furthermore, they had to speak in Spanish ("Christian") as the *mestizo* settlers often demanded, echoing the Spanish imposition by which *conquistadores* required natives to speak their language in order to teach them "the word" of their god.

Today, Salasaca new migrants continue to shed their ethnic identity while also claiming to "feel ashamed" of being Indigenous or simply opting for a silent strategy of ethnic declassification in the archipelago. For example, it is frequent today to come across people in Puerto Ayora whose surname is Masaquiza but deny their Salasaca origin, claiming they rather come from the *mestizo* cities of Ambato, Pelileo, or Quito.[13] In such way, they attempt to become more white and more urban—in short, more fit to become members of *galapagueño* society. Even so, on the islands, they are relegated to occupy a zone of "cultural invisibility," in Rosaldo's words, in which immigrants and socially mobile individuals "appear invisible because they were no longer what they once were and not yet what they could become" (1993[1989], 209).

Meanwhile, most of the sons and daughters of Salasaca parents who were born in the Galápagos adopt a *mestizo* or *galapagueño* identity. They speak with a coastal accent, are more outgoing than the stereotyped Indigenous person, they dance *salsa* instead of Peruvian *cumbia,* and prefer eating *encebollado* (fish soup) rather than *cuy* (guinea pig) or *guatita* (beef stripe stew), which are typical of the highlands. Moreover, they claim they are *"mestizos"* even though they have Indigenous parents. This is troubling for some Salasaca parents, as a friend of mine told me. She said she was worried about her daughter's determination to see herself as a *mestiza.* "I rebuke her . . . I tell her: you are an Indigenous person and should be proud of being one." However, her daughter answers back: "No, I am a *mestiza* because I was born in the Galápagos," as she described the situation. Probably, by enacting a *mestizo* identity, her daughter could become identified by others as a *"chola,"* acknowledging her progress in becoming more white on the island. In doing so, she gets closer to become recognized as a *galapagueña.* Conversely, if she had chosen to maintain the ethnic markers of her Salasaca descent, she would have to face greater discrimination on an everyday basis in the Galápagos.

Ironically, as *mestizos* judge or discriminate, they also deny and despise their obvious Indigenous ancestry. The aspiration to become more white is expressed in the practice of silencing Indigenous pasts that start in one's own family and then extend to society to the point of shaping the production of history. In the Galápagos, the conservationist project that aims to erase human pasts and presence in the archipelago overlaps with the local project of the white *mestizo* elite to "purify" and "sanitize" their country by whitening it. This not only defines the production of history and *galapagueño* identity but also the policy of deportation in the Galápagos.

Conservation Work

To belong or not belong to the Galápagos is the subject of heated disputes among local people. On the islands, *galapagueños* seem to agree that membership and rights are proportional to the years of hard work, suffering, and isolation involved in the initial settling of the islands. They thus think that the pioneering families belong to the Galápagos and have the most rights on the islands. However, by removing vernacular categories like "*colonos*" from colloquial use and from the legal framework, conservation law refuted local notions of membership.

New migrants often ignore these histories. Their concern is centered instead on claiming their rights, as Ecuadorian citizens, to live and work in the Galápagos. When discussing which groups of humans belong to the Galápagos, locals tend to use conservationist arguments and borrowings from the scientific lexicon. They settle in the end on appealing to the moral authority of conservationism, which led them to their own confinement and separation from Galápagos nature. By tracing the most emblematic conservation campaigns, I examine the way conservation science frames membership to the archipelago and how this definition permeates cultural life in the Galápagos.

Protected Species: Pure vs. Hybrid

Conservation work in the Galápagos began with a survey of all nonhuman species and their classification as endemic, introduced, or invasive. Scientists then ascribed them value based on the the attribution of endemism and specificity—closely attached to evolutionary ecology thinking (Choy 2011, Chernela 2012). They thus agreed on the appropriate scheme for their management, involving the reproduction, control, or extermination of each species.[14] Within this hierarchy, the iconic tortoises of the Galápagos are of high conservation value. First, because of their pre-historic bodies (which can be traced back 250 million years ago to the age of the dinosaurs, at the end of the Triassic Period), capable of transporting tourists to another time and place—to an untouched, pre-human, pristine kind of "Eden."[15] The Galápagos species are one of only two remaining lineages whose ancestors are thought to have floated out on the sea currents until arriving in the archipelago at least two million years ago. Once there, far from their parent population and in the absence of predators, the tortoises evolved into fifteen autochthonous species, each on different islands. Mayr (1942) calls this sort of genetic drift the "founder effect."[16]

The value of the giant tortoises is further heightened by the place they occupy in the evolutionary landscape of the Galápagos. This is because evolutionary processes can only be observed if each species (or "race") of tortoises is correctly placed on its ancestral island, and if the purity of their lineages there is preserved. Then scientists can recreate the landscape which inspired Darwin—where evolution was "discovered"—and where modern science found a place to locate its origin.

Caring for Galápagos tortoises therefore aims to protect the racial purity of the ancestral species, which includes: the selective reproduction of endemic species at in situ centers; the repatriation of tortoises which are bred in captivity to their island of origin; and their isolation in order to conserve the pure lineages of the Galápagos.

Following Hennessy (2014), the management of hybrid tortoises is the most problematic. They not only trigger the Western historical fear of degeneration, of which ideas of human "race suicide" form a part (Spiro 2008) but they also disrupt existing categorizations.[17] Western obsession with racial purity can be traced back to naturalists of the Victorian age who thought that border-crossing species should be forbidden "by divine or natural law to produce further offspring" (Ritvo 1997, 90). These anxieties further extended to policymaking, justifying eugenics, and restrictive immigration policies in the early twentieth-century United States. In the Galápagos, they also shaped classificatory and curatorial practices, the administration of human and non-human populations, and conservation campaigns in the archipelago.

Although at first sight the hybrid tortoises are as charismatic as the purebred ones, they threaten racial purity while unveiling histories of human translocation (Caccone et al. 2012, 2018). In so doing, they point to a non-natural evolutionary occurrence within the "natural park."[18] Efforts to control hybrids in the Galápagos are therefore mainly directed towards sterilization. And yet over the past decade, the utility of hybrids on the islands has been reassessed. "Alien" tortoises are now being used as "ecological engineers," capable of restoring keystone plant species throughout different islands (Gibbs et.al. 2010, Hunter and Gibbs 2014), and might even be the living hope to resuscitate imperiled species of tortoises through back-breeding techniques (Garrick et al. 2012), even if contrary to evolutionary processes.[19] All in all, from the conservationist perspective, full membership to the archipelago is restricted to species belonging to the ancestral lineages that have inhabited the islands for several million years. The conservationist time frame is thus set to include nonhumans only, specifically those that are capable of demonstrating evidence of evolutionary processes during their existence in the Galápagos.

Eradication of Invasive Species

It was clear for scientists that invasive species in the Galápagos should be completely exterminated because they compete with or predate on native populations. As a result, since the Darwin station and the Galápagos National Park began operations, the largest share of their resources was allocated to the implementation of campaigns to massively eradicate goats, pigs, dogs, and donkeys on the islands. As such, the job of caring as Puig de la Bellacasa (2012, 197) notes is, at once, "a vital affective state, an ethical obligation, and a practical labour that, nonetheless, does not guarantee a harmonious world." On the islands, caring for the giant tortoises entailed the use of violent means implicit not only in the eradication of rival species, but also in breeding the protected ones in captivity and in techniques to force their reproduction (Constantino 2007, Hennessy 2013, Bocci 2017).

So far, for the scientific community, the most ambitious campaign in the Galápagos is "Proyecto Isabela" (Isabela Project), which sacrificed more than 150,000 goats—by land and by air—between 1998 and 2006. More than 90 percent of the exterminated goats died during the initial stages, victims of aerial attacks by sharpshooters. To get rid of the rest, the campaign used: first, "Judas goats" released with radio collars, which would seek out a pack, leading hunters to group kills. Even more effective were the "Mata Hari" goats, sterilized females in chemically induced oestrous who lured the remaining male goats (see Bocci 2017).[20] Yet for the local population, this project did not take into account the waste of meat (since thousands of dead goats were thrown off cliffs into the ocean), or the excessive growth of the density of cacti, resulting in "thorns" that made some islands impenetrable post-eradication, as I was told by some of my interviewees.

Furthermore, *galapagueños* do not recall *Proyecto Isabela* as the conservationist campaign with the greatest impact in the archipelago. Whenever I asked locals about their knowledge of or relation with conservation work, they all referred instead to the eradication of dogs and cats within settlement areas. This task has been deployed through nocturnal campaigns in which officials of the Agency for the Regulation and Control of Bio-Security and Quarantines in the Galápagos (ABG) periodically threw poison mixed with ground glass to exterminate dogs and cats, which otherwise might eat the eggs or the babies of reptiles native to the Galápagos.[21]

The poisonings started in the 1970s when the station and the park engaged in the extermination of packs of feral dogs in different islands (see for examples, *Noticias de Galápagos* 1972–1980). But from the 1990s onwards, the practice was extended to dogs and cats in residential areas, including private properties.[22] All of those whom I interviewed lost at least one of their pets in such campaigns. One of them even felt a moral duty in line with the campaign, and took matters into his own hands after he found his son's pet with a dead iguana in its mouth. "I had to drown her . . . it was Paolo's cat but I had to do it, it was eating that little iguana," he told me (Interview, Puerto Ayora, September 2017). Those years were "the beginning of the period of repression" in the Galápagos, as one of the environmentalists I talked to called it (Interview, Puerto Ayora, August 2017). In that same decade, the park and the station were also drafting the Special Law for the Galápagos.

The poisoning of pets continues to this day. During my stay in Puerto Ayora, on two occasions, I observed protests of pet owners after their pets had been killed. An official of the municipality attributed these occurrences to a "crazy man" who had no authority to eradicate the animals (Interview, Puerto Ayora, July 2018). However, locals claim that officials of the Agency

Figure 6.5. Protests by pet owners. A few days before, their pets were poisoned during a nocturnal eradication campaign. They carried posters that said: "Yes to sterilization, no to mass killing," "I was condemned to a slow and painful death," and "We are not guilty of damage to the ecosystem." Puerto Ayora, Galápagos, July 2017. *Source*: Photo. P. Sánchez.

for the Regulation and Control of Bio-Security and Quarantines (ABG) in the Galápagos are behind these proceedings.

According to the logic of conservation, humans on the islands would fall in the category of "introduced" species—that is, non-native to the Galápagos. As in biology, some introduced species could be deemed beneficial, however, while others are detrimental to the endemic fauna. The latter are known as "invasive." Yet as Davis (2011) notes, scientific distinctions between the different categories ("native," "introduced," or "invasive") are often crisscrossed by cultural standards of belonging, citizenship, and morality, and by the blurred boundaries of the time frames which uphold them (Constantino 2007). Time frames are particularly troubling because, following Helmreich (2009, 257) in his study of microbial oceanography in Hawaii, "if you go back far enough everything is an introduction." This is the same argument that *galapagueños* use when discussing the rights of different human groups to the archipelago.

Moreover, *galapagueños* resort to the same categories of conservation to label different groups of people in the archipelago. From this perspective, the raids against "illegal" *Salasacas* might be seen as part of the "repression" and eradication campaigns that are promoted by the Darwin station, but enforced by local authorities (mainly the Galápagos Government Council) through their own understandings of race. Additional punitive actions (which include changing the legal status of local people and imposing more fines and sanctions on them) ultimately make clear that endemic nonhuman species are more valuable than humans on the archipelago, particularly those who do not belong to *galapagueño* society, nor are recognized as "full citizens" of the Ecuadorian state.

TRANSLATING CONSERVATION LAW

Conservation work in the Galápagos (with its classificatory practices, eradication efforts, and sanctions) have gradually shaped the moral sense of *galapagueños* to the extent that, today, they appropriate categories and arguments to use them in the course of their everyday discussions. I often heard and was told about verbal conflicts that followed a particular reasoning. For example, a taxi driver described to me how he had to defend his rights as a migrant with a client (a native *galapagueña*) who confronted him for being illegal on the island:

> They [the *galapagueños*] say that there is no room for us [the migrants]. I have lived here for the past ten years . . . And just because they've lived here a year more, they think they own the place!
>
> A lady one day told me: 'we are the owners because we got here first.'
> So, I answered: 'If anyone is the owner, it is the tortoises, *señora*!
> (Puerto Ayora, February 2018).

The reasoning in this conversation is a typical example of the arguments by which the inhabitants of the Galápagos defend their right to remain on the archipelago. The first point under discussion is how long the person has lived on the islands. Sometimes they also inquire if the person comes from a family of *colonos* (first settlers). In this case, the taxi driver was the son of a *galapagueño*, but had been born and raised "outside" in the city of Ambato on the mainland. To the woman in question, he was merely an "*afuereño*" (foreigner, from the continent). She thus resorted to the fact that she has lived on the archipelago for a longer time than the man. He, the taxi driver, finally ended the argument by saying that if you followed her reasoning to the end, then the tortoises would be the only owners of the archipelago because they arrived first.

I heard the same reasoning from Gaspar Masaquiza (a Salasaca *colono* and park ranger on Santa Cruz) when we were talking about the pioneers of the Galápagos. On that occasion, Gaspar told me: "the only owners of the islands are the tortoises, because there were no humans [when they arrived] here. We [the humans] are all introduced." In saying that, locals affirm what they learned from conservationists: strictly speaking, all humans are "introduced" in the archipelago. This confirms the adoption of hegemonic ideas that for decades have asserted that the Galápagos Islands are a territory of nonhumans— that is, it pertains to conservation.

Indeed, due to the archipelago's isolation, the Galápagos has no Indigenous (or aboriginal) human population. The Salasaca people are Indigenous to the Andes, but they are migrants in the Galápagos. However, they were part of the first squads of people sent to the islands and were one of the earliest groups who had permanently settled on Santa Cruz. Meanwhile, although there are no native (aboriginal) peoples of the Galápagos, there are many individuals who could aspire to achieve full citizenship rights on the grounds that they were born in the archipelago. Yet from a Western purview, reflected in the 1998 law, they are all "introduced" or "aliens" in the Galápagos. In turn, every time someone says that "the only owners of the Galápagos are the tortoises," they reaffirm what conservation work taught them: the islands belong to nonhumans; therefore, no one—including pioneering families and their descendants—born in the archipelago can have access to full property and citizenship rights. Furthermore, in saying so, they take the islands back to its status as a "no-man's-land" (or *res nuillius*), forgetting the nearly two centuries of colonization and human labor involved since their annexation to Ecuador in 1832. The Galápagos therefore continues to be the subject of legitimate dispute and possible appropriation by different parties.

At the same time, foreign scientists are perceived as the only legitimate experts in the management of nature and the care of giant tortoises in the archipelago. Six decades of conservationist rule have further heightened anxieties among locals about being constantly watched over and condemned for their "non-ecological" conduct. Conservation policy and public morality, for example, condemn locals for using fireworks in New Year's Eve celebrations, for playing with colored foam in the islands' carnivals, for the limited knowledge of some when recycling, and, in general, for disobeying or challenging the norms of the Galápagos National Park and the Darwin station. Moreover, locals feel compelled to police others' behavior, often calling for the expulsion of "undesirable elements" (like drugs dealers or thieves). In that way, the Galápagos Islands turn into a scene of conflict in which the solution to unwanted people, following the conservation rationale, is expulsion from the archipelago.

At the same time, a sort of xenophobia emerged in the islands which is not a matter of nationals versus foreigners but an internal one between Ecuadorian migrants and between *mestizos* and Indigenous people. These tensions, aggravated by the ratification of the Special Law, have become more acute in recent years with the growth of the local population. This was noted by one of my interviewees: "before they called us outsiders [*afureños*], but they never shouted at the other: "Get out of here!" as they do now" (Interview Puerto Ayora, May 2017). In the same vein, constant complaints and verbal conflicts are often heard between islanders and Ecuadorians of the mainland, with the latter resenting the fact that they do not have the same rights to the islands as the *galapagueños*. They further claim that *galapagueños* do in fact have the same rights as themselves in continental Ecuador.

For their part, *galapagueños* resist conservationist rationale by identifying themselves as "Carapachudos" or "Tortugueños" (a play on the words *caparazón*; *carapace* from the tortoise shell, and *tortuga*, tortoise), thus placing themselves alongside the iconic Galápagos tortoises. They also do so by telling and retelling the stories of the pioneers, by recalling the lists of Santa Cruz *colonos'* surnames, or by participating in campaigns that assert their pride in being "100 percent *galapagueños*." However, in these gestures, local people tend to exclude the *Salasacas* from the list of *colonos* and show little interest in recovering the history of the Salasaca community in Santa Cruz Island. Instead, they deny Indigenous presence because, in their view, it contaminates the superior racial status linked to *galapagueño* identity (closer to the Ecuadorian coast and to white European settlers, as well as visitors and scientists).

Overlapping Regimes

The interaction of conservation and state law involves a number of acts of translation—from science to law, and to the actual administration of local population. Foreign ideas "need to be remade in the vernacular" in order to be effective (Merry 2006). Such processes entail—on the islands—situating conservation ideas within contexts of power and meaning that make sense at the local level. In the Galápagos, this process is informed by science and the *hacienda* order. The way these two systems of law interact can be observed through the emergence of new types of insults that target the Salasaca people on the archipelago. For example, across the Andean region, the word *"indio"* ("Indian," and also the word *"longo"* in Ecuador) is used to insult persons of Indigenous descent or to offend someone who behaves rudely. On the Galápagos Islands, however, colloquial language borrowed terms from the lexicon of conservationism to insult others by calling them "introduced," "predator," or "intruder." These insults overlap and are frequently used to humiliate Salasaca Indigenous persons on the island. Discrimination especially targets those *Salasacas* who make visible their indigeneity. This is the case of Ivonne and Paulina, two Salasaca girls in Santa Cruz, who told me about being bullied at their high school:

> Ivonne: "When I started high school, some of my fellow students bothered me when I wore my Salasaca dress . . . They threw stones at me, they called me a *longa vaga* [Indian bum] or *longa tonta* [stupid Indian] or *"introduced"*; they looked at me with hatred . . ."

> Paulina: "There were times when I dressed as a Salasaca. But they hit me. Once, a *mestizo* boy grabbed my private parts . . . I folded over my *bayeta* [shawl] and fought back!"

> Ivonne: "We want peace . . . They say we are *"introduced,"* but I was born here and have spent my whole life here."
> (Puerto Ayora, September 2017).

By combining such insults as *"longa"* and "introduced," the *mestizo* students at the high school turned the Salasaca children into subjects with no rights on the islands and objects of abuse. In this case, both Ivonne and Paulina were born in the Galápagos and are the daughters of Salasaca *colonos*. Nevertheless, they sometimes wore their ethnic clothing to their high school. This act signals their resistance to "whiten" themselves, or to the imposition of mainstream society: to feel ashamed because of their Indigenous origins.

Along the same lines, the officials of the Government Council equate the members of the Salasaca Indigenous community who remain as "illegals" with the introduced species that pollute local society and should therefore be eradicated from the Galápagos. They thus persecute the most vulnerable members of the collective, "the dumbest ones" (*los más cojudos*), as an environmentalist I interviewed once told me (Interview, Puerto Ayora, June

2015); in particular, people like Víctor who come to the island in search of work (but without a job contract) and go to the Miraflores marketplace every morning in hopes of finding a job in the informal sector of the economy. Due to their precarious economic conditions and Indigenous race, *Salasacas* have become the target of conservation measures which have made internal migration their most significant enemy.

TWO PEOPLES

Conservation law created two different kinds of Salasaca people in the Galápagos (the legal and the illegal), thus dividing the collective in the claims and the rights they would need to pursue in the archipelago. I attended several meetings led by leaders of the collective (both legal and illegal residents), which aimed to negotiate the terms for a union of the whole collective on Santa Cruz Island. The first common goal was to unite all *Salasacas* "living in the Galápagos" (quoting the invitations sent by the leaders of the Salasaca Association), regardless of their legal status, for the celebration of New Year's Eve. During those months, I went back and forth with letters and invitations from the Salasaca Association to the Salasaca Soccer League across the Miraflores neighborhood. However, after many negotiations, the Salasaca leaders couldn't reach an agreement—not even regarding their partnership for the celebration of the end of the year *fiesta.* Two *fiestas* were held, with the one of the Salasaca Soccer League gathering by far the biggest crowd.

The two conflicting agendas are reflected in the use of space within the Miraflores neighborhood.[23] Whereas the soccer stadium and the *ecuavoley* court serve as a kind of "central plaza for the *Salasacas* on the island" (as a Salasaca *colona* noted in an interview, Puerto Ayora, December 2018), congregating them all in one place, the community center built by the Salasaca Association is frequently used by first settlers (*colonos*) and legal residents.

Furthermore, each space plays a different role for the *Salasacas.* The soccer stadium and the *ecuavoley* court primarily work as a means for Indigenous migrants to undergo cultural whitening on Santa Cruz Island. Leaders of the collective tacitly encourage this whitening by instilling sports discipline through a system of rules, rewards, and sanctions, which primarily aim at reducing alcohol intake among the young *Salasacas.* It also prompts punctuality, competitiveness, and sportsmanship within the collective. Both Amable Pilla (founder of the Salasaca Soccer League) and Vicente Masaquiza (who built the *ecuavoley* court) referred to these values as the key drivers for the creation of these spaces in Miraflores (Interviews, Puerto Ayora, December 2018, January 2019). In turn, the soccer cup tournament is also critical in

Figure 6.6.   Salasaca leaders of the Association (Daniel Masaquiza, the principal of the Runa Kunapak school, and Gaspar Masaquiza) and the soccer league. *Source*: Photo: P. Sánchez, Puerto Ayora, Galápagos, November 2018.

building a community network sustained by weekly gatherings around Miraflores stadium and the Salasaca Cup. It also gathers a very attractive mass of voters for candidates competing for the mayor's office on Santa Cruz Island.

For its part, the community center acts as a place to reaffirm the cultural roots and find a political voice for Indigenous peoples on the Galápagos. This path is, however, only possible for Salasaca legal residents in the Galápagos who can, in theory, make themselves visible as Indigenous peoples in order to claim rights on the archipelago to the Ecuadorian state. Their voice is, however, debilitated by *mestizo* politicians who don't take their claims seriously, in part because of their racism, and in part because they know that they cannot fully represent the larger group of *Salasacas* who remain illegal in the archipelago. Instead, they encourage the legal residents to denounce the illegal ones because they should "start protecting" themselves and prevent the loss of their jobs, as the representative of the national government stated in the meeting with the Salasaca Association that I described earlier.

Divided by law, Salasaca settlers of the Galápagos have to find different paths to claim their rights in the archipelago. Whereas Salasaca *colonos* can find a way within the pluralist frame of formal rules and political strategies available, illegal *Salasacas* on the Galápagos Islands, like Víctor, need to whiten themselves and hide in order to evade official harassment and deportation. Finally, the way local authorities and *mestizo* citizens enforce conservation law reflect their own anxieties to erase their Indigenous pasts and become more white.

NOTES

1. I relate the experiences of Victor Caizabanda (whose name has been anonymized) with his permission.

2. The minimum monthly wage in the Galápagos Islands is $870 (USD)—that is, more than twice of mainland Ecuador. However, the cost of living on the islands is pretty high. For example, while a bottle of potable water there costs $2.50, the same sells for $1 on the mainland. Similarly, a bottle of Ecuadorian beer costs $4 on the islands, compared to $1.30 on the mainland.

3. Both groups of *Salasacas* (legal and illegal) go to the stadium. By contrast, most of the Salasacas who gather together at the community center are legal residents.

4. In Santa Cruz, the only vehicles that circulate are taxis (white pickup trucks) and some electric cars, which have licenses. Most people use bikes to get around Puerto Ayora.

5. Eighteen soccer teams compete for the Salasaca Cup. Each represents one of the eighteen communities of the Salasaca Indigenous nation in Tungurahua. All of the players must be of Salasaca origin. In addition, they can only play for the team that represents their community in their hometown.

6. The *poncho* was returned to him by a friend who later traveled to Salasaca (Tungurahua).

7. Except for a department on biology, geography, and related subjects from a private university of Quito, which is located in San Cristóbal Island.

8. Such racist remarks about hygiene ("they are dirty" or "they don't wash themselves") are frequently made by *costeños* (coast-dwellers) to criticize Indigenous persons and the inhabitants of the highlands (*la sierra*) in general. They go in hand with discourses of cleanliness and progress that underlie the making of white-*mestizo* cities and "urban regeneration projects" in Quito and Guayaquil. The urban Indigenous are deemed to be "backward," "rural," and "dirty"—a disturbance in the project to develop a proper urban space (Swanson 2010, 92–3), particularly if they occupy public space (as beggars or street vendors) where white-*mestizos* congregate (Pareja 2018, 35–6). While cultural whitening and *mestizaje* is promoted by a national discourse, "social cleansing" is part of renovation projects that result in the creation of generic cityscapes more suitable for the attraction of tourism (Andrade 2007, 107–43).

9. Alcoholism is widespread, both in the Indigenous and *mestizo* population in the whole of Ecuador. Meanwhile, Indigenous and Afro-Ecuadorian women are, indeed, the groups who suffer the most gender violence in Ecuador. They also constitute the most vulnerable groups in the country.

10. This is an internal "technical report" of the Charles Darwin Station. It was not published.

11. In 1918, after the abolishment of the *concertaje* system and the introduction of a free labor system, Indigenous peoples in Ecuador became increasingly integrated into national society through labor intensive activities such as agricultural production (mainly in *haciendas* located in the highlands in Chimborazo, Pichincha, and Imbabura), cattle production (the Saraguro and Lojano), the manufacturing of Panamá hats (the Cañar) and weaving (the *Salasacas* and Otavalos). These changes are, however, a "rethorical modernization of Indian exploitation" (Clark and Becker 2007, 10).

12. In 2018, nine thousand tons of waste were collected in the Galápagos. 6,100 were collected in Santa Cruz; 50 percent of the waste of this island could be recycled and exported to the mainland of Ecuador.

13. The surname Masaquiza is exclusively used by members of the Salasaca nation.

14. For example, in 1990, the Darwin station summed up its main achievements on the archipelago, among which stand out: the discovery of a way to manipulate the sex of the tortoises' eggs by controlling the temperature at the time of their incubation (1984); the repatriation to its ancestral land of the one-thousandth tortoise bred in captivity (1988); the elimination of dogs from the coastal area by means of poisoning (1987); and the eradication of between eighty thousand to one hundred thousand goats on five islands (*Noticias de Galápagos*, 1984–1990).

15. From the time of Beebe (1924), the Galápagos have been associated with an "Eden" for science, geology, and biology (Dawkins, quoted in Stewart 2007, 6) and for making an evolutionary landscape (Hennessy and McCleary 2011). To go back to Eden is furthermore the vision of the Darwin station work, as described in the previous chapter.

16. Oceanic archipelagos became "excellent theaters" of evolution insofar as their populations, being physically distanced from their parent populations, tend to go through a dramatic decrease in genetic diversity that, given enough time, can eventually lead to the formation of new, autochtonous species (MacArthur and Wilson 2001 [1967], 152–80). This finding was central to the theory of island biogeography, which revolutionized ecology in 1967 by suggesting that the biota of any island is a dynamic equilibrium between immigration and extinction of species, on which processes of evolution act (Simberloff 1974). The theory, formulated by MacArthur and Wilson, posits that islands and archipelagos like the Galápagos Islands are ideal sites to perform "natural experiments" by which evolutionary theses could be tested.

17. "Race suicide" was used to describe the declining birth rate of "old stock Americans in the face of increased migration." It was based on the belief that "miscegenation between higher and lower peoples does not produce a blend of the two races but rather a specimen that reverts to a mentally inferior—and probably infertile—type" (Spiro 2008, 101).

18. For example, through genetic studies, conservationists in the Galápagos were able to trace the genotypes of eighty-four Volcano Wolf tortoises to a purebred *Chelonoidis elephantopus* who was involved in hybridization events that have been occurring over the past two hundred years, since human translocation became common (Garrick et.al. 2012, R10–11). The "alien" tortoises, which were believed in the past to be natives of Wolf Island, were actually hybrid individuals whose ancestors were likely collected by whaling crews elsewhere in the archipelago, and dumped on

Wolf while they sailed toward the fertile whaling grounds of the Galápagos. At the time, Wolf Island was a popular stopover. Whalers deposited excess tortoises there to be retrieved upon return (Caccone et al. 2012 [2018]). Today, Wolf has hybrids with all sorts of mixtures.

19. Since back-breeding could take nearly eighty to one hundred years, hybrids with high conservation value (with more than half alleles of a purebred) are being selected for breeding and repatriation so they can be useful both in their role as dominant herbivores, and in the part they play in bringing back to life extinct species of the Galápagos.

20. *Proyecto Isabela* (PI) was allocated more than fifteen million dollars and resources like helicopters, sharpshooters, local hunters, hunting dogs, and veterinarians to eliminate the goats. Bocci (2017) points to the ways people resisted PI. For example, local hunters sometimes recorded some kills when in fact they had let goats go; they said they were "ok to kill goats," but not to eradicate the whole species. The goats themselves developed survival strategies, like remaining immobile when they heard the helicopters approaching.

21. In prior decades, this job was done by employees of the Darwin station and, later, by rangers at Galápagos National Park. The ABG was created by the Galápagos National Park.

22. The poison is put into pieces of meat that are thrown onto the street, empty lots, and private yards.

23. The Miraflores district began to be built in the mid-1980s on a terrain at the outskirts of Puerto Ayora that was originally used as a garbage dump by the island dwellers. There in the mid-1980s, the mayor of Santa Cruz ceded some lots to seven Salasaca *colonos* who worked for the municipality. In a short time, the Miraflores neighborhood extended much further, with new migrants arriving and invading nearby lands. In Miraflores, the Salasaca pioneer families built their houses, the *ecuavoley* court (where the weekly marketplace takes place on Sundays), and, later, the community center. Between these spaces, the municipality built the soccer stadium in 2006, where I began my fieldwork. None of these projects was meant to be a profit-making one. They instead enabled the community to build a space of its own, free of racism, for the Salasaca people on Santa Cruz Island.

Conclusion

This Other Eden

The question of who owns and who belongs to the Galápagos Islands criss-crosses human history and continues to be a central concern for *galapagueño* society. Multiple communities challenge and compete for these rights. The first is the *colono* (first settler) population. It is made up of the pioneer families and their descendants in the four inhabited islands of the Galápagos. They arrived to the archipelago as *hacienda* laborers and debt prisoners. Due to its race (Indigenous origin) and the legacies of a labor system that enslaved and criminalized native populations since the Spanish Conquest, they were treated as convicts. Their presence in the archipelago can be traced back to the group of eighty Ecuadorian men who were recruited on the mainland by General Villamil between the 1830s and the 1850s. Other groups arrived with don José Valdizán, Manuel J. Cobos, and Antonio Gil from the 1860s onwards. A few decades later, with the arrival of the first women, came the first generation of native *galapagueños* who were born in the oceanic archipelago since the 1880s.

Colonos of the Galápagos built a unique identity based on feelings of difference towards Ecuadorians from the mainland. This was marked, in Ospina's (2001) words, by their lonely fight to humanize a hostile territory with almost no fresh water, in the cruelest solitude and state abandonment. Later on, they further appropriated the nickname "*carapachudos*" in order to index their belonging to the archipelago—living in oceanic isolation, enclosed like the endemic giant tortoises of the Galápagos—under their own carapaces (*carapachos*). For them, people who don't belong to the Galápagos—including Ecuadorians from the mainland—are known as: "*afureños*" (foreigners).

Although colonization of Santa Cruz happened a century later, the first settlers of this island are also considered members of the *colono* community of the archipelago. Most arrived after the 1960s, following the creation of the

205

Galápagos National Park and the Charles Darwin Station that transformed the Galápagos from being a state property into becoming a national park and a conservation territory. Ironically, the arrival of conservation rule to protect the 'nonhumans' in the archipelago triggered drastic growth in human population, turning the once desolate Santa Cruz into the most populated island in the archipelago. In particular, Salasaca people played a crucial role in building the city of Puerto Ayora and providing the services that conservationism, the tourism industry, and the state bureaucrats needed in the Galápagos.

A series of norms and social arrangements grant citizenship and property rights to *colonos* of the Galápagos, recognizing their sacrifice and labor. This rationale can be framed in Lockean terms, which state that "a person who labors upon resources that are either unowned or held in common . . . has a natural property right to the fruits of his or her efforts and the state has a duty to respect and enforce that natural right" (Chander and Sunder 2004, 1343–44). Accordingly, the Ecuadorian state backed the rights of those who first settled in what was known as a "no-man's-land." It did so by adopting the "*colono*" label as the official category to identify and protect their rights. It, however, restricted their territory to the 3 percent of the lands of the archipelago when creating the Galápagos National Park. Furthermore, the Ecuadorian state took charge of delimiting the new natural property, patrolling its borders, and maintaining locals out.

The second community is made up by Ecuadorian citizens who claim their right to own the Galápagos. In theory, state law grants all citizens the right to migrate, live, and work within the national territory. And yet, although Ecuadorians from the mainland are perceived as "*afuereños*" in the islands, they could eventually aspire to belong to the *galapagueño* society as earlier migrants did in the past. Furthermore, in theory, they gained equal rights to own, profit, and enjoy the 97 percent of the land after being declared a "national park."

From the 1970s onwards, multiple systems of law were put in place to challenge the rights of both *galapagueños* and Ecuadorian citizens over the islands in order to favor emergent and powerful social actors. The creation of new forms of property and transnational governance regimes preceded this move. For example, the introduction of the concept of "heritage" in international law which, following Hafstein (2004), not only created new forms of property but also gave tools and techniques to transnational communities to organize themselves as "imagined national communities" in Anderson's (1983) terms. In the Galápagos, this was ratified through the 1978 declaration of the archipelago as a World Heritage site in UNESCO's first list of natural properties. It thus granted common rights over the archipelago to a newly created collective: the "humankind"—mainly composed of wealthy (white) tourists and forty-five tourism operators. It also gave them the ethical duty to safeguard endemic species in the islands while making their descendants the natural heirs of Galápagos nature and territory. Critical to this construction is the imagery of the Galápagos as a nonhuman territory, a "no-man's-land." At the very same time, the recently created collective (the 'humankind') needed to establish an international authority—a network of experts in conservation and science to govern the natural heritage. All those who are not holders of a tourism license or are not able to afford the costs of traveling across the Galápagos waters are excluded from the rights to enjoy, own, or profit from the natural park, including *colonos* of the archipelago who live nearby.

In such context, the fourth community that competes for rights over the archipelago is made up of scientists and conservation agencies that were entitled to set the guidelines for managing nature and society in the Galápagos. Through the 1998 Special Law, they were able to translate conservation ideas into law, transforming *colonos* into "residents" in their homeland, and Ecuadorian nationals into "tourists" or potential "illegal" subjects if exceeding the time limit allowed in their islands. The Ecuadorian state ratified their right as experts, admitting that—from there on—*colonos,* native *galapagueños,* and Ecuadorian citizens were considered 'aliens' in the archipelago. State law thus granted foreign conservationists the authority to define who belongs to the Galápagos. For the group of conservationists, only the ancestral lineages of endemic species (as the purebred giant tortoises), which enact the evolutionary landscape that inspired Charles Darwin, belong to these islands. In their view, all humans are outsiders or in conservationist lexicon: "introduced species." Some might be beneficial for the environment due to their expertise and care for nature, conservationism, and evolutionary science. In turn, others (for example, all locals who do not hold jobs in conservation agencies) are considered harmful to—or "invasive" in—the Galápagos. Moreover, they framed the major threat in the quest to protect nature as a Malthusian problem linked to Ecuadorian colonization.

The views of Western scientists reflect their long-standing beliefs on race and cultural development that were built upon evolutionary ideas of Social Darwinism, which situated nonwhite, hybrid races, and colonized 'others' as inferior, primitive, and uncivilized. Accordingly, early European visitors in the archipelago labeled locals as: "colored," "blacks," "Indians," "*mestizos,*" and "inferior," thus preferring not to associate with them in any way. More recently, the work of scientists of the Charles Darwin Research Station is marked by the neglect of the local population and their knowledge on the management of Galápagos nature, the absence of dialogue, and their resistance to conceive social issues as linked to the goals of conservation in the archipelago. In turn, the Ecuadorian state bureaucrats also express their own racial prejudices when they stigmatize all *galapagueños* as "the descendants of convicts," as publicly stated in the political discourses at the inaugural event of the Darwin station and in the recent remarks of assemblymen when discussing the 2015 reform to the 1998 law. In the interaction of the overlapping systems of law and race, the *Salasacas* of the Galápagos are perceived as misplaced not only for being human, nonwhite, and Ecuadorian intruders but also for being Indigenous, Andean *serranos* (highlanders) who historically resisted state-making projects, notably *mestizaje*. Local *mestizos* translate conservation ideas and adopt the scientific lexicon to designate Indigenous Salasaca people in the archipelago as "introduced," "invasive," and transgressors of conservation law. Authorities, too, translate these views when making Salasaca "illegal" subjects in the archipelago the main target of deportation.

Finally, the fifth community that competes over ownership and control of the islands is made up of state bureaucrats who direct conservation agencies in the archipelago—the most prominent being the Galápagos National Park, while also receiving most of the revenues generated by admission fees to the park. Their interests are protected by an institutional and legal framework backed by state law, including the 1998 Special Law, the 2009 presidential decree, and the 2015 reform to the 1998 Law. These set of laws eliminated the voice of *galapagueños* with their right to decide on their provincial government (through the election of a local governor or "*prefecto*") and their democratic representation within entities that govern, manage, and profit from the archipelago. In turn, the creation of the Governing Council (*Consejo de Gobierno*) responds to the agenda of forcing locals out of the archipelago, either by demographic control or by the neglect to provide the basic infrastructure that a population of 30,000 citizens require to live. As a result, the *galapagueños* continue to lack basic services (potable water, wastewater, and sanitation services), and have no access to good health services and college education; all of this despite living at the margins of one of the fastest growing economies of the world: the Galápagos National Park (Taylor et al. 2006). Furthermore, restrictions on local agriculture plus their dependence on a system of supply of goods, potable water, and food from the continent ensure the almost complete subordination of the inhabitants of the Galápagos to the central government on the mainland. The fifth community thus represents the interests of the Ecuadorian political and economic elite—mainly the descendants of *hacienda* owners who govern the country from Quito.

In theory, the Salasaca people take part in the first two communities either as *colonos* of the archipelago or as Ecuadorian nationals. However, members of these groups stigmatize and exclude the *Salasacas* for being Indigenous, and worse still, for having rejected their whitening. They thus must create their own strategies (like sharing their residency permits) in order to claim rights to live and work in the Galápagos. Conservation law, however, created two different groups of Salasaca people. In recent years, few can opt to re-indigenize themselves in order to gain political access and visibility. The rest rather need to go through a process of cultural whitening, which ultimately aims to complete the colonial project; that is, to erase Indigenous peoples. This aspiration, combined with the interests of conservation rule, made the Salasaca pioneers disappear not only from the legal framework (as *colonos*) but also from the historical accounts of the archipelago. In turn, Salasaca migrants constantly 'disappear' from the islands through deportation.

The case of the Salasaca people is interesting not only because of the fascinating history that surrounds their journey from the Andean highlands to the Galápagos Islands or their large presence and significance in *galapagueño* society. More importantly, their history and everyday life illustrate the ways multiple, and sometimes contradictory, systems of law and race shape social order in the Galápagos. In this book, I chose to talk about the "Indigenous Settlers of the Galápagos" in order to emphasize the racial condition of the earliest colonizers of the archipelago and the way this shaped the production of historical accounts and popular imagery that continue to stigmatize them to the present day. "Indigenous settlers" also embraces the group of Salasaca people who became first settlers of Santa Cruz Island a century later. In the last chapters, I described the complexities in which many *Salasacas* live, being immersed in oppressive forms of racism and new colonialist, exploitative regimes that unfold in the name of civilization and the protection of nature. However, I tried to be careful not to represent them as the passive recipients of state policies and conservation measures. Far from being the case, the Salasaca people have developed an array of strategies to resist, reject, adapt, or change in order to participate as members of the *colono* community in the Galápagos. Furthermore, in spite of living under constant harassment and threat of physical and symbolic violence, their history illustrates the numerous times they have reinvented themselves. They continue to do so every time they shift identities as Indigenous members of a traditional ethnic group in the highlands, as environmentally conscious subjects in the Galápagos, or as political and economic agents with the ability to mobilize resources and changes both in the islands and in the highlands.

Through their voices, this book thus aimed to start listening to the human pasts of the Galápagos, highlighting the role of Indigenous peoples in the construction of city, nature, and society in the archipelago. To talk about the complex social and racial issues within "protected areas" does not dismiss the urgency to address environmental problems, but rather calls for inquiry about alternative, more equitable approaches to the governance of nature and society in treasured sites such as the Galápagos. This is particularly important at a time when 192 state parties committed to follow the IUCN (International Union for Conservation of Nature) mandate on what nature is and should be, concurring with the urgency required to expand both nationally and internationally designated "protected areas" on their territories—a primordial task that the World Commission on Protected Areas (WCPA) currently progresses. At present, the United Nations List of Protected Areas already accounts for 209,000 natural sites, which represent thirty-three million square kilometers (15 percent of the world's land and 3 percent of the oceans)—an area larger than the African continent. In so doing, the UN 2014 list followed the trend of every edition, doubling the number of sites that the previous list records. It further notes that the world's land is already divided in "ecoregions" crisscrossing national boundaries for the preservation of species and ecosystems. The drastic growth of protected areas urge for more work that attends not merely to the social construction of nature but also to the material effects of its production, and the social impacts or the livelihood change of people living in these areas (West et al. 2006). This work responds to this call by specifically examining how foreign ideas (like conservation thought) travel and are translated differently in host territories. It further aims to offer a novel perspective to questions surrounding the mutual exchange between science and culture (Martin 1998), which takes place in the Galápagos through the repertoire—linguistic, performative, and political—made by Indigenous and non-Indigenous settlers from conservation ideas and practices.

Bibliography

Abercrombie, Thomas. 1998. *Pathways of Memory and Power: Ethnography and History among an Andean People*. Madison: Univ. of Wisconsin Press. xxiv, 18, 494.

——. 2016. "The Iterated Mountain: Things as Signs in Potosí." *The Journal of Latin American and Caribbean Anthropology*, 21(1): 83–108.

——. 1998. "Tributes to Bad Conscience: Charity, Restitution, and Inheritance in Cacique and Encomendero Testaments of 16th-century Charcas." *Dead Giveaways*. Susan Kellog and Mathew Restall, (eds.). University of Utah Press. 249–89.

——. 1996. "Q'aqchas and La Plebe in Rebellion: Carnival vs. Lent in 18th-century Potosí." *The Journal of Latin American and Caribbean Anthropology*, 2(1): 62–111.

Acosta, Alberto and Martínez, Esperanza, (eds.). 2011. *La Naturaleza Con Derechos: De La Filosofía a La Política*. Quito, Ecuador: Ediciones Abya-Yala.

Albers, Patricia. 1996. "Changing Patterns of Ethnicity in the Northeastern Plains, 1780–1870." *History, Power, and Identity: Ethnogenesis in the Americas 1492–1992*. Jonathan D. Hill, (ed.). Iowa City: University of Iowa Press. 90–18.

Alfaro, Olmedo. 1930. *Las Islas Galápagos y su Situación Actual*. Guayaquil: La Opinión Pública. 16–17.

Anderson, Benedict. 2016 [1983]. *Imagined Communities*. New York: Verso.

Andrade, X. 2007. "Más Ciudad, Menos Ciudadanía: Renovación Urbana y Aniquilación del Espacio Público en Guayaquil." *Ecuador Debate*, 68: 107–97.

Arboleda, María. 2001. "Género y ambiente en Galápagos: Roles productivos, reproductivos y comunitarios de las mujeres en relación con los hombres y posición de las mujeres frente a los temas ambientales." ProGenial Ecuador/Banco Mundial.

Bailey, RG. 1989. "Explanatory Supplement to ecoregions Map of the Continents." *Environmental Conservation*, 16: 307–09.

Becker, Mark. 1995. "Indigenismo and Indian Movements in 20th century Ecuador." Pittsburgh: LASA. 2.

———. 2011. *Pachakutik!: Indigenous Movements and Electoral Politics in Ecuador.* Lanham, Maryland: Rowman and Littlefield Publishers.

Beebe, William. 2012 [1924]. *Galápagos World's End.* Mineola: Dover Publications. 243.

Beer, Gillian. 2009. *Darwin's Plots: Evolutionary Narrative in Darwin, George Elliot and Nineteenth Century Fiction.* Cambridge University Press.

Bender, Barbara. 2002 "Time and Landscape." *Current Anthropology* 43 (Supplement): 103–112.

Bensted-Smith, Powell, Dinerstein (eds.). 2002. "Back to Eden—One Last chance." *A Biodiversity Vision for the Galápagos Islands.* Charles Darwin Foundation and World Wildlife Fund. Puerto Ayora, Galapagos. 1–5.

Bensted-Smith, Robert. 1998. "The Special Law for the Galápagos," *Noticias de Galápagos*, No. 59:6.

Berger, John. 1991 [1980]. *About Looking.* New York: Vintage International.

Bocci, Paolo. 2017. "Entangled Care: Killing Goats to Save Tortoises on the Galápagos Islands." *Cultural Anthropology.* 32(3): 424–49.

Bognoly J., Espinosa J. M. 1905. *Las Islas Encantadas o el Archipiélago de Colón.* Guayaquil: Imprenta del Comercio. 54–212.

Bonifaz, C. 1963. "El Ecuador y las Islas Galápagos." *Noticias de Galápagos*, 1: 1–3.

Bowler, Peter. 1988. "Anthropology and Evolution." *Isis.* 79 (1):104–07.

Bowman, Robert. 1960. *Report on A Biological Reconnaissance of the Galápagos Islands during 1957.* Paris: UNESCO.

———. 1966. *The Galápagos: Proceedings of the Galápagos International Scientific Project.* Oakland, California: University of California Press. 3, 282–85.

Bromley, Ray. 1979. "Urban Rural Demographic Contrasts in Highland Ecuador: town recession in a period of catastrophe." *Journal of Historical Geography,* 3(5): 281–95.

Buschges, C. 1997. "Las leyes del honor: honor y estratificación social en el distrito de la Audiencia de Quito (siglo XVIII)". *Revista de Indias*, Vol: 57, No. 209: 55–84. https://doi.org/10.3989/revindias.1997.i209.795.

Caccone, A., Gentile, G., Gibbs, J., Fritts, T., Snell, H., Betts, J., Powell, J. 2002. "Phylogeography and History of Giant Galápagos Tortoises." *Evolution*, 56: 48, 2018–66.

Cañizares- Esguerra, Jorge. 2006. *Nature, Culture, and Nation.* Redwood City, California: Stanford University Press. 14–45.

Carrasco, Eulalia. 1982. *Salasaca: la Organización Social y el Alcalde.* Quito: Mundo Andino. 31.

Cassagrande, Joseph B. 1981. "Strategies for Survival: The Indians of Highland Ecuador." In Cultural *Transformation and Ethnicity in Modern Ecuador*, edited by Norman E. Whitten Jr., ed. Urbana: University of Illinois Press. 160–77.

———. 1981. "Strategies for Survival: The Indians of Highland Ecuador," in *Cultural Transformations and Ethnicity in Modern Ecuador.* Norman E. Whitten, Jr., ed. Urbana: University of Illinois Press. 260–77.

Challener, Richard. 2016 [1973]. *Admirals, Generals, and American Foreign Policy, 1898–1914.* Princeton Legacy Library. Princeton, New Jersey: Princeton University Press. 106.

Chander and Sunder 2004. "The Romance and Public Domain." In *California Law Review,* Vol. 92: 1331–73.

Chernela, Janet. 2012. "A Species Apart: Ideology, Science, and the End of Life." In Sodikoff, G. (ed.). *The Anthropology of Extinction.* Bloomington, Indiana: Indiana Univ. Press, pp: 18–38.

Chiriboga R., Maignan S., Fonseca. 2006. "Caracterización de los sistemas de producción en Galápagos en relación con el fenómeno de las Especies Invasoras Proyecto ECU/00/G3." *Especies invasoras de las Galápagos.*

Choque Quishpe, María Eugenia. 1992. *La estructura de poder en la comunidad originaria de Salasaca.* Master's thesis, Facultad Latinoamericana de Ciencias Sociales, Ecuador. 81–92.

Choy, Timothy. 2011. *Ecologies of Comparison: An ethnography of endangerment in Hong Kong.* Durham: Duke University Press.

Cicala, Mario. 1994 [1771]. *Descripción histórico-topográfica de la Provincia de Quito de la Compañía de Jesús.* Quito: Biblioteca Ecuatoriana Aurelio Espinosa Polit.

Clark, Kim, and Becker, Marc. 2007. *Highland Indians and the State in Modern Ecuador.* Pittsburgh, Pennsylvania: University of Pittsburgh Press. 9–10.

Cohn, Bernard. 1996. "Law and the Colonial State in India." *Colonialism and its Forms of Knowledge.* Princeton, New Jersey: Princeton University Press. 57–77.

Colloredo-Mansfeld, Rudi. 2012. "Rafael Correa's Multicolored Dream Shirt: Commerce, Creativity and National Identity in Post-Neoliberal Ecuador." In *Latin American and Caribbean Ethnic Studies,* 7(3): 275–94.

Constantino, Jill. 2007. Fishermen, Turtles and Darwin: Galápagos Lives in Evolution's Laboratory. Phd Dissertation. Ann Arbor: University of Michigan. 207–37.

Corr, Rachel. 2018. *Interwoven: Andean Lives in Colonial Ecuador's Textile Economy.* The University of Arizona Press. 3–4, 144–62.

———. 2013. *Ritual and Remembrance in the Ecuadorian Andes.* Tucson, Arizona: University of Arizona Press.

Corr, Rachel and Powers, Karen. 2012. "Ethnogenesis and Cultural Refusal: The Case of the Salasacas in Highland Ecuador." *Latin American Research Review.* 47 (Special Issue): 5–57.

Costales Peñaherrera, Jaime. 1975. *El obraje de San Ildefonso,* Tesis de licenciatura, Pontificia Universitaria Católica del Ecuador, Quito.Cronon, William. 1983. *Changes in the Land: Indians, Colonists, and the Ecology of New England.* New York: Hill & Wang.

———. 1992. *Nature's Metropolis: Chicago and the Great West.* New York: W. W. Norton & Company.

———. 1996. *Uncommon Ground: Rethinking the Human Place in Nature.* New York: W. W. Norton & Company.

Cronon, William. 1996. *Uncommon Ground: Rethinking the Human Place in Nature.* W.W. Norton & Company.

————. 1992. *Nature's Metropolis: Chicago and the Great West.*

————. 1983. *Changes in the Land: Indians, Colonists, and the Ecology of New England.* New York: Hill & Wang.

Curry-Lindhal, K. "Twenty years of conservation." *Noticias de Galápagos*, No. 68: 9.

Darwin, Charles. 2003[1859]. *The Origin of Species: 150th Anniversary Edition.* Kolkata: Signet.

————. 2013 [1835]. *The Voyage of the Beagle.* Lexington KY. 220–398.

Davis, M., M. Chew, R. Hobbs, A. Lugo, J. Ewel, G. Vermeij, J. Brown. 2011. "Don"t Judge Species on their Origins." *Nature,* 474 (7350): 153–54.

de Castro, Fabio, Hogenboom, Barbara, Baud, Michiel. 2016. *Environmental Governance in Latin America.* London: PalGrave MacMillan.

de Costales, Peñaherrera, Piedad, and Costales Samaniego, Alfredo. 1959. *Los Salasacas: Investigación y elaboración.* Llacta 8. Quito: Instituto Ecuatoriano de Antropología y Geografía.

de la Cadena, Marisol. 2015. *Earth Beings: Ecologies of Practice Across Andean Worlds (The Lewis Henry Morgan Lectures).* Durham: Duke University Press.

————. 2000. *Indigenous Mestizos: The Politics of Race and Culture in Cuzco, Peru, 1919–1991.* Duke: New Ed. Edition [2000]. 1.

de la Torre, Carlos. 2015. *De Velasco a Correa. Insurrecciones, Populismos y Elecciones en Ecuador. 1944–2013.* Universidad Andina Simón Bolívar. Editora Nacional.

————. 1993. *La Seducción Velasquista.* Quito, Ecuador: Libri Mundi. 31.

Delaunay, D., León J., and Portais M. 1990. *Transición demográfica en el Ecuador.* Quito, Ecuador: Talleres Gráficos del IGM.

Descola, Phillipe. 2013 [2005]. *Beyond Nature and Culture.* Chicago: University of Chicago Press.

Diamond, J. M. 1975. "Assembly of species communities." In M. L. Cody and J. M. Diamond (eds.). *Ecology and Evolution of Communities.* Harvard Univ. Press, Cambridge, Massachusetts. 342–444.

Diener, P. 1974, "Ecology or Evolution." *American Ethnologist,* 1: 601–18.

Dorst, J. 1963. "Future Scientific Studies in the Galápagos Islands", in *Galápagos Islands: A Unique Area for Scientific Investigation.* San Francisco, California Academy of Science. Occasional Papers of the California Academy of Science: 30, 147–54.

————. 1959. *Rapport sur une mission en Équateur concernant l'établissement d'une station de recherche «Charles Darwin» dans les îles Galápagos.* París: UNESCO. 10–35.

————. 1961. "Where Time Stood Still: The Galápagos Islands and their prehistoric creatures." *UNESCO Courier.* 8, 28–32.

d'Ouzville, Noemi. 2008. "Water Resource Management in Galápagos: the case of Pelican Bay Watershed." *Galápagos Report 2007–2008.* GNP, CDF, and INGALA: 158–64.

Drayton, R. 2000. *Nature's government: Science, Imperial Britain and the Improvement of the World.* Hyderabad, Teleangana: Orient Blackswan.

Durham, William. 2008. "Fishing for Solutions: Ecotourism and Conservation in Galápagos". In *Putting Ecotourism to Work in the Americas*, A. Stronza & W. Durham (eds.). CAB International. 85.

Eibl-Eibesfeldt, Irenaus. 1958. "Galápagos: Wonders of a Noah's Ark Off the Coast of Ecuador." UNESCO Courier. January 1958. 19–23.

Endler, John A. 1986. *Natural Selection in the Wild.* Princeton, New Jersey: Princeton University Press. 3–51.

Epler, Bruce, 2007. "Tourism, the Economy, Population, Growth and Conservation in Galápagos." Puerto Ayora: Charles Darwin Foundation, September. pp. 12–26.

Escobar, Arturo. 1995. *Encountering Development: The Making and Unmaking of the Third World.* Princeton studies in Culture/Power/History. Princeton, New Jersey: Princeton University Press.

Garcés, Reino and Arturo, Pedro. 2004. "La Comarca de Capote: Cevallos." *Municipiode Cevallos.* Tungurahua, Ecuador: I. Municipio de Cevallos-Tungurahua.

———. 2002. *Tisaleo Indígena en la Colonia.* Ambato, Ecuador: Editorial Maxtudio. 106.

Garrick, R., Benavides, E., Russello, M., Gibbs, J., Poulakakis, N., Dion, K., Hyseni, C., Kajdacsi, K., Márquez, L., Bahan, S., Ciofi, C., Tapia, W., and Caccone, A. 2012. "Genetic rediscovery of an 'extinct' Galápagos giant tortoise species." *Current Biology*, 22, R10–11.

Gavilán, Vivian y Pablo Ospina 2000. "Mujeres y hombres en Galápagos. Demografía, mercado laboral y migraciones. Una mirada desde las relaciones de género". En J. Cevallos y C. Falconí (coords.). *Informe Galápagos 1999–2000.* (Quito: Fundación Natura / WWF).

Geertz, Clifford. 1983. *Local Knowledge: Further Essays in Interpretive Anthropology.* New York: Basic Books. 184.

Gibbs, J. P., E. J. Sterling, and F. J. Zabala. 2010. "Giant tortoises as ecological engineers: a long-term quasi-experiment in the Galapagos Islands." *Biotropica*, 42: 208–14.

Gobierno Autónomo Descentralizado Municipal de Santa Cruz, 2019. "Dejando Huellas: Tributo a los pioneros de Santa Cruz". https://www.youtube.com/watch?v=ItiXFnirdEU.

Goffman, Erving. 2007 [1959]. *La Presentación de la Persona en la Vida Cotidiana.* Buenos Aires: Amorrortu.

Goldstein, Daniel. 2012. *Outlawed: Between Security and Rights in a Bolivian City.* Durham: Duke University Press.

Grant, Madison. 1919. *The Passing of the Great Race*, New York: Charles Scribner's sons.

Grant, Thalia and Estes, Gregory, 2009. *Darwin in Galápagos: Footsteps to a New World.* Princeton, New Jersey: Princeton University Press.

Grenier, Christopher, 2007 [2002]. *Conservación Contra Natura: Las Islas Galápagos.* Quito: Abya-Yala. 78–194, 244–70.

Griffiths, Alison. *Wondrous Difference: Cinema, Anthropology & Turn of the Century Visual Culture.* New York: Columbia University Press. 46–85.

Grove, Richard H. 1996. *Green Imperialism: Colonial Expansion, Tropical Island Edens and the Origin of Environmentalism, 1600–1860.* Cambridge: Cambridge University Press.

Guarisco, Claudia. 1995. *El Tributo Republicano: Indios y Estado en el Ecuador (1830–1857).* Master's thesis, Facultad Latinoamericana de Ciencias Sociales: Ecuador. 86.

Gudynas, Eduardo, 2011. "Buen Vivir: Today's Tomorrow." *Society for International Development*, 54(4). https://www.researchgate.net/publication/241764771_Buen _Vivir_Today%27s_Tomorrow.

———. 2009. *El Mandato Ecológico: derechos de la naturaleza y políticas Ambientales en la nueva constitución*: Quito, Ecuador, Abya-Yala: Universidad Politécnica Salesiana.

Guerrero, Andrés. 2003. "The Administration of Dominated Populations under a Regime of Customary Citizenship: The Case of Postcolonial Ecuador," in *After Spanish Rule,* Mark Thurner and Andrés Guerrero (eds.). Durham: Duke Univ. Press. 1, 272–85.

Guevara, Carlos E. 2015. "Rebelión en Galápagos: la hacienda "El Progreso" de Manuel J. Cobos en la isla San Cristóbal (1879–1904). Informe de investigación. Universidad Andina Simón Bolívar.

Hafstein, Vladimar. 2004. *The Making of Intangible Cultural Heritage: tradition and authenticity, community and humanity.* PhD dissertation, University of California Berkeley.

Haila, Yrjo. 1997. "Wilderness' and the Multiple Layers of Environmental Thought." *Environment and History*, 3(2): 129–47. http://www.jstor.org/stable/20723037.

Haraway, Donna. 1985. "Teddy Bear Patriarchy: Taxidermy in the Garden of Eden, New York City, 1908–1936." Social Text 11: 20–64.

Hardin, Garrett. 1968. "The Tragedy of the Commons." *American Association for the Advancement of Science.* 162: 1243–8.

Harrison, Paul. 1947. *Study of the U.S.A. Forces "Galápagos Island."*HCR. "Galápagos: fuerte cruce de acusaciones en la Asamblea," Diario La Hora, June 10, 2015. https://issuu.com/la_hora/docs/diario_la_hora_loja_10_de_junio_201_ca96df fa6ea9fd/11.

Helmreich, Stefan. 2009. *Alien Ocean: Anthropological Voyages in Microbial Seas.* Berkeley: University of California Press. 12, 257.

Hennessy, Elizabeth. 2013. "Producing pre-historic life: Conservation breeding and the remaking of wildlife genealogies" in *Geoforum*, 49: 71–80.

———. 2014. *On the Back of Tortoises: Conserving Evolution in the Galápagos Islands.* Phd Dissertation. University of North Carolina at Chapel Hill.

Hennessy, Elizabeth and McCleary, Ann. 2011. "Nature's Eden? The Production and Effects of 'Pristine' Nature in the Galápagos Islands." *Island Studies Journal*, 6: 131–56.

Herzog, Tamar. 2013. "Colonial Law and 'Native Customs': Indigenous Land Rights in Colonial Spanish America." In *The Americas*, 69: 303–21.

Heyerdahl, Thor and Skolsvold, Arne. 1956. "Archaeological Evidence of Pre-Spanish Visits to the Galapagos Islands." *American Antiquity*, V22, No. 2, Part 3.

Hirschkind, Lynn. 1995. "History of the Indian Population of Cañar." *Colonial Latin American Review,* 4 (3):1311–42.

Hoff, Stein. 1985. Drømmen om Galapagos: En Ukjent Norsk Utvandrerhistorie. [translation: *The Galápagos Dream: An Unknown History of Norwegian Emigration.*] Oslo: Grødahl & Søn Forlag. A.s.Holdgate, Martin. 2017 [1999]. *The Green Web: A Union for World Conservation.* Oxfordshire, England: Routledge. 22.

Holm, Olaf, 1986. "Navegación precolombina." *Revista del Instituto de Historia Marítima,* 2:7–13; 2:97–108; 3:148–160.

Honey, M. 2008. *Ecotourism and sustainable development: who owns paradise?* Washington DC: Island Press.

Humphreys, Robert. 1981. *Latin America and the Second World War, Volume One 1939–1942.* University of London. 122.

Hunter, E. A. & J. P. Gibbs. 2014. "Densities of Ecological Replacement Herbivores Required to Restore Plant Communities: A Case Study of Giant Tortoises on Pinta Island, Galápagos." *Restoration Ecology,* 22(2): 1–9.

Huxley J., 1992 [1964]. *Evolutionary Humanism.* Amherst, New York: Prometheus books. 92.

———. 1954. *Scientific Humanism, Evolution, and Human Destiny.* Calif. American Humanist Association. 9.

Ibarra, Hernán. 1992. "Ambato: las Ciudades y Pueblos de la Sierra Central Ecuatoriana (1800–1930) en Kingman, Eduardo (ed.), *Ciudades de los Andes: Visión Histórica y Contemporánea.* Lima: Institut français d'études andines.

———. 1987. *Tierra, Mercado y Capital Comercial en la Sierra Central: el Caso de Tungurahua (1850–1930).* Master's thesis, Facultad Latinoamericana de Ciencias Sociales, Ecuador. 85.

Jaramillo, P. Tapia, W., Romero & Gibbs. 2017. *Galápagos Verde 2050: Restauración de Ecosistemas Degradados y Prácticas Agrícolas Sostenibles usando Tecnologías Ahorradoras de Agua.* Puerto Ayora: Charles Darwin Foundation. 1–130.

Jelin, Elizabeth. 2003. *State Repression and the Labors of Memory.* Minneapolis: University of Minnesota Press.

Kingman, Eduardo. 2006. *La Ciudad y los Otros, Quito 1860–1940: Higienismo, Ornato y Policía.* Facultad Latinoamericana de Ciencias Sociales, Ecuador. 61, 158–240.

Kolata, Alan. 2013. *Ancient Inca.* Cambridge, England: Cambridge Univ. Press. 54.

Lanning, Edward. 1969. "South America as Source for Aspects of Polynesian Cultures." In *Studies on Oceanic Culture History,* ed. by Green and Kelly, 175–185. Honolulu B. P. Bishop Museum.

Larson, Edward. 2001. *Evolution's Workshop: God and Science in the Galápagos Islands.* New York: Basic. 57–178.

Latorre, Octavio. 2011. *Historia Humana de Galápagos: Nuevos Descubrimientos.* Quito, Ecuador: Academia Nacional de Historia. 20–253.

———. 2013 [1992]. *La Maldición de la Tortuga.* Latorre Torres Ediciones. 2: 16–83.

———. 1991. *Manuel J. Cobos: Emperador de Galápagos.* Ecuador: Fundación Charles Darwin para las Islas Galápagos. 25–60.

———. 1996. *Tomás de Berlanga y el Descubrimiento de Galápagos.* Quito, Ecuador: Autores Varios Cel. 47.

Latour, Bruno. 1993. *We Have Never Been Modern.* Cambridge: Harvard University Press.

Livingstone, D. N. 1992. *The Geographical Tradition.* Malden, MA: Basil Blackwell.

Losos, J.B. and R.E. Ricklefs. 2009. *The Theory of Island Biogeography Revisited.* Princeton Univ. Press.

Luna Tobar, Alfredo. 1997. *Historia Politica Internacional de las Islas Galápagos.* Quito, Ecuador: Ediciones Abya-Yala.18–309.

Lundh, J. 2006. "History of the farm area on Santa Cruz in 1932-1965." *Noticias de Galápagos*, No. 64:12–25.

Lundh, Jacobo. 1995. "Breve Relato sobre ciertos Primeros Habitantes de la isla Santa Cruz." *Noticias de Galápagos*. 37, 60–1.

———. 2001-2. *Galápagos: A Brief History.*MacArthur, Robert and Wilson, Edward O. 2001 [1967]. *The Theory of Island Biogeography.* Princeton, New Jersey: Princeton University Press. 152–80.

Malpezzi, Stephen. 2013. "Population Density: Some Facts and Some Predictions." *Cityscape: a Journal of Policy Development and Research,* 15(3): 183–201.

Many, Gabriel. 2006. *Finanzas, Cultura y Poder en la Comunidad Salasaca: un Análisis de la Experiencia del Microcrédito y Cooperativas Indígenas.* Facultad Latinoamericana de Ciencias Sociales, Ecuador. 96.

Martin, Emily. 1998. Anthropology and the Cultural Study of Science. *Science, Technology & Human Values*, Vol. 23 (1): 24–44.

———. 2001 [1987]. *The Woman in the Body: A Cultural Analysis of Reproduction.* Beacon Press.

Martinez, Carmen. 2014. "Managing Diversity in Post-Neoliberal Ecuador." *The Journal of Latin American and Caribbean Anthropology,* 19(1):103–125. DOI: 10.1111/jlca.12062.

Masaquiza, Rumiñahui. 1995. "Los Salasacas." In Vinueza, José (ed.), *Identidades Indias en el Ecuador Contemporánea.* Quito, Ecuador: Ediciones Abya-Yala. 230–36.

Mayr, Ernst. 2005 [1942]. *Systematics and the Origins of Species.* Columbia Univ. Press, New York.

Melville, Herman. 2002 [1854]. *The Enchanted Isles*. London: Hesperus Press Limited.

Merry, Sally Engle. 2000. *Colonizing Hawai'i: The Cultural Power of Law.* Princeton, New Jersey: Princeton University Press.

———. 1986. "Everyday Understandings of Law in Working-class America." *American Ethnologist*, Vol. 13, No. 2: 253–70.

———. 2006. *Human Rights and Gender Violence: Translating International Law into Local Justice.* Chicago: University of Chicago Press.

———. 2003. "Human Rights Law and the Demonization of Culture (and Anthropology along the way)", *Political and Legal Anthropology Review*, Vol. 26 (1): 55–76.

———. 1988. "Legal Pluralism." *Law & Society Review* 22: 869–96.

———. 2016. *The Seductions of Quantification.* The University of Chicago Press.

Mestanza, Juan Carlos. 2015. "Galápagos necesita 6000 toneladas de víveres mensualmente." *Diario El Comercio,* February 22, 2015. https://www.elcomercio.com /actualidad/ecuador/viveres-galapagos-productos-barcos-avion.html.

Mignolo, Walter. 2002. "Introduction to Jose de Acosta's Historia Natural y Moral de las Indias." in *Natural and Moral History of the Indies (Chronicles of the New World Encounter),* Mangan J. (ed.). Duke University Press. 212.

Minchom, Martin. 1994. *The People of Quito 1690–1810: Change and Unrest in the Underclass.* Boulder: Westview Press.

Mitchell, Adrian. 2010. *Dampier's Monkey: The South Sea Voyages of William Dampier.* Cambridge, Massachusetts: Wakefield Press.

Moreno Yáñez, Segundo E. 1988. "Formaciones Ppolíticas tribales y señoríos étnicos." In *Nueva Historia del Ecuador*, Ayala Mora, Enrique (ed.). 2:11–134. Quito: Corporación Editorial Nacional, Grijalba.

———.1976. *Sublevaciones Indígenas en la Audiencia de Quito.* Quito: Universidad Católica de Quito.

Moscoso, J. Villacrés.1985. *Las Ambiciones Internacionales por las Islas Galápagos.* Guayaquil, Ecuador: Casa de la Cultura. 87–176.

Nader, Helen, 1993. *Liberty in Absolutist Spain: The Habsburg Sale of Towns, 1516–1700.* Introduction. The John Hopkins Univ. Studies in Historical and Political Science.

Naveda, B. 1952. *Galápagos a la vista.* Quito: Casa de la Cultura Ecuatoriana.

Nicholls, Henry, 2007 [2006]. *The Life and Loves of the World's Most Famous Tortoise,* London: Pan Macmillan. 17–32.

Norris, Robert. 2004. *El Gran Ausente: Biografía de Velasco Ibarra.* Quito: Ecuador. Libri Mundi. 58–9.

Oberem, Udo. 1981. "Los Cañaris y la Conquista Española de la Sierra Ecuatoriana: Otro Capítulo de las Relaciones Interétnicas en el siglo XVI." *Contribución a la Etnohistoria Ecuatoriana.* In Moreno, S. And Oberem U., (eds.). 129–92, 315.

Olwig, Kenneth. 1996. "Reinventing Common Nature: Yosemite and Mount Rushmore—A Meandering Tale of a Double Nature." In Cronon ed. *Uncommon Ground: Rethinking the Human Place in Nature.* 379–408.

Orbe, Tania. 2019. "Agua en Galápagos, un recurso en riesgo." *Scidevnet.*

Ortiz de la Tabla. 1977. "El obraje colonial ecuatoriano: aproximación a su estudio." Madrid: *Revista de Indias*, No: 149–150: 471–541.

Ospina, Pablo. 2006. *Galápagos, Naturaleza y Sociedad: Actores Sociales y Conflictos Ambientales en las Islas Galápagos.* Quito, Ecuador: Corporación Editorial Nacional. 9– 10.

———. 2001. *Identidades en Galápagos. El sentimiento de una diferencia.* Quito, Ecuador: Ediciones Trama. 8.

Pareja, Pamela. 2018. *De Mestizas a Indígenas: Reindigenization as a Political Strategy in Ecuador.* Master's Thesis, University of South Florida. 35–36.

Parks, Taylor and Rippy, Fred. 1940. "The Galápagos Islands: A Neglected Phase of American Strategy Diplomacy," *Pacific Historical Review,* 9(1): 37–45.

Pérez, Aquiles R. 1962. *Los seudopantsaleos.* Llacta 14. Quito: Instituto Ecuatoriano de Antropología y Geografía and Talleres Gráficos Nacionales.

Platt, Tristan. 1982. *Estado Boliviano y Ayllu Andino: Tierra y Tributo en el Norte de Potosí.* Instituto de Estudios Peruanos.

Poeschel, Ursula. 2001. *No quisimos soltar el agua: formas de resistencia indígena y continuidad étnica en una comunidad ecuatoriana 1960-5.* Quito: Abya-Yala. 67.

Powers, Karen. 1991. "Resilient Lords and Indian Vagabonds: Wealth, Migration, and the Reproductive Transformation of Quito's Chiefdoms, 1500–1700." *Ethnohistory,* 38 (3): 225–49

Pratt, Mary Louise. 2008 [1992]. *Imperial Eyes: Travel Writing and Transculturation.* Oxfordshire, England: Routledge. 37, 123.

Proctor, James. 1996. "Whose Nature? The Contested Moral Terrain of Ancient Forests". In Cronon ed. *Uncommon Ground: Rethinking the Human Place in Nature.* 269–97.

Puig de la Bellacasa, 2012. "Nothing comes without its world: Thinking with care." *Sociological Review,* 60(2): 197–216.

Quiroga, Diego. 2009 "Crafting nature: the Galápagos and the making and unmaking of a 'natural laboratory.'" *Journal of Political Ecology,* 16: 123–40. https://doi.org/10.2458/v16i1.21695.

Radin, Margaret Jane. 1987. Market Inalienability. *Harvard Law Review.* Vol. 100 (8): 1849–1937.

Raffles, Hugh. 2002. *In Amazonia: a Natural History.* Princeton, NJ: Princeton University Press.

———. 2004. "Social Memory and the Politics of Place-Making in Northeastern Amazonia." *Berkeley Workshop on Environmental Politics.*

Ramos, Wacho. 2016. "Causa de Colonización y Migración hacia Galápagos: Efectos en el Desarrollo Sostenible de Santa Cruz". *Congreso Online Internacional de Migración y Desarroll*: 36-19

Rappaport, Joanne. 2014. *The Disappearing Mestizo: Configuring Difference in the Colonial New Kingdom of Granada.* Durham: Duke Univ. Press. 127–9, 217.

Reyes, M. F., Trifunovic, N., Sharma, S. and Kennedy, M. 2017. "Estimación y predicción de la demanda de agua en Puerto Ayora," *Informe Galápagos 2015–2016,* Cayot y Cruz ed., DPNG, CGREG, FCD y GC, Puerto Ayora, Galápagos, Ecuador.

Ritvo, Harriet. 1997. "The Point of Order." *The Platypus and the Mermaid and Other Figments of the Classifying Imagination.* Cambridge, MA: Harvard University Press. 1–50.

Rodas, Paola, and Vivanco, Adriana. 2012. *Galápagos: Prisión de Basalto, Terror y Lágrimas en la Isla Isabela (1946–1959).* Quito, Ecuador: Fondo Editorial, Ministerio de Cultura del Ecuador. 190–203, 290–92.

Rosaldo, Renato. 1994. "Cultural Citizenship and Educational Democracy." *Cultural Anthropology,* 9(3): 402–11.

———. 1993 [1989]. *Culture & Truth.* Boston, Massachussetts: Beacon Press Books. 209.

Rothschild, M. 1983. *Dear Lord Rothschild: Birds, Butterflies, and History.* Distributed by ISI. 171.

Salomon, Noah. 2011. "The Ruse of Law: Legal Equality and the Problem of Citizenship in a Multireligious Sudan." In *After Secular Law.* Sullivan, Winnifred (ed.). Redwood City, California: Stanford Law Books. 200–20.

Santos, Boaventura de Sousa. 2002. *Toward a New Legal Common Sense.* Cambridge, England: Cambridge University Press. 437.

Sarmiento de Gamboa, P. (1942). *Viajes al Estrecho de Magallanes.* Rosenblat, A (ed). Madrid: Instituto de Estudios Políticos.

Schwartz, Stuart and Salomon, Frank. 1999. *New People.* New York: Cambridge University Press. 478.

Scott, James C. 2009. *The Art of Not Being Governed: An Anarchist History of Upland Southeast Asia.* New Haven, CT: Yale University Press. 20.

Seed, Patricia. 1993. "Are These Not Also Men?: The Indian Humanity and Capacity for Spanish Civilization." *Journal of Latin American Studies,* 25(3): 140, 629–652.

Sevilla, Elisa. 2017. "Darwinians, Anti-Darwinians, and the Galápagos (1835–1935)." In *Darwin, Darwinism, and Conservation on the Galápagos Islands: The Legacy of Darwin and its new applications.* Quiroga and Sevilla (eds.). New York: Springer. 30–38.

Silva P., 1992. "Las islas Galápagos en la historia del Ecuador." En *Nueva Historia del Ecuador.* Quito, Ecuador: Corporación Editora Nacional, Vol. 12: 253–303.

Simberloff, Daniel. 1974. "Equilibrium Theory of Island Biogeography and Ecology". *Annual Review of Ecology and Systematics,* 5: 161–82.

Snell, Tye, Causton, Powell, Dinerstein, Allnut and Bensted-Smith. 2000. "Projections of the Future: A Terrestrial Biodiversity Vision." *A Biodiversity Vision for the Galápagos Islands:* 48–59. CDF & WWF.

Snow, David. 1964. "Research Station in the Galápagos." In *The International Journal of Conservation,* 7(6): 4, 275–76.

Spencer, Herbert. 2013[1864]. *The Principles of Biology.* Madrid, Spain: HardPress Publishing.

Spiro, Jonathan. 2015 [2008]. *Defending the Master Race: Conservation, Eugenics, and the Legacy of Madison Grant.* Burlington: University of Vermont Press.

Stewart, Alban. 1911. *A botanical Survey of the Galápagos Islands.* San Francisco: California Academy of Sciences.

Stocking, George. 1991. *Victorian Anthropology.* New York: The Free Press.

Stutzman, Ronald. 1981. "El Mestizaje: An All-inclusive Ideology of Exclusion." In *Cultural Transformations and Ethnicity in Modern Ecuador,* edited by Norman E. Whitten, Jr. Urbana (eds.). Champaign, Illinois: University of Illinois Press. 45–94.

Swanson, K. 2010. *Begging as a Path to Progress: Indigenous Women and Children and the Struggle for Ecuador's Urban Spaces.* The University of Georgia Press.

Tardieu, Jean Pierre. 2012. "Negros e Indios en el obraje de San Ildefonso. Real Audiencia de Quito 1665–6." *Revista de Indias,* 72(255): 527–50.

Taylor, Elizabeth. 2014. *On the Back of Tortoises: Conserving Evolution in the Galápagos Islands.* Phd Dissertation. University of North Carolina at Chapel Hill. 63–8, 84–89.

Taylor, J. E., Hardner J., and Stewart M. 2006. "Ecotourism and Economic Growth in the Galápagos: An Island Economy-wide Analysis." *Agriculture and Resource*

Economic Working Papers, Department of Agricultural and Resource Economics. UC Davis.

Toral-Granda, M. V., Causton, C. E., Jäger, H., Trueman, M., Izurieta J. C., Araujo E., et al. 2017. "Alien species pathways to the Galapagos Islands." Ecuador. *PLoS ONE,* 12(9): e0184379. https://doi.org/10.1371/journal.pone.0184379.

UNESCO Institute for Statistics (UIS), 2007. State Report. https://whc.unesco.org /en/soc/994.

Vervloet, Lis. 2013. "Salasacas en Santa Cruz: Aspectos Culturales, Sociales y Ambientales." Informe Técnico. Fundación Charles Darwin. 15–18.

von Hagen, Victor. 1941. *The Galápagos Revisited.* Oxford, England: Oxford University Press. 171.

Walsh, Stephen, McCleary, Amy, and Heumann, Benjamin. 2010. "Community Expansion and Infrastructure Development: Implications for Human Health and Environmental Quality in the Galápagos." *Journal of Latin America Geography,* 9(3): 137–59.

West, Paige, Igoe, J., and Brockington D. 2006. "Parks and Peoples: The Social Impact of Protected Areas." *Annual Review of Anthropology,* 35: 251–77.

Whiston, Anne. 1996. "Constructing Nature: The Legacy of Frederick Law Olmsted." In Cronon ed. *Uncommon Ground: Rethinking the Human Place in Nature.* 91–113.

Whitehead, Hili. 1985. "Studying Sperm Whales on the Galápagos Grounds," in *Noticias de Galápagos,* 42: 18–21.

Whitten, Jr., Norman E. 1981. *Cultural Transformations and Ethnicity in Modern Ecuador.* Chicago: University of Illinois Press. 12–13.

Williams, Raymond. 1975. *The Country and the City.* Oxford Univ. Press

Wittmer, Margaret. 2014 [1989]. *Floreana: A Woman's Pilgrimage to the Galápagos.* Moyer Bell.

Worster, Donald. 1994 [1977]. *Nature's Economy: A History of Ecological Ideas.* Cambridge, England: Cambridge Univ. Press. 202.

Wulf, Andrea. 2015. *The Invention of Nature: Alexander Von Humboldt's New World.* New York, New York: Knopf. 66.

Index

About the Author

Pilar Sánchez Voelkl is author of *Indigenous Settlers of the Galápagos and Masculinities in Corporate Elites in Colombia and Ecuador*. She holds a PhD in Cultural Anthropology from New York University. She has done ethnographic research in the Galápagos since 2014. Her research has examined the translation of science into law and everyday life; the emergence of new forms of property-like natural heritage sites; and the relationship between gender, race, and power in the corporate world.

www.ingramcontent.com/pod-product-compliance
Lightning Source LLC
Chambersburg PA
CBHW022309280326
41932CB00010B/1037